THE NEW MERMAIDS

Three Sixteenth-Century Comedies

THE NEW MERMAIDS

General Editor

BRIAN GIBBONS
Professor of English Literature, University of Zurich

Previous general editors of the series have been:

PHILIP BROCKBANK
BRIAN MORRIS
ROMA GILL

Three Sixteenth-Century Comedies

GAMMER GURTON'S NEEDLE
ROISTER DOISTER
THE OLD WIFE'S TALE

Edited by

CHARLES WALTERS WHITWORTH

*Lecturer in English and
Associate Fellow of the Shakespeare Institute,
University of Birmingham*

LONDON/ERNEST BENN LIMITED

NEW YORK/W. W. NORTON AND COMPANY INC.

First published in this form 1984
by Ernest Benn Limited
Sovereign Way, Tonbridge, Kent TN9 1RW

©Ernest Benn Limited 1984

Published in the United States of America by
W. W. Norton & Company, Inc.
500 Fifth Avenue, New York, N.Y. 10110

Printed in Great Britain

British Library Cataloguing in Publication Data

Three sixteenth century comedies.—(The New mermaids)
1. English drama—Early modern and Elizabethan,
1500–1600
I. Whitworth, Charles   II. Series
822'.3'08   PR1263

ISBN 0–510–33509–8

FOR
ELISABETH, DIMITRI, JESSICA

CONTENTS

ACKNOWLEDGEMENTS

I AM GRATEFUL to Dr Roma Gill, a former general editor of this series, who proposed this volume of plays to me and to Professor Brian Morris, another general editor, for picking up where she left off and offering help from the wealth of his experience. Many colleagues have willingly imparted advice to a novice editor and their expertise has made rough places plain. For the roughness that remains, the novice must as willingly bear the blame. Dr Russell Jackson and Dr Ian Small, experienced Mermaidmen both, have given practical guidance. Conversations at various times with Dr Stanley Wells, Dr R. L. Smallwood, Mr I. A. Shapiro, Professor Glynne Wickham, Dr O. B. Hardison, Dr Jean-Marie Maguin, Professor John Velz and Dr J. A. B. Somerset have illuminated facets of the plays, their texts and contexts. The Director and Fellows of the Shakespeare Institute, with whom I am privileged to be associated, invited me to give a paper on *Gammer Gurton's Needle*. Another colleague, Dr J. W. Binns, a Renaissance Latinist, has responded readily to appeals for help. The Institute librarian, Dr Susan Brock, has been consulted almost daily and has as frequently been helpful. Dr Richard Axton and Dr Marie Axton replied promptly to queries. I owe general debts of long standing which, alas, cannot be repaid, to the late Professors Geoffrey Shepherd and T. J. B. Spencer, whose support and counsel began years ago when I was a postgraduate student and ended only with their untimely passing.

   Acknowledgement is made to the following for their welcome and assistance: the librarians and curators of the Pierpont Morgan Library and the Carl H. Pforzheimer Library in New York; the Beinecke Rare Book and Manuscript Library, Yale University; the Houghton Library, Harvard University; the Folger Shakespeare Library, Washington, D.C.; the Charles Patterson Van Pelt Library, University of Pennsylvania; the Bodleian Library, Oxford; the Victoria and Albert Museum (Dyce Collection). The following institutions answered enquiries and supplied material: the Lilly Library, Indiana University; Eton College; and a special acknowledgement is due Mr Robert L. Volz, Custodian of the Chapin Library, Williams College, for exemplary promptness, efficiency and courtesy. I am grateful to the Chapin Library also for permission to reproduce the titlepage of *Gammer Gurton's Needle*, and to the British Library for permission to reproduce that of *The Old Wife's Tale*. The late Ms Virginia Knight kindly provided slides and notes on her production of *Gammer Gurton's Needle* at Shorter College. Mrs Anne Buckley has decoded tangled manuscripts and typed the entire text of this volume expertly, sometimes in trying personal circumstances. The British Academy and the Arts Faculty of the University of Birmingham gave financial assistance, *sine qua non*.

Birmingham   C.W.W.

St. Swithin's Day, 1983

ABBREVIATIONS

I. Texts; editions collated and cited

Q	(In notes to each play, Q refers to the sixteenth-century quarto used as copy text. For details, see 'This Edition', below.)
1661	The reprint that year of the 1575 *GGN* quarto
GGN	*Gammer Gurton's Needle*
OWT	*The Old Wife's Tale*
RD	*Roister Doister*
Adams	Joseph Quincy Adams, ed., *Chief Pre-Shakespearean Dramas* (1924) (*GGN, RD*)
Baskervill, *et al.*	C. R. Baskervill, V. B. Heltzel, A. H. Nethercot, eds., *Elizabethan and Stuart Plays* (New York, 1934) (*GGN, RD, OWT*)
Binnie	Patricia Binnie, ed., *The Old Wives Tale*, The Revels Plays (Manchester and Baltimore, 1980)
Boas	F. S. Boas, ed., *Five Pre-Shakespearean Comedies* (1934; repr. 1970) (*GGN, RD*)
Bradley	Henry Bradley, ed., *Gammer Gurton's Needle*, in Gayley
Brett-Smith	H. F. B. Brett-Smith, ed., *Gammer Gurtons Nedle*, The Percy Reprints (Oxford, 1920)
Brooke and Paradise	C. F. Tucker Brooke and N. B. Paradise, eds., *English Drama 1580–1642* (Boston, 1933) (*OWT*)
Bullen	A. H. Bullen, ed., *The Works of George Peele*, 2 vols (1888), I (*OWT*)
Creeth	Edmund Creeth, ed., *Tudor Plays* (New York, 1966) (*GGN, RD*)
Dyce	Alexander Dyce, ed., *The Dramatic and Poetical Works of Robert Greene and George Peele* (1861) (*OWT*)
Flügel	Ewald Flügel, ed., *Roister Doister*, in Gayley
Gayley	Charles Mills Gayley, ed., *Representative English Comedies* (1903) (*GGN, RD, OWT*)
Greg (*OWT*)	W. W. Greg. ed., *The Old Wives Tale*, MSR (Oxford, 1909)
Greg (*RD*)	W. W. Greg, ed., *Roister Doister*, MSR (Oxford, 1935)

Gummere	F. B. Gummere, ed., *The Old Wives' Tale*, in Gayley
Hazlitt	W. Carew Hazlitt, ed., *A Select Collection of Old English Plays*, fourth edition, 15 vols (1874–6), III (*GGN, RD*)
Hook	Frank S. Hook, ed., *The Old Wives Tale*, in *The Life and Works of George Peele*, 3 vols, gen. ed. C. T. Prouty, III (New Haven, 1970)
Manly	J. M. Manly, ed., *Specimens of the Pre-Shakesperean Drama*, 2 vols (Boston, 1897), II (*GGN, RD*)
McIlwraith	A. K. McIlwraith, ed., *Five Elizabethan Comedies* (1934, etc.) (*OWT*)
Neilson	W. A. Neilson, ed., *The Chief Elizabethan Dramatists* (1911) (*OWT*)
Scheurweghs	G. Scheurweghs, ed., *Roister Doister* (Louvain, 1939)
Williams and Robin	W. H. Williams and P. A. Robin, eds., *Ralph Roister Doister*, The Temple Dramatists (1901)

II. Reference works and scholarly works cited frequently

Boas, *UD*	F. S. Boas, *University Drama in the Tudor Age* (Oxford, 1914)
Chambers, *ES*	E. K. Chambers, *The Elizabethan Stage*, 4 vols (Oxford, 1923)
Chambers, *MS*	E. K. Chambers, *The Medieval Stage*, 2 vols (1903)
Craik	T. W. Craik, *The Tudor Interlude* (Leicester, 1958)
DNB	*Dictionary of National Biography*
ODEP	*The Oxford Dictionary of English Proverbs*, compiled by William George Smith, third edition, ed. F. P. Wilson (Oxford, 1970)
OED	*Oxford English Dictionary*
Southern	Richard Southern, *The Staging of Plays before Shakespeare* (1973)
Tilley	Morris Palmer Tilley, *A Dictionary of the Proverbs in England in the Sixteenth and Seventeenth Centuries* (Ann Arbor, Michigan, 1950)
Wickham, *EES*	Glynne Wickham, *Early English Stages 1300–1660*, 3 vols (1959–1981): I (1959; second edn., 1980); II, pt. i (1963), II, pt. ii (1972); III (1981)

Wilson   F. P. Wilson, *The English Drama 1485–1585*,
                      Oxford History of English Literature, IV, pt.
                      i (Oxford, 1969)
Young   Karl Young, *The Drama of the Medieval
                      Church*, 2 vols (1933)

III. Journals and series

AUMLA   *Journal of the Australasian Language and
                      Literature Association*
EETS   Early English Text Society
ELN   *English Language Notes*
ELR   *English Literary Renaissance*
ES   *English Studies*
MLR   *Modern Language Review*
MP   *Modern Philology*
MSC   Malone Society Collections
MSR   Malone Society Reprints
N&Q   *Notes and Queries*
O.S.   Original Series
ShS   *Shakespeare Survey*
UTSE   *University of Texas Studies in English*

IV. Other abbreviations

ed.   this edition   ⎫ in textual notes;
eds.   some other editions   ⎭ elsewhere, 'editor(s)'
Fr.   French
L.   Latin
s.d.   stage direction
s.p.   speech prefix

Works by Classical authors are cited in the Loeb Classical
Library editions, Shakespeare in the Peter Alexander edition,
other dramatists in the New Mermaid editions, unless otherwise
indicated. Place of publication is London, unless otherwise
indicated.

INTRODUCTION

THE CONTEXT

THE THREE PLAYS in this volume were included in Charles Mills Gayley's *Representative English Comedies from the Beginning to Shakespeare*, published in 1903. Gayley defended his choice of plays (seven in all) on the grounds of 'their importance in the history of comedy'. The language of his preface is marked by borrowings from the language of science: 'specimens', 'scientifically', 'evolution', 'permutation', 'genus', 'species', 'scientific value'. The study of literature is 'literary science', a text is a 'specimen' or 'species', a genre is a 'genus'.[1] Gayley was writing at the time when the rudiments of Darwin's theory of the evolution of animal species were being appropriated by scholars in fields of study remote from biology. Literary and dramatic history too was being described as such an evolutionary process.[2] In 1903, the year Gayley's volume appeared, E. K. Chambers published *The Medieval Stage*, a work of immense importance and influence: the serious study of early English drama dates from its publication. Chambers too subscribed to the evolutionary view, and he traced the growth, 'the main line of development', as he saw it, of English drama from the embryo, the liturgical tropes, or sung texts, in which the visit to Christ's sepulchre by the three Marys on Easter morning was performed in the tenth-century English church, to its splendid maturity in the high Elizabethan drama of Marlowe, Jonson and above all, Shakespeare. In such a view, naturally, all that preceded Shakespeare not only led to him, but was found to be primitive in comparison with him. This was inevitable; earlier drama was to be studied for what it revealed about his antecedents. The postulate determined the choice of data; the 'specimens' would have to demonstrate the theory. John Addington Symonds, writing at about the same time as Chambers, stated the concept baldly: 'The more we study Shakespeare . . . the more we perceive that his predecessors, no less than his successors, exist for him . . . . Having him, we could well dispense with them'.[3]

[1] Compare the title of J. M. Manly's collection: *Specimens of the Pre-Shakesperean Drama*.

[2] An excellent exposition and critique of the evolutionary view is in the first chapter of O.B. Hardison, Jr.'s *Christian Rite and Christian Drama in the Middle Ages* (Baltimore, 1965), pp. 1–34. My summary is indebted to this work.

[3] *Shakespere's Predecessors in the English Drama* (1900), pp. 14–15.

Chambers himself began accumulating 'facts' about early drama because he wanted to write a book about Shakespeare and the conditions under which he wrote, and 'it seemed natural to put first some short account of the origins of play-acting in England and of its development during the Middle Ages'.[4] So Chambers's view, and that of scholars and historians who followed him, was backward from the Shakespearean promontory across the centuries to the primitive beginnings and halting advances of English drama as it strove toward self-realization. This teleological view was implicit in major works on early drama as late as 1955, when Hardin Craig's *English Religious Drama of the Middle Ages* was published.[5]

Interest, then, in pre-Shakespearean drama was, for the most part, historical, antiquarian, archaeological, and ulterior. Mystery plays, saint plays, moralities, interludes, sword plays, mummings, Robin Hood plays, farces, the first true comedies and tragedies—all were specimens, fossil remains pointing the way along the evolutionary trail to the Elizabethans. The religious drama, particularly, became extinct, like the dinosaur, and was replaced by hardier, secular species. The fossils were exhumed and displayed in collections like Gayley's and Manly's and Joseph Quincy Adams's *Chief Pre-Shakespearean Dramas* (1924).[6] Some collectors began only in the sixteenth century, with the immediate ancestors of Shakespeare. They always included *Gammer Gurton's Needle* and *Roister Doister*, rivals for the title of 'first regular English comedy'. The comedies were judged to be clever enough, but simple in construction, lightweight in substance, crude in their verse, and frequently in dubious taste; *Gammer Gurton's Needle* was not dubious—it was positively coarse. One could easily see from this viewpoint how Shakespeare's immediate predecessors—Gascoigne, Lyly, Greene, Peele—refined the comic drama they had inherited, handing it on to Shakespeare fit for his use. The very sub-titles of the anthologies, with their reference to Shakespeare as *terminus ad quem* ('pre-Shakespearean', 'from the beginnings to Shakespeare', 'down to Shakespeare'), betray the

---

[4] Chambers, *MS*, I, v. Chambers apologizes for his failure to reach an 'austere standard of scientific completeness' (p. viii).

[5] It appears to be implicit in Arnold Williams, *The Drama of Medieval England* (East Lansing, Michigan, 1961), but it had already begun, and continued, to be challenged from various directions, e.g., by H. C. Gardiner, *Mysteries' End* (New Haven, Conn., 1946); Eleanor Prosser, *Drama and Religion in the English Mystery Plays* (Stanford, Cal., 1961); Hardison; and Wickham, *EES*, I.

[6] The collecting of 'old plays' had begun much earlier. Robert Dodsley's *Select Collection of Old Plays* (1744) was re-issued, with additions, by Isaac Reed (1780), J. P. Collier (1825) and W. C. Hazlitt (1874-6).

bias. It was thus inevitable that earlier drama should look and sound primitive, even to scholars who approached it with good will and with the genuine desire to make it accessible and comprehensible to their students.

When collectors of early plays were being selective, they naturally chose the best, most interesting 'specimens' of the genus they were dealing with. So Gayley's 'representative' comedies are not really representative, in the sense of being typical of a class; they are in fact atypical. The reasons for presenting three of them here, in a new edition, have nothing to do with their representativeness. Each is unique, out of the ordinary and, most important, highly entertaining. Each is eminently worth knowing for its own sake. All three are comedies, but each is a different kind of comedy. None of them is a watershed in the history of English drama, for none of them gave rise on its own, directly or visibly, to other plays and to schools and traditions.

This is not to suggest, of course, that these comedies were written in a vacuum or that their authors owed nothing to other dramatists of their own and previous times. Some specific debts, as well as parallels and analogies with, and possible influences by and upon other drama, earlier and later, are noted in the commentaries. The authors of these comedies knew the drama of their contemporaries and of their predecessors, including the distant Romans, Plautus and Terence. In this they were not unlike the authors of other sixteenth-century plays, whether they wrote for the entertainment of a private household, for the edification (mixed with mirth) of schoolboys, the holiday diversion of sophisticated university students or Inns of Court men, or the less discriminating audiences who gathered to watch the travelling players in inn-yard or town square. For the variety of English drama, and of comedy in particular, in the middle of the sixteenth century is much greater than one might be led to expect by the traditional account of its inexorable progress from church altar to Elizabethan public stage. A. P. Rossiter parodies the evolutionists' imagery:

> From the reign of Henry VIII (1509–47) to that of Elizabeth, the dramatic world is like a seething primordial swamp in which local time is, so to speak, accelerated, and a confused wealth of forms emerge, few of which last long.[7]

A brief survey of the dramatic and theatrical landscape of mid-Tudor England will establish the setting in which the three

[7] A. P. Rossiter, *English Drama from Early Times to the Elizabethans* (1950), p. 108.

comedies in this volume were composed and produced. Then, because of the distinctness of each and the peculiar problems that each presents, it will be sensible to consider each play separately. To generalize about English drama of the sixteenth century from these three plays would be as misleading as to conceive of that drama as an organism, a penultimate link in an evolutionary chain.

Recognisable dramatic events, if not fully-fledged plays, seem to have existed in England for some six hundred years by the time *Gammer Gurton's Needle* and *Roister Doister* were written in the middle of the Tudor century.[8] This is a considerably greater span of time than that which separates us from them. It was barely four hundred years ago that James Burbage built The Theatre in Shoreditch, England's first genuine theatre building, expressly designed for the staging of plays before the public. In the same year, 1576, Richard Farrant, Master of the Children of Windsor Chapel, leased part of a house in the Blackfriars precinct, which had before the Reformation been a large Dominican religious community. The house became the Blackfriars theatre, where boys from the Chapel Royal and St. Paul's choir schools performed plays.[9] Thus in the same year, the first of each of the two principal kinds of permanent Elizabethan theatre buildings in London were established: the large, outdoor, partially covered theatre, holding several thousand spectators, of which Shakespeare's Globe was just one example, and the smaller, more intimate and more exclusive indoor theatre, seating a few hundred at most. But momentous as these occurrences of 1576 were in the history of English drama, they should be seen rather as the natural culmination of several centuries of the acting and staging of plays, than as a quantum leap which instantaneously made possible what had been unimaginable before, namely, the vital

---

[8] The birth of drama in England is usually assigned to the year 975 or thereabouts, when Ethelwold, bishop of Winchester, in *Regularis Concordia*, instructed the monks in his diocese to enact the visit of the three Marys to the tomb of Christ as part of the Easter Sunday Mass. See Wickham, *EES*, III, 26–9; Chambers, *MS*, II, 306–9; Young, I, 249–50, 581–3. For a full discussion of the *Quem quaeritis*, see Hardison, Essays V and VI.

[9] Chambers has very full accounts of the acquisitions, by Burbage and Farrant, of The Theatre and Blackfriars, in *ES*, II, 383–400, 475–515. See also Reavley Gair, *The Children of Paul's* (1982).

new drama of Kyd, Marlowe and Shakespeare.[10] The more we learn about the performing of plays before the first theatres were built, the easier it is to see how the players' habits and techniques of staging in the various kinds of venues, indoor and outdoor, in which they were used to performing, influenced the designs of the new theatres. Professional acting troupes, with both men and boys in them, had been performing in England for a very long time before 1576.

The great medieval cycles of miracle plays, of which so few survive, were performed, in part at least, on pageant wagons at successive stops in a procession through the town.[11] The pageant wagon, often elaborately decorated, was also used for civic and royal pageants, and was adapted by the touring troupes, providing them with both transport for their equipment and a rolling stage which could be pulled up in courtyards and village squares. Another kind of outdoor playing place, more like a theatre or amphitheatre, in that it was fixed, is exemplified in an illustration in the Macro manuscript of the oldest extant complete morality play, *The Castle of Perseverance* (*c.* 1425).[12] This 'place-and-scaffold' theatre had several scaffolds at intervals around a flat 'place' or *platea* in which the play was performed. The scaffolds were part of the set, and the spectators usually sat on the stepped bank which encircled the 'place'. These outdoor theatres may have been built upon existing circular or semi-circular mounds such as Iron Age hill forts. Such theatres continued in use well into the sixteenth century: Sir David Lindsay's Scottish morality play, *Ane Satyre of the Thrie Estaitis*, contemporaneous with *Gammer Gurton's Needle* and *Roister Doister*, calls for just such a theatre, with 'place', scaffold, hill and a moat or ditch filled with water.[13]

A third kind of outdoor stage was the 'booth-and-trestle'. Boards were placed on trestles or barrels to elevate the stage several feet above ground level, and a curtained booth erected at the rear of it to provide a house or 'inner stage' as needed, or a

[10] The year 1576 is, however, a watershed in other respects. As Wickham points out, it marks the end of 'what may reasonably be called "a public service theatre"' and the beginning of 'what thereafter may with equal fairness be described as "a commercial theatre"' (*EES*, II, pt. i, xii).

[11] The following summary is derived from Richard Hosley, 'Three Kinds of Outdoor Theatre before Shakespeare', *Theatre Survey*, 12 (1971), 1–33.

[12] See *The Macro Plays*, ed. Mark Eccles, EETS, O.S. 262 (1969), frontispiece. Also reproduced in Richard Southern, *The Medieval Theatre in the Round*, second edn. (1975), p. 18.

[13] See Hosley, pp. 11–12; and the edition by Peter Happé in *Four Morality Plays* (1979).

backstage area or tiring house. This kind of stage may have been set up in inn-yards and courtyards or market-places, perhaps in conjunction with a wagon, with spectators watching from windows and galleries of the surrounding buildings, as well as from the ground around the stage. The booth, or curtained area, was doubtless the forerunner of the 'discovery space' of the Elizabethan playhouse.[14] Such a feature appears to be required for Sacrapant's cell in *The Old Wife's Tale*.[15]

This cursory survey of some of the kinds of outdoor theatre in use in England in the sixteenth century does not include the simple unadorned outdoor areas like the village green in which folk plays, such as Robin Hood, sword, and mummers' plays were performed. Nor does it take account of other kinds of formal, partly dramatic and often visually elaborate outdoor entertainments, such as tournaments and civic and royal pageants. But all of these, as Chambers, Wickham and others have shown, contributed to the development and diversification of English drama proper throughout the later Middle Ages and the Renaissance.[16]

Besides the many forms of outdoor drama and other more or less dramatic entertainments, there were various kinds of indoor theatre and spectacle which survived and flourished well into the seventeenth century, and which also provided the playwright, from the mid-sixteenth century onwards, with ready-made techniques and devices. Udall and 'Mr S.' made use of them in the 1550s, as had Henry Medwall, John Skelton, John Heywood, John Bale and others before them. Feasts, receptions for foreign dignitaries, seasonal festivities, barriers (an indoor version of the tournament), masques and plays were regular pastimes of the

[14] Most scholars are now sceptical about an 'inner stage', but most also accept a 'discovery space' of some kind. See Hosley, 'The Discovery-Space in Shakespeare's Globe', *ShS*, 12 (1959), 35–46; Wickham, *EES*, II, pt. ii, 198–203; and Michael Hattaway, *Elizabethan Popular Theatre* (1982), pp. 27–9.

[15] Particular questions about sets and staging are discussed below, under 'Staging', and in notes on the plays.

[16] Chambers, *MS*, I, and his *The English Folk-Play* (1933; repr. 1964); Wickham, *EES*, I. See also Alan Brody, *The English Mummers and their Plays* (1969), and Robert Withington, *English Pageantry*, 2 vols (1918–20; repr. 1963). The many studies of the native English inheritance of Elizabethan drama include Willard Farnham, *The Medieval Heritage of Elizabethan Tragedy* (1936); Glynne Wickham, *Shakespeare's Dramatic Heritage* (1969); David Bevington, *From 'Mankind' to Marlowe* (Cambridge, Mass., 1962); and Bernard Spivack, *Shakespeare and the Allegory of Evil* (1958).

Tudor Court.[17] As early as the 1480s, players (*lusores*) of interludes were retained by English noblemen, including Richard, Duke of Gloucester, afterwards Richard III. Henry VII had four players, and his entertainment-loving son, Henry VIII, doubled their number. Henry's elder brother, Arthur, when Prince of Wales, had his own company, and Henry himself, as Prince of Wales, also had one (Chambers, *MS*, II, 186–8). These players are clearly distinguished in the records from minstrels, *joculatores* (jesters) and other entertainers. Henry VII's *lusores* are identified in 1494 as 'pleyars of the Kyngs enterluds'.

The precise meaning of 'interlude' has been debated at length, inconclusively. Chambers (*MS*, II, 181–3) queried the earlier view that it was a dramatic performance which took place between the courses of a banquet, and suggested that *inter-* referred to the participation of more than one performer of the *ludus* (play, entertainment). That is, it was a dialogue or a more complex dramatic event.[18] F. P. Wilson concludes:

> It is impossible, however, to tie the word 'interlude' to any one meaning, for in one place or another it is found attached to every kind of drama known to the Middle Ages.

The word *interludium* is found as early as the thirteenth century in the title *Interludium de Clerico et Puella*, a fragmentary piece of dialogue about a university student who, pining away for a beautiful girl whose favours he is unable to obtain, goes to an old bawd for help.[19] So whatever they were, interludes had existed for two centuries or more before the Tudor age. Furthermore, they were, partially at least, comical or farcical or suitably amusing, in any case, to provide seasonal entertainment. *Sir Gawain and the Green Knight*, written in the second half of the fourteenth century, refers to 'enterludez' at court at Christmas (1. 472).

The dividing line between interlude and morality play in the sixteenth century is indeterminate, and Craik, Wickham and others pre-empt debate by talking of 'moral interludes'. 'Morality'

---

[17] The magnificence of court spectacles from the fourteenth century onwards is amply documented by Wickham, *EES*, I; Withington, *English Pageantry*, I; and Enid Welsford, *The Court Masque* (1927). The poet John Lydgate wrote a number of pageants for the court of Henry VI. Shakespeare and Fletcher made dramatic capital of Henry VIII's fondness for masquing in *Henry VIII*, I.iv.

[18] Other discussions of the word's possible meanings, as it was used in the sixteenth century, are in Wickham, *EES*, I, 234–5; Craik, p. 1; Wilson, pp. 10–11.

[19] Wickham gives parallel texts in *English Moral Interludes* (1976), pp. 199–203. He cites the *Interludium* as 'making nonsense of the idea, current for so long among critics and historians, that religious drama had to be "secularized" before art of any merit in dramatic form could develop' (p. 196).

sounds weightier, more solemn and didactic, while the association of 'interlude' with banqueting and merriment gives a rather lighter, if not necessarily purely secular, impression. Nor will length suffice as a simple criterion. *Roister Doister* is called 'our comedy or interlude' in the Prologue, and it is a full-length play, while *Mankind* and *Everyman*, the two most famous English moralities, run to barely 900 lines each in the New Mermaid edition.[20] 'Interlude' continued to be used throughout the century, even when other more precise labels like 'comedy', 'tragedy' and 'history' would appear to have superseded it.

While many of the longer morality plays, such as *The Castle of Perseverance* and *Ane Satyre of the Thrie Estaitis*, were written for performance outdoors and would seem to have been played to audiences who gathered for the sole purpose of seeing them, many interludes were played in banqueting halls, frequently as part of the entertainment of the diners on special occasions. The great Tudor banqueting halls, which are so prominent an architectural feature of the period, ranged from those in the relatively modest homes of country gentry, to those of colleges and guildhalls, to the spacious halls of the great palaces of nobility and royalty. One of the largest, the great hall of Hampton Court palace, was forty feet wide and 108 feet long, with forty-two-foot high walls.[21] It was in these halls, small and large, and places like them, that the interluders played. The great hall, with its screens and entrances at one end, tables ranged along the two long walls and a raised dais with the high table at the other end, dictated to the dramatists of the first three-quarters of the sixteenth century many of their staging techniques.[22] Barely a hundred plays of all kinds (including masques, royal entertainments, etc.) survive from that period. More than twice that number are known to have been written, but are lost. How many others perished without leaving even the trace of a passing reference? For the last quarter of the century, from which more plays survive than from the preceding seventy-five years, losses, works whose titles only

[20] G. A. Lester, ed., *Three Late Medieval Morality Plays* (1981). The other play in this volume, *Mundus et Infans*, is also between 900 and 1000 lines in length.
[21] Richard Hosley, 'Three Renaissance English Indoor Playhouses', *ELR*, 3 (1973), 166–82 (p. 171). Richard Southern gives the dimensions of the slightly smaller Lambeth Palace hall (93′ × 38′) in *The Revels History of Drama in English*, II: 1500–1576 (1980), by Norman Sanders, Southern, Craik, and Lois Potter (p. 74), and see Plates 1 and 5.
[22] The fullest study of staging in the Tudor halls is Southern, with numerous drawings. See 'Staging', below.

remain, still outnumber survivals by nearly two to one.[23] Thus any generalization from the surviving body of dramatic material must necessarily be made cautiously and provisionally. Excluding such dramatic forms as masques, tilts, royal entries, mummings, and so forth, and considering only plays proper, we may observe that morality plays and moral interludes predominate in the first half of the sixteenth century.[24]

A few moralities were unremittingly serious, more like dramatized treatises than stage plays. *Everyman* is the outstanding example of this kind. But they are a minority. Writers of morality plays inherited a long tradition of secular as well as sacred drama, and even the latter had, for several centuries, exploited the titillating effect of visible, vivid, grotesque and foul-mouthed wickedness incarnate. Devils had appeared in religious drama very early; for example, in a Latin play of the Wise and Foolish Virgins, probably of the eleventh century (Young, II, 361–9). While death, damnation and the Final Judgement were terrifying prospects to medieval man, the Christian promise of salvation and eternal bliss meant that the human story, for all its tedium and woe, had a happy ending. This fundamentally comic, or more precisely, tragicomic form of the Christian myth, in both its universal aspect, that is, the ultimate triumph of Christ over Satan, and its individual dimension, Everyman's hope of everlasting joy in Heaven, informed the Christian liturgy. It also informed liturgical drama: the earliest trope to be performed as drama was, after all, the *Quem quaeritis*, the visit by the three Marys to the empty tomb of the risen Christ on Easter morning.[25]

If the devil and human vice, which came to be personified as the Vice, were ultimately to be vanquished, one could enjoy their skulduggery, their bluster and blasphemy and bawdry in the meantime. Dramatists were quick to exploit that natural tension between moral consciousness and human nature. Shakespeare's Richard III and Falstaff, Marlowe's Barabas, Jonson's Volpone and Mosca are descendants of Nichol Newfangle, Mischief,

---

[23] These figures are approximate and are based on Alfred Harbage, *Annals of English Drama* 975–1700, revised edn. by S. Schoenbaum (1964).

[24] On morality plays generally, see Robert Potter, *The English Morality Play* (1975) and W. Ray Mackenzie, *The English Moralities from the Point of View of Allegory* (1914).

[25] It is Wickham's illuminating observation that tragicomedy is the fundamental form of Christian drama and thus of all drama which derives, wholly or partially, from it (*EES*, III, 173–8). See also Hardison, pp. 284–92: 'the archetypal form of Christian drama is not tragic . . . but comic' (p. 291).

Titivillus and their fellows.[26] So too, in part, are Mr S.'s Diccon of Bedlam and Udall's Matthew Merrygreek. Comedy and the comic were inherent in English drama by the sixteenth century, and other influences, notably from classical drama and the Renaissance theory based upon it, enhanced comedy's already broad appeal to mid-century dramatists, for whomever they wrote their plays.[27] Much more might be said about the varieties of interlude, morality, farce, classical imitation, dialogue and jesting practised in the early Tudor period, to illustrate the rich soil in which Mr S., Nicholas Udall and their contemporaries worked, and which Peele, Lyly, Greene and Shakespeare inherited several decades later.[28] But the plays in this volume, to which I have attempted to sketch the outlines of a background, must now be brought into closer focus.

GAMMER GURTON'S NEEDLE

Few sixteenth-century titlepages can have raised such troublesome questions as this one: 'A Ryght Pithy, Pleasaunt and merie Comedie: Intytuled *Gammer gurtons Nedle*: Played on Stage, not longe ago in Christes Colledge in Cambridge. Made by Mr S. Mr of Art.'[29] There is no date, but that omission is remedied in the printer's colophon on the last page of the quarto: 'Imprinted at London in Fleetstreate beneath the Conduite, at the signe of S.

[26] The Devil and the Vice are not to be conflated, and I do not mean to imply that they are in mentioning, in the same breath, Titivillus, the devil in *Mankind*, and Nichol Newfangle and Mischief, the Vices in *Like Will to Like* and *Mankind* respectively. But while Falstaff may be 'that reverend vice, that grey iniquity' (the Vice in *King Darius* (1565) is named Iniquity), Richard of Gloucester is 'a fiend', 'foul devil', the 'minister of hell', 'unfit for any place but hell', though he likens himself to 'the formal vice, Iniquity'. The fullest study is L. W. Cushman, *The Devil and the Vice in English Dramatic Literature* (1900; repr. 1970). On the Vice, see also Wilson, pp. 59–66; Peter Happé,' "The Vice" and the Popular Theatre, 1547–80', in *Poetry and Drama 1570–1700: Essays in Honour of Harold F. Brooks*, ed. Antony Coleman and Antony Hammond (1981), pp. 13–31; and Spivack, *Shakespeare and the Allegory of Evil*.

[27] Those other influences are discussed more fully by Wickham, *EES*, III, 173–218; Enid Welsford, *The Fool* (1935); Leo Salingar, *Shakespeare and the Traditions of Comedy* (Cambridge, 1974); and Arnold Williams, 'The Comic in the Cycles', in *Medieval Drama*, ed. M. Bradbury and D. Palmer, with Neville Denny, Stratford-upon-Avon Studies, 16 (1973), pp. 109–23.

[28] See, besides works cited previously, M. C. Bradbrook, *The Growth and Structure of Elizabethan Comedy* (1955).

[29] Compare the title-page reproduced in the present volume: 'and' is misprinted 'anp'. See note on 'This Edition', below.

John Evangelist, by Thomas Colwell. 1575'. For two hundred years, educated guesses have been made as to the identity of 'Mr S.'. And what theatre-historical significance attaches to the claim 'played on stage'? This is the earliest extant play for which the explicit claim that it was played 'on stage' is made.[30]

The questions do not stop there: 1575 is the publication date, but there is an entry in the Stationers' Register licensing Thomas Colwell to print a play called *Dyccon of Bedlam* in the year 1562–3, twelve or thirteen years before the quarto of 1575 (Q), the only extant sixteenth-century edition, was published. Diccon is the principal character of *Gammer Gurton's Needle*, Colwell its printer, and the coincidence seems too great to be only that. On the titlepage of Q, the type in which the words '*Gammer gurtons Nedle*' are printed is different from that of the lines immediately around it, and even of part of the same line. It is italic, compared with the surrounding blackletter, and the typeface is smaller. This suggested to an early modern editor of the play, Henry Bradley, that the title had been changed from *Diccon of Bedlam* to *Gammer Gurton's Needle* and the new, longer title reduced in size to fit the vacancy.[31] How long ago, then, and from when, is 'not long ago'? Would a titlepage set up in type in 1563 be held for twelve years, awaiting printing? Were there editions of the play, as *Diccon of Bedlam* or *Gammer Gurton's Needle*, before 1575? If so no traces remain, yet Q survives in eleven copies, an exceptionally high number (compare *Roister Doister's* one and *The Old Wife's Tale's* four). The next known edition, of 1661, seems to have been printed directly from Q, preserving most of its errors. A scene in Francis Merbury's *The Marriage Between Wit and Wisdom* (1579) is modelled closely on action in *Gammer Gurton's Needle*, and many years later it was still being referred to familiarly as if it were well known.[32] And what could possibly have elicited a re-issue in 1661, the year after the Restoration, when plays like

---

[30] This aspect of the play is discussed in the section on 'Staging', below.

[31] Bradley's edition is in Gayley, pp. 195–261. The suggestion about the title-page is on p. 199. The only other extant play printed by Colwell, William Ingelend's *The Disobedient Child* (c. 1560), has the title in uniform type, unlike *GGN*, but also lacks the date.

[32] Bradbrook quotes the satirical play *Histriomastix* (1599), in which there is a reference to '*Mother Gurton's Needle*, a tragedy' in the repertoire of Sir Oliver Owlet's men (*Growth and Structure*, p. 41).

Gammer Gurton's Needle must have appeared quaint, to say the least?[33] There is a hidden history to *Gammer Gurton's Needle* of which occasional glimpses are caught, but which it is probably vain to hope to discover in full. Definite answers to the questions of authorship, date, staging conditions, and printing history are impossible, given the evidence available to us. But the needle was found at last; so too may be these lost data. None of these questions need be answered, or even asked, for the play's vitality, neatness of construction and earthy jocularity to be appreciated. As so much discussion has been generated by them, however, since the play first attracted the attention of those eighteenth- and nineteenth-century antiquaries, it is appropriate in a new edition to canvass the chief attempts to answer them.

With only the initial 'S' for guidance, and although the play's titlepage claims only that it was played at Christ's College, not that it was written by a member of that college, scholars have looked for a member of the college whose surname began with 'S', who was known to be involved in college dramatic activities, and whose tenure at the college could be interpreted as being 'not long' before 1562–3, assuming that the titlepage's 'played not long ago' dates from then and not from 1575. John Peile, when writing a history of the college, found in the Christ's College bursar's accounts that a certain 'Sir Stephenson' received payments for plays in 1550–1, 1551–2 and 1553–4.[34] Bradley was given access to the records and found a further reference to 'Mr Stevenson's play', in 1559–60. This clear proof that someone called Stevenson was involved in the production of plays at Christ's in the 1550s led Bradley to the 'highly probable' conclusion that 'Mr S.' was Stevenson. A William Stevenson was in fact a Fellow of the College, as a Bachelor of Arts (hence 'Sir', i.e., *dominus*) from 1550 to 1553 and again, as Master of Arts ('Mr') in 1559–60. He disappears from the list of Fellows (after March, 1554) and from the dramatic records (after Christmas,

<hr />

[33] The 1661 edition was published by, among others, Francis Kirkman (1632–c. 1680), author, publisher, bookseller and collector of old plays. It could well have been his copy of Q that provided the text for the reprint. See R. C. Bald, 'Francis Kirkman, Bookseller and Author', *MP*, 41 (1943–4), 17–32 (pp. 23–4). I am grateful to Mr Gervase Hood for this reference.

[34] John Peile, *Christ's College*, University of Cambridge College Histories (1900), p. 54. In fact, the 1553–4 entry reads 'Expended by Mr. Stephenson at setting furth of his plaie . . . '; Stevenson received his M.A. in 1553. Bradley was the first commentator to have the benefit of Peile's findings. 'The Academic Drama at Cambridge: Extracts from College Records' was edited by G. C. Moore Smith in *MSC*, II, pt. 2 (1923); the Christ's records, covering the years 1531 to 1568, are on pp. 204–9.

1553) in the interim. This was a time of persecution of Protestant Reformers under Queen Mary, and a number of Cambridge men were among the 'Marian exiles' in Europe during her reign. Christ's College was Edwardian (and later positively Puritan), in its sympathies. The Master, Richard Wilkes, was ejected in 1553 and there was a rapid turnover of personnel in the years immediately following. Very possibly Stevenson left or was forced out, returning in 1559 after the accession of Elizabeth had put an end to Bloody Mary's persecutions. He soon left the University for good, however, having received his B.D. in 1560. He was named to a prebend in Durham Cathedral in January, 1561, and he died in 1575, the year the play was published.[35].

Stevenson has been accepted as the play's author by a majority of scholars since Bradley. It should be noted that the Christ's College records do not say that Stevenson *wrote* plays. He received payment for disbursements connected with the *production* of plays. The Christ's records do not name plays. Some other colleges' accounts do, and there are many entries which take the form of those in the Trinity College records: 'Item paid to Mr Legge for ye expenses abought the settinge forthe of *Medea*' or 'to Master Shaclocke for the charges of *pseudolus*' (MSC, II.2, pp. 161, 163). The plays named are Roman plays, by Seneca and Plautus respectively, and Legge and Shacklock produced them. There are occasional references to unnamed 'English plays', and those may have been written as well as produced by members of the colleges. The evidence for Stevenson is strong, but entirely circumstantial. If *Gammer Gurton's Needle* is one of the plays mentioned in connection with his name in the accounts, it must have been written and produced between 1550 and 1553, or in 1559–60. The phrase 'in the king's name' in the play (V.ii, 234), if taken to refer to the actual state of affairs in England, would indicate a date of composition not later than mid-1553, when Edward VI died. On the other hand, a span of ten years or more does not sound like 'not long ago', while 1559–60 would be 'not long' (not many years anyway) before 1562–3, if the titlepage information is taken to date from the year of the S.R. entry. And 'in the king's name' may be no more than author's license; it is a play, after all, and may be deliberately set in a vaguely recent past. There is little or no topical allusion in the play, so dating from internal evidence is not possible.

Before Stevenson was nominated, two other candidates had been proposed. One, John Still, Bishop of Bath and Wells, was

---

[35] Details in *Biographical Register of Christ's College 1505–1905*, 2 vols (1910), I, 40–41.

suggested by Isaac Reed in 1782, and was disposed of in 1897; some library catalogues still enter the play under Still's name.[36] Stevenson's strongest rival is John Bridges, Dean of Salisbury Cathedral, later Bishop of Oxford, who left several theological treatises and translations. Against Bridges are the facts that he was not a Christ's College, but rather a Pembroke Hall man, and that his name does not, obviously, begin with 'S'. It ends with 's', and the suggestion has been made that this was a deliberate decoy to safeguard the author's anonymity.[37] The chief evidence for Bridges's authorship comes in the attribution made by 'Martin Marprelate', pseudonymous author of a series of Puritan pamphlets in the late 1580s in which the Anglican episcopate was virulently attacked. These pamphlets and the equally virulent (and scurrilous) rejoinders from the Anglican side, written by John Lyly and Thomas Nashe among others, constitute the notorious 'Marprelate Controversy'.[38]

One of the marred prelates was Dr John Bridges. He was by then Dean of Salisbury, and had written forcefully in defence of the Anglican cause against both Catholics and Puritans. His *Defence of the Government Established in the Church of England for Ecclesiastical Matters*, published in 1587, attracted the wrath of Martin. In 'The Epistle', published in October, 1588, Martin (possibly John Penry, who had written other anti-episcopal tracts in his own name) addresses Bridges:

> 'You have been a worthy writer, as they say, of a long time; your first book was a proper interlude, called *Gammer Gurton's Needle*. But I think that this trifle, which showeth the author to have had some wit and invention in him, was none of your doing, because your books seem to proceed from the brains of a woodcock, as having neither wit nor learning.'   (modernized; Boas, *UD*, p. 83)

This is scarcely an unambiguous ascription. Is emphasis to be put on the statement, 'your first book was . . . *Gammer Gurton's Needle*', or upon Martin's claim to disbelieve that Bridges was capable of the 'wit and invention' evinced in the play? However we choose to answer that, Martin must have had a reason for

---

[36] C. H. Ross, 'The Authorship of *Gammer Gurton's Needle*', *Anglia*, 19 (1897), 306–11.

[37] Joseph Hunter, quoted by Boas, *UD*, p. 84. Boas argues for Bridges's authorship, as does Ross (see n. 36).

[38] There are many accounts of the controversy. For a brief summary, see J. Dover Wilson, in *The Cambridge History of English Literature*, III: *Renascence and Reformation* (1908; 1932), pp. 374–98. Fuller treatments are William Pierce, *An Historical Introduction to the Marprelate Tracts* (1908), and Donald J. McGinn, *John Penry and the Marprelate Controversy* (New Brunswick, N.J., 1966).

mentioning (whether to affirm or to deny) Bridges's alleged authorship of the play. This was, after all, thirteen years after the publication of the only known edition of the play, and more than a quarter of a century after its probable date of composition. That it is not simply an isolated, wild shot is clear from two further specific allusions to the play in the sequel to 'The Epistle', called 'The Epitome', which appeared a month later. It too is addressed to Bridges. Martin threatens him:

> Let me take you again in such a prank, and I'll course you, as you were better to be seeking Gammer Gurton's needle, than come within my fingers. (Boas, *UD*, p. 84)

Later, Martin rebukes Bridges for asserting something without citing an authority for it, and asks where he found it: 'What if he found it in Hodge's breeches, seeking for Gammer Gurton's needle?' (*UD*, p. 84).

It is difficult to imagine why Martin would invent Bridges's authorship of the play. Even if that were credible as an interpretation of the first passage—he wished to damage Bridges's reputation by charging that he had written a coarse, decidedly unbishoplike play, or he pretended to have heard it said that Bridges wrote a play known to be witty, only so that he could declare it beyond the capacity of someone with the 'brains of a woodcock'—he would have little reason to continue to insist, by implication, upon the fabrication in his next pamphlet. The joke would have lost its point. It seems likely, then, that Bridges's name was associated with *Gammer Gurton's Needle*, even if only in university, church and literary circles; they would have been the main readership of the Marprelate tracts. Martin presumably hoped to score points by reminding his readers of the learned dean's less staid, more frivolous days as a young Cambridge don. Martin may have been mistaken. But John Penry, probable author of 'The Epistle' and 'The Epitome', had been supplied with slanderous material on important churchmen by those who engaged him to write the pamphlets. They may well have dug up the embarrassing fact that Bridges had had a hand in *Gammer Gurton's Needle* years earlier. Again, why would anyone bother to invent it? What would the title *Gammer Gurton's Needle* mean to readers twenty or thirty years after it was written if it were simply plucked from the air by Martin Marprelate and blindly ascribed to Bridges? There is no record of a denial by Bridges or anyone else.

As Boas points out, Bridges might well have had his play performed at Christ's or elsewhere, if his own college, Pembroke Hall, did little or nothing in that vein. Richard Legge, when master of Gonville and Caius College, had his Latin play, *Richardus Tertius*, performed at St. John's. Pembroke is not among the colleges for which dramatic records from the period survive. Bridges took his B.A. in 1556, his M.A. in 1560. 'Mr of Art' and 'not long ago', if the titlepage dates from 1562–3 at the latest, would make sense if they referred to Bridges and to a performance of the play at Christ's within the preceding two or three years. So Bridges, like Stevenson, was at Cambridge at the right time, and he did write; we have no evidence that William Stevenson did. The stumbling block is Martin Marprelate's credibility in a polemical pamphlet in which Bridges is his principal target and hits were to be scored by whatever means possible.

No one, so far as I know, has taken up Bradley's passing suggestion that Bridges may have revised Stevenson's earlier work, possibly for a revival in the early 1560s (Gayley, p. 200). Whether revision, collaboration, recasting or a case of Stevenson the producer putting on Bridges the author's play, *Gammer Gurton's Needle* may have been touched by both men. One might even speculate that publication of the play was deferred for so many years out of regard for the reputations of Stevenson and Bridges, both churchmen, and that when it was published in 1575, the year of Stevenson's death, Bridges was already so prominent in his profession that he wished not to acknowledge the play, or it was simply published without his express approval. If Stevenson did have anything to do with the play, alone or in collaboration, its publication in the year of his death, so many years after it seems to have been written and entered for printing, is another tantalizing bit which may or may not be a piece of the jigsaw puzzle.

As F. P. Wilson remarked with reference to another excellent anonymous play of the period, *Respublica*: 'There is a natural reluctance to allow a work that stands above the ruck to remain anonymous. We do not like to see valuables lying about unattached' (Wilson, p. 42). Despite our wish to father so lively a child on an identifiable individual, the evidence, either way, is simply not conclusive. Stevenson has 'become' the author by common assent in recent decades, but there is no proof that he wrote anything at all. It is only that his name begins with 'S', and that he appears in the Christ's College dramatic accounts between two and twelve years prior to the play's entry in the Stationers' Register, which constitute his claim. Bridges, a prolific writer, is named as author by a contemporary witness, whose credibility may be suspect but is not therefore necessarily to be discounted out of hand, and he appears not to have denied the attribution.

But the facts that 'S' is the wrong letter and Christ's the wrong college must be explained away. I am afraid that, unless further evidence comes to light, the author of *Gammer Gurton's Needle* must remain simply 'Mr S. Mr of Art'. 'S', after all, may stand for neither Stevenson nor Bridges, but only 'Somebody'.

This leaves the date uncertain as well, with 1550–53 and 1559–62 both possibilities. The latter is the *terminus a quo* if one prefers Bridges, and seems more likely if 'not long ago' means anything. But if 'in the king's name' is taken as referring to the actual English monarch at the time the play was written, the earlier date is forced upon us; no king reigned in England for fifty years after July, 1553. The play's glib irreverence toward saints, relics and the Virgin Mary, and the slight hints of anti-clerical satire (Prologue, 11. 9–10, and the treatment of Doctor Rat) make Mary's reign (mid-1553–58) seem somewhat less likely than either the latter years of Edward's or the first years of Elizabeth's. Common practice has attached 'c. 1553' to *Gammer Gurton's Needle* and, all in all, there seems no compelling reason to change to any other equally speculative date; 'c. 1550–60' may, however, better indicate the uncertainty.[39]

Martin Marprelate was right at least about *Gammer Gurton's Needle*'s 'wit and invention'. It is a *tour de force*, the clever, spirited, outrageous production of a witty, inventive, gifted dramatist. It is university students' entertainment, doubtless performed during some such time of seasonal merrymaking as the Christmas holidays when the Lord of Misrule, or Christmas Lord, presided. Such festivals of hierarchical inversion and licensed anarchy survived in universities and Inns of Court long after the church had suppressed them (Wickham, *EES*, III, 84). A very rare example of a university play in the vernacular, *Gammer Gurton's Needle* is pure low comedy, farce really, devoid of even the moderately corrective bias of Roman comedy, let alone the spiritual and moral didacticism of the moralities. In this respect, it is atypical of the majority of the comedies of the period, which retain something of the moralities' homiletic character.

Mr S. obviously knew the comedies of Plautus and Terence: he adopted their five-act structure, imposing it upon his native, vernacular and very homely matter.[40] The 'homely world of village japes and jealousies' recalls those of John Heywood's farces earlier in the century and of John Lydgate's *Mumming at Hertford*

---

[39] My own hesitant inclination, worth only a cautious footnote in view of the problems set out above, is toward Bridges and a date c. 1560.

[40] More will be said about Roman comedy's, particularly Terence's, influence in the introduction to *RD*, below.

from the early fifteenth century (c. 1425; *EES*, III, 208). The plot of *Gammer Gurton's Needle* is twofold. Gammer Gurton loses her needle. This domestic mischance sets her household in an uproar. Diccon, the 'Bedlam', comes upon the chaotic scene, and deliberately instigates further chaos 'for sport'. The dénouements of both plots, the finding of the needle and the exposure and 'punishment' of Diccon for his mischief-making, are neatly brought off concurrently in the finale, the longest scene of the play (V.ii). Gammer Gurton and her bellicose neighbour, Dame Chat, Gammer's slow-witted field hand, Hodge, the bibulous village curate Doctor Rat, the bailiff Master Bailey, the other servants and maids are the inhabitants of any small English village, 'the primitive human scenery of the English countryside'. Gammer Gurton's household are distinguished from the other characters by their dialect, the stage rustic which had become conventional by this time. The eponymous heroine herself may already have been a type of the provincial English countrywoman when the play was written.

The most interesting character, Diccon, exhibits the variety of influences and dramatic traditions which converge in the play. Though called 'the Bedlam', that is, a former inmate of St. Mary of Bethlehem Hospital in London, an insane asylum, he is far from mad.[41] Indeed, he has more wits than anyone else except Master Bailey. He lives by his wits, as he gleefully informs us in I.i, 1–6, 22–4. He may be a beggar, wandering from place to place, but he is clearly known to the villagers (II.ii, 22; II.iv, 7; V.ii, 151–3). In the farcical context of this play's world, Diccon is mischievous, no worse, but he owes as much to the Vices of the English moralities and interludes and the cheeky servants of the mystery cycles (e.g., Pikeharness in the Wakefield *Mactatio Abel*) as to the duplicitous, mocking pages, valets and messengers of Roman comedy.[42] He is also the presenter, the master of ceremonies, solicitous of his audience's enjoyment, calling for music between the acts. He thus straddles the boundary between play and audience, turning to the latter to explain and prepare, returning to the play to perform his catalytic role as trouble-maker. He speaks the brief epilogue.[43]

When Diccon, by his barefaced lies, has set Dame Chat and Gammer Gurton at odds, he clears off, having promised his

---

[41] See note on Diccon in Dramatis Personae, and compare Edgar's masquerade as Mad Tom in *King Lear*.

[42] Compare Merrygreek in *RD*, and see n. 26, above.

[43] In a recent production (1982) by the Medieval Players, Diccon also spoke the Prologue, which was accompanied by a dumb show, and then went straight into his own speech in I.i.

audience rare sport if once the two incensed dames should meet
(II.v). Their titanic battle, imitated from French farce and
fabliau, via such native examples as Heywood's *The Pardoner and
The Friar*, is the play's centrepiece (III.iii).[44] It is the first stage
fight in English drama between two pantomime dames (*EES*, III,
88). Not yet satisfied, Diccon lures Doctor Rat, the curate, into a
trap set at Diccon's suggestion by Dame Chat to catch a chicken
thief whom she supposes to be Hodge. Thus new characters, new
intrigue and more farcical knockabout are introduced in Act IV.
Act V brings in Master Bailey and his silent catchpole Scapethrift,
and sees the untangling of Diccon's well-spun web. The
construction is masterly, the work of a scholar well versed in
classical drama and its theory. The characters, language and
holiday hilarity are English through and through. The bumpy,
irregular verse, sometimes hexameters, sometimes fourteeners,
frequently not easily identifiable as any particular metre at all, is
an apt vehicle for the play's patently inconsequential matter.
There is some attempt to vary the prevailing long, 'tumbling' line,
as when Hodge and Diccon speak in six-line tail-rhyme stanzas in
II.i (continued, with a slightly longer line, by Diccon in II.ii), and
when Doctor Rat speaks in mainly four-stress lines at the end of
IV.iv.

Gammer Gurton's Needle has not always been well regarded. Its
obvious merits as high-spirited entertainment have been obscured
in the view of some critics by its crude language and especially by
its gleeful scatology. Its first modern editor, Bradley, sniffed at
'the very rudimentary kind of humour which turns on physically
disgusting suggestions no longer amusing to educated people'.
There was too much of 'this poor stuff' for Bradley's taste, but he
did discern 'real comedy, not quite of the lowest order' in some
scenes (Gayley, pp. 202–3).[45] Educated Victorians may not have
been amused; at least they would not have shown it. But neither
ought we to suppose, as patronizing critics used to do, that
educated Elizabethans were capable of appreciating only that
'very rudimentary kind of humour'. The play's excrementitious-
ness is a vital part of its holiday, anarchic, world-turned-upside-
down mood. It is college men's uproarious fun, loudly coarse,
childishly naughty. It is as misguided for post-Freudian critics to
descant archly upon 'the aesthetics of scatology' as it was for

[44] The Medieval Players performed *The Pardoner and the Friar* in a programme
with *GGN*. For the latter the actors wore masks, evoking a *commedia dell'arte* style.
[45] Compare another editor of the play, Brett-Smith: 'Scholarly persons, living in
academic celibacy, have often a singular taste for the manners of low life, and find
in the crude humour and gross speech of the rustic a diversion from the niceties of
classical culture' (p. vii).

Bradley, Brett-Smith and others primly to cluck their tongues, or for William Hazlitt to speculate solemnly upon the impact of the loss of Gammer Gurton's 'valuable instrument of household industry' on the socio-economic system of the parish.[46] An old English proverbial expression, that something is 'not worth a needle', provides the key to the play's 'meaning'.[47] It is a trifle, written, one may imagine, on a college common room wager: 'I'll bet you that I can write a classical five-act comedy about anything you care to name.' 'You're on. How about a needle?' Mr S. would have won his wager handsomely.

ROISTER DOISTER

To turn from *Gammer Gurton's Needle* to its near contemporary, *Roister Doister*, is to turn from a play that, in the opinion of more than one critic, sinks to the 'physically disgusting', to 'one of the cleanest comedies in the sixteenth century'.[48] *Roister Doister* was written for schoolboys, not university men, and in it Roman comedy is masterfully adapted to the moral aims of Humanistic education in Reformation England.

The sole surviving copy of *Roister Doister*, in the Eton College library, has no titlepage. (One may well share F. S. Boas's inclination to wish that the extant copies of *Gammer Gurton's Needle* had, like the Eton copy of *Roister Doister*, lost their titlepages, in view of the knotty scholarly problems posed by the former (Boas, pp. xiv–xv)). The lucky survival of one copy of the play is matched by the lucky chance of a reference in another sixteenth-century book which identifies its author beyond doubt. Thomas Wilson was no Martin Marprelate. A close friend and former Eton pupil of Nicholas Udall's, he wrote important books on rhetoric and logic, an attack upon usury which is of great interest to social historians, and he translated Demosthenes. He also had a parliamentary, legal and diplomatic career, becoming a secretary of state in Elizabeth's reign. Udall wrote a prefatory verse for Wilson's *Art of Rhetoric*, published in 1553. The first recorded use of the word 'roister' occurs in Wilson's *Rule of Reason*, a treatise on logic, first published in 1551. In the third

---

[46] William B. Toole, 'The Aesthetics of Scatology in *Gammer Gurton's Needle*', *ELN*, 10 (1973), 252–8; Hazlitt, *Lectures on the Dramatic Literature of the Age of Elizabeth* (1820), Lecture V, in *The Complete Works of William Hazlitt*, ed. P. P. Howe, 21 vols (1930–34), VI, 286.

[47] As in *Ancrene Wisse*, ed. Geoffrey Shepherd (1959), p. 25., l. 39.

[48] W. L. Edgerton, *Nicholas Udall*, Twayne's English Authors Series, (New York, 1965), p. 23.

edition of this work, dated 'January, 1553' on the titlepage, Wilson quotes in full both versions of the letter written by Ralph and misread by Merrygreek (III.iv, v), citing them as, respectively, 'an example of such doubtful writing, which by reason of pointing may have double sense, and contrary meaning, taken out of an interlude made by Nicholas Udall', and 'the contrary sense of the same in the same words'.[49] W. L. Edgerton (pp. 90–93) has shown that the date on the titlepage of Wilson's book refers to the calendar year 1553 and not, as had been thought, to the legal year which began on March 25th, which would have made 'January, 1553' mean January, 1554. Thus both the author's identity and the latest possible date of composition of the play are supplied fortuitously, and fortunately, by Wilson's choice of illustration.

In the year 1566–7 Thomas Hackett was licensed to print 'a play intituled *Rauf Ruyster Duster*', and the surviving copy was probably published at that time.[50] Udall's fame is sufficient explanation for the sudden publication of his play a decade after his death. The personal pronouns in the prayer to the queen which ends the play would have been altered to the feminine, since the original addressee was probably King Edward VI. Wilson's quotation from the play in a book published six months before Mary Tudor came to the throne in the summer of 1553 makes it obvious that it was not written for her entertainment at court at Christmas that year. That used to be the accepted occasion for the probable first performance of *Roister Doister*.[51] It seems likely, however, that it was performed at Windsor Castle in September, 1552, before the young, ailing King Edward. Udall had been made a canon of St. George's Chapel, Windsor, in December, 1551, and took up residence there in the summer of 1552. *Roister Doister* calls for several songs, a peal of bells, a psalmody and a mock-requiem. Windsor Chapel, with its choristers and choirmaster, John Marbecke, a person of some consequence in the history of English church music, afforded Udall the requisite forces, and the king's visit a few months after Udall's arrival at Windsor provided the occasion for his comedy.[52]

---

[49] *The Rule of Reason, conteinyng the Arte of Logique. Sette furthe in Englishe, and newly corrected by Thomas Wilson.* Anno Domini. M.D.LIII. Mense Ianuarij. Fols. 66v–67v.

[50] Another, 'immaculate', copy may have existed as recently as 1922. See Edgerton, p. 104.

[51] See, e.g., William Peery, 'The Prayer for the Queen in *Roister Doister*', *UTSE*, 27 (1948), 222–33. Earlier scholars assumed that the play was written during Udall's time at Eton (e.g., Flügel and *DNB*). Details of Udall's career are from Edgerton.

[52] On the date of *RD*, see also Scheurweghs, pp. lv–lx; he too argues for 1552.

Nicholas Udall would be a figure of considerable stature in the Tudor literary landscape even if he had not written this comedy or it had not survived at all. Born in Southampton about 1504, he attended Winchester College, then Corpus Christi College, Oxford, 'a beehive of humanism'. There he was taught by and associated with some of the leading Humanists of the time: Thomas Lupset, Edward Wotton, John Leland, the Spaniard Juan Luis Vives. He received his B.A. in 1524 and became Fellow and lecturer in logic and Greek in 1526. Udall's literary career probably began at Oxford. He may well have written plays, including possibly the comical interlude *Thersites*, which is known to have been performed some years later, in 1537, at court.[53] His earliest known writings are verses, in Latin and English, for the coronation of Anne Boleyn in 1533.[54] His first substantial work was *Flowers for Latin Speaking Selected and Gathered out of Terence* (1534). In the same year, Udall became headmaster at Eton, a post he retained for seven years.

The second-century B.C. Roman dramatist Terence was a staple of the school curriculum throughout the Middle Ages. As early as the tenth century, a German nun, Hrotswitha, wrote plays explicitly modelled on Terence's. His comedies were felt by schoolmasters to be rather more wholesome and edifying than those of Plautus, and his Latin rather more eloquent.[55] Udall's aim, in culling the best passages from Terence and translating them into English, was to provide pupils with examples for memorization and emulation. Udall shared the Humanists' intense concern that the modern, vernacular languages be shown to be as rich, expressive and eloquent as the classical languages. Udall was not alone in particularly admiring Terence: both Erasmus and the German Reformer Philip Melanchthon wrote commentaries on his comedies. Udall's translating and annotating of the 'best bits' from Terence, appears, in retrospect, a logical preliminary to the writing of a full-length Roman-style comedy, indebted to both Terence and Plautus, but in English and

[53] A prayer at the end of the surviving text of *Thersites* contains a reference to the queen and the infant prince Edward: Edward VI was born on 12 October 1537 and his mother, Jane Seymour, died twelve days later.

[54] Udall complimented Anne by making her the surprise recipient of the golden apple in a pageant of the Judgement of Paris. George Peele was to honour Anne's daughter Elizabeth in the same terms half a century later.

[55] The vast importance of Terence and Plautus in the Renaissance is fully treated by T. W. Baldwin in *Shakespere's Five-Act Structure* (Urbana, Illinois, 1947), which contains detailed discussion of Udall's use of Roman comedy. In *William Shakespere's Small Latine and Lesse Greeke* (Urbana, 1944), Baldwin demonstrates the importance of *Flowers for Latin Speaking* in Tudor education.

adapted specifically to the education and entertainment of contemporary English schoolboys. *Flowers for Latin Speaking* became a standard school textbook.

Udall's tenure at Eton ended abruptly in 1541, when he was dismissed for reasons that remain unclear, despite contemporary documents that ought to clarify them. He appears to have committed an offence, which may have been as scandalous as engaging in homosexual relations with boys at the school, or as (relatively) venial as conniving at the sale of stolen school property. Whatever he did, he spent only a short time in the Marshalsea, and his reputation suffered no lasting damage.[56] Within a short time he was undertaking scholarly work under the patronage of Queen Catherine Parr. He published his *Apophthegmes*, translated from Erasmus, and began working on translations of Erasmus's Latin commentaries on the New Testament. A collaborator on the latter project was Princess Mary Tudor. This early association may help to explain Udall's indemnity, even advancement, when the ardently Catholic Mary became queen.

Udall was thus extending the popularizing effort of the greatest Humanist scholar of the age, who had digested and summarized the masses of learned commentary on the Bible. Udall's English text of the paraphrases, printed alongside that of the English Great Bible, was published in 1549. He had both overseen the whole project and himself translated the paraphrases on Matthew, Luke and possibly Acts. Like his *Flowers for Latin Speaking*, *The Paraphrase of Erasmus* was immensely successful. It became, by a royal injunction issued even before the work was completed, the prescribed biblical commentary, to be owned and used by 'every parson, vicar, curate, chantry-priest and stipendiary' in the country. The English Bible, the *Book of Common Prayer* and *The Paraphrase of Erasmus* in Nicholas Udall's English translation, lay together in the pulpit of every church in England.

Udall wrote other works, including a lost play, *Ezechias*, which was performed at Cambridge before Queen Elizabeth eight years after its author's death. This is not so surprising, since Udall had chosen his Old Testament character, the godly king Ezechias (Hezekiah) with Henry VIII in mind. He had exhorted the young Edward VI in his lengthy preface to the king in the first volume of the *Paraphrase*, to follow the example of the righteous boy-king, Josiah, Hezekiah's great-grandson, and not that of

---

[56] See *DNB*, Scheurweghs, pp. xxiv–xxxiii, and Edgerton, pp. 37–48. Edgerton argues, not entirely convincingly, that the word 'buggery' in the Privy Council Register is a mistake for 'burglary'.

Josiah's wicked grandfather and father, Manasseh and Amon. Zealous Protestants in the early years of Elizabeth's reign would have seen further parallels, between the papist Mary and wicked Manasseh, who restored the pagan gods, and between Henry's true heir, Protestant Elizabeth, and the good king, Josiah. Other plays have been attributed to Udall. They include the interlude *Jack Juggler*, the biblical play *Jacob and Esau*, and the excellent pro-Marian morality, *Respublica*.[57]

Thus Udall's work as a Humanist educator and Reformation apologist lived after him. He ended his days a schoolmaster once again. He was appointed headmaster of Westminster School in 1555 and died a year later, in December, 1556. His best-known work, *Roister Doister*, should be seen in the light of his entire literary and scholarly career. The play may stand out in the history of English drama, but it is very much of a piece with Udall's other writings. It may not be a typical English play, even of its period, but it is typical of the Humanist, Reformer, classicist and educator, Nicholas Udall.

Terence, who was, in T. W. Baldwin's words, 'at the very foundation of the grammar school', may or may not have divided his plays into five acts. Donatus thought he did, and it was Donatus, a fourth-century grammarian who wrote commentaries on Terence, whose 'rules' were inherited by Renaissance students along with the plays themselves. Other classical theorists, including Horace and Aristotle, were interpreted in the light of Donatus. With Terence pre-eminent and Plautus to complement him, and Donatus's rules for authority, it is scarcely surprising that classical comedy was imitated and adapted by Renaissance vernacular writers before classical tragedy. Udall seems to have been the first English dramatist to write a 'regular' (i.e., according to Donatus's rules) vernacular comedy. But *Roister Doister* is not only modelled upon the Roman comic structure. It also draws upon and echoes particular Roman comedies. Those recollections and echoes would have been part of the fun for the Windsor Chapel boys who first rehearsed and performed this first regular English comedy.

The Roman plays to which *Roister Doister* is most indebted are Plautus's *Miles Gloriosus* (*The Braggart Warrior*) and Terence's

---

[57] See G. Dudok, 'Has *Jacke Juggler* been written by the same person as *Ralph Roister Doister*?', *Neophilologus*, 1 (1915), 50–62; W. H. Williams, 'The Date and Authorship of *Jacke Jugeler*', *MLR*, 7 (1912), 289–95; W. W. Greg, ed., *Respublica*, EETS, O.S. 226 (1952), pp. viii–xviii; and Marie Axton, ed., *Three Tudor Classical Interludes* (Cambridge, 1982), pp. 2–3.

Eunuchus (The Eunuch).[58] Terence's subplot provided Udall with the main features of his plot. The cowardly braggart Thraso, aided and abetted by the parasite Gnatho, woos Thais, who remains faithful to her absent lover Phaedria. There is an abortive assault by Thraso upon Thais's house, and then a reconciliation, with Thraso invited to Phaedria's house. Udall substitutes a chaste, dignified Christian widow for the sprightly, conniving Roman girl. Her very name, Christian Custance, suggests fortitude and fidelity. She likens her plight, when her betrothed, Gawin Goodluck, suspects her of encouraging Roister Doister in his advances, to those of biblical heroines Esther and Susanna (V.iii). Udall also expands Gnatho's role as a fun-maker. Matthew Merrygreek is only nominally a parasite, and is as near a relation to the morality Vices as to the Roman freeloaders. He enters singing, like the Vice, and after announcing his intentions in I.i, spends the rest of the play mocking, insulting and gulling Roister Doister, and then brings about the comic dénouement with the reconciliation of his foolish, fearful victim to Goodluck and Dame Custance.

Udall's anglicized names and liberal use of English proverbs, songs and colloquialisms make the play unmistakably English, despite its Roman antecedents, but it is as free from coarseness as *Gammer Gurton's Needle* is full of it. He further introduces Dame Custance's three chirpy, chatty maids in place of the courtesan's knowing maidservant of Roman comedy. As the Prologue assures us, there is not a hint of bawdiness: 'All scurrility we utterly refuse'. The ridiculous Roister Doister never even looks like posing a serious threat to Dame Custance's virtue. Thus defused, Udall's adaptation retains none of the sexual innuendo and occasional nastiness of its prototypes. Roister Doister himself, though the titular target of the comedy's invective against vainglory, needs Merrygreek's incessant reminding to bear himself like a proud, bold hero. He is like a rag doll, propped up or knocked about at will by the ebullient Merrygreek. The 'serious' characters—Dame Custance, Goodluck, Sim Suresby the faithful servant, Tristram Trusty the loyal friend—are never allowed to waver. The bourgeois morality of the solid London citizenry triumphs. By making them as 'straight' as possible, and turning the *miles gloriosus* into a nincompoop and the parasite into a good-humoured prankster who has the confidence of the

---

[58] Detailed analysis of parallels between *RD* and its Roman models is made by D. L. Maulsby, 'The Relations between Udall's *Roister Doister* and the Comedies of Plautus and Terence', *Englische Studien*, 38 (1907), 251–77. See also Baldwin, *Five-Act Structure* (n. 55); Edgerton, pp. 94–101; Scheurweghs, pp. lx–lxxi.

heroine and her friends and of the audience, Udall achieved his two aims of instructing and entertaining. He was well acquainted with Horace's dictum that poetry should be both *utile* and *dulce*, should both teach and delight. 'Mirth with modesty' and 'very virtuous lore' are claimed for the play in its Prologue. There are, besides, a practical lesson in punctuation in the letter episode, several songs, a mock-requiem, sham battles and much marching about with drums. A mêlée in which Roister Doister is the recipient of Merrygreek's intentionally errant blows recalls Heywood's farces and *Gammer Gurton's Needle*. The boy players, as well as the audience, were meant to enjoy themselves.

The play performs better than it reads. Although the hexameter is the dominant line, the verse of Roister Doister is as difficult to scan as that of *Gammer Gurton's Needle*. In Merrygreek's first speech, for instance, many lines could be read as either pentameters or hexameters, and few lines maintain a single metre throughout. These lines near the end of Merrygreek's speech might be read as irregular trochaic hexameters or as anapestic tetrameters (following an initial iamb):

> I can when I will make him merry and glad,
> I can when me lust make him sorry and sad.   (I.i, 59–60)

Both Udall and Mr S. were writing when the syllabic-stress system of English verse scansion was not yet established; compare the irregular metres of *Tottel's Miscellany* (1557), for example. Dramatists in the first half of the sixteenth century, seeking a more natural medium, broke away from the formal stanzas of much of the cycle drama, and many of them employed a wide variety of verse forms and line lengths. Udall, like Mr S., sticks largely to the long-lined rhymed couplet, but maintains somewhat more consistently a dominant metre, the hexameter. He may have been attempting to approximate the Latin *senarius* (iambic hexameter, in which much variation was permitted). In passages of stichomythia, like the battle scenes (IV.vii, viii), there is clearly no attempt to preserve regular metre.[59]

It would be misguided to judge Udall's dramatic verse, or that of Mr S., by the standard of Marlowe's or Shakespeare's blank verse, although we may, with F. P. Wilson, 'be thankful that before the century was out the poets found a law of metre within which they could permit themselves an infinite liberty of rhythm' (Wilson, p. 15). The unpredictability of Udall's and Mr S.'s 'tumbling verse' is at least preferable to the 'monotonous

---

[59] On the verse of *RD* and *GGN*, see J. E. Bernard, Jr., *The Prosody of the Tudor Interlude* (New Haven, 1939; repr. Hamden, Conn., 1969), pp. 215–19.

certainties' of the dramatic verse of the 1560s, '70s and early '80s. Sackville and Norton were the first to use blank verse for a play; their *Gorboduc* was written c. 1561. But blank verse remained an inert medium until Marlowe demonstrated its potential in the late 1580s. The technical innovations of the 1560s and 1570s in the writing of plays were as important in the subsequent history of English drama as the building of The Theatre and the purchase of Blackfriars in 1576 were for the playing of them. Mr S. and Nicholas Udall excelled as playwrights with the tools at their disposal, but they happened to stand on the far side of those crucial decades. George Peele stood on the near.

THE OLD WIFE'S TALE

The third play in this volume is 'odd man out' (perhaps 'odd woman' is more appropriate). Much of what was said in the first part of this introduction was intended to indicate the context in which mid-century dramatists like Mr S. and Udall wrote, and to dispel the persistent notion that English drama between the religious cycles and moralities and the arrival on the scene of Marlowe and his contemporaries was a non-event. The decades between the 1550s and the 1590s, in drama as well as poetry, were a period of experimentation, expansion, absorption and adaptation. Tragedy and historical drama, pastoral, mythological drama and the masque followed comedy in becoming acclimatized. The theatrical milieu which George Peele entered in the early 1580s was vastly different from that of the early 1550s. The acting companies, men's and boys', had permanent homes in the London theatres and the royal chapels and choir schools, although they continued also to tour in the provinces as their predecessors had done. By the time Peele wrote *The Old Wife's Tale*, Marlowe, Kyd, Lyly and Greene had written most if not all of their dramatic works.[60] Marlowe and Greene, and perhaps Kyd, were dead. Shakespeare had written several comedies and history plays. Peele's play belongs, chronologically and qualitatively, to the Elizabethan Golden Age.

Peele came by his gift naturally. His father wrote pageants for the city of London and, in a more mundane vein, treatises on

[60] I assume, as scholars have done for two hundred years, that the titlepage's 'G.P.' is Peele. The ascription was first made in writing by Isaac Reed in 1782.

bookkeeping.[61] Peele studied in the school of Christ's Hospital where his father was clerk, and at Christ Church, Oxford. He took his B.A. in 1577 and his M.A. in 1579, having successfully petitioned the university to reduce the three-year residence period normally required of candidates for the higher degree. Like Udall, he undoubtedly wrote while at Oxford. A translation of one of Euripides's Iphigenia plays is lost, its existence attested to by surviving commendatory Latin verses by Peele's kinsman, William Gager, who also wrote Latin plays. Peele married an heiress whose inheritance embroiled him in a series of lawsuits. In the highly litigious Elizabethan age, it was only to be expected.[62]

Peele's earliest surviving dramatic work was a mythological extravaganza presented at court before Queen Elizabeth in or sometime after 1581. In *The Arraignment of Paris*, the first English play to call itself 'a pastoral', Peele flattered the queen through the same device Nicholas Udall had used half a century earlier to flatter her mother, Anne Boleyn. The play was unsuccessful, no royal patronage was forthcoming, and Peele eked out a living writing civic pageants as his father had done, and plays for the public theatres in the second decade or so of their existence. He was not a schoolmaster like Udall, nor a young don providing idle entertainment for colleagues and students, but one of the first generation of professional authors in England, depending solely on his pen for his livelihood.[63] A 'University Wit' like Marlowe, Greene, Lodge and Nashe, he brought his learning to his profession as a public entertainer. Like them too, he tried a variety of literary and dramatic forms. He did not follow Greene, Lodge and Nashe into prose romance, satirical pamphlets and underworld potboilers, but he did write narrative poems, occasional pieces for royal tournaments and an Order of the Garter investiture, as well as the civic pageants and poems for anthologies such as *The Phoenix Nest*. In drama, he tried anti-Spanish patriotism in *The Battle of Alcazar*, seizing, like many others, the opportunity for such stuff afforded by the famous defeat of the

---

[61] Biographical data are from David H. Horne, *The Life and Minor Works of George Peele*, vol I in the Yale edition of *The Life and Works of George Peele*, gen. ed., C. T. Prouty (New Haven, 1952), pp. 1–131. L.R.N. Ashley's *George Peele* in Twayne's English Authors Series (New York, 1970), is sometimes inaccurate.

[62] For the extraordinary tangle of lawsuits in which Peele's contemporary fellow-poet, Thomas Lodge, was involved, see Charles J. Sisson, 'Thomas Lodge and his Family', in *Thomas Lodge and Other Elizabethans*, ed. Sisson (Cambridge, Mass., 1933), pp. 1–164.

[63] His wife's inheritance may have been consumed by lawsuits. At any rate, he was borrowing money by 1587, and in 1596 sent his ten-year-old daughter to present his poem, *The Tale of Troy*, to Lord Burleigh with a plea for financial aid.

Armada in 1588. He wrote an English history, *Edward I*, and one of the last biblical dramas of the age, *David and Bethsabe*.

None of these plays, however, is as brilliant or as curious as *The Old Wife's Tale*, entered in the Stationers' Register in April, 1595, and published that year.[64] The titlepage claim that it was 'played by the Queen's Majesty's players' is impossible to verify, and the play has much in it that suggests child rather than adult actors. The Queen's Men broke up in May, 1594, according to Philip Henslowe, and they would probably have sold the plays in their possession to publishers before then.[65] There is a close relationship between *The Old Wife's Tale* and Greene's *Orlando Furioso*, but that play too cannot be dated with any degree of certainty.[66] It was published in mid-1594 but the suggestion that Peele knew and borrowed from that quarto must be set against the theory that *The Old Wife's Tale* was disposed of by the Queen's Men when they dissolved shortly before *Orlando Furioso* was printed. Peele may have seen Greene's play performed some time before it was published and have made his 'borrowings' from memory. Greene's play contains a clear allusion to the defeat of the Armada and so was written after 1588; it is usually dated c. 1592. If, as seems likely, Peele owed something to *Orlando Furioso*, his play may reasonably be assigned to the year c. 1593–4.

Titlepage claims that Elizabethan plays were performed by one or another of the leading companies of the day are of questionable validity. Publishers wanted to sell books and might stretch the truth even when they did not prevaricate outright. The number of plays glibly attributed to Shakespeare in the early seventeenth century is an example of the license play publishers allowed themselves in advertizing their wares. We cannot know that *The Old Wife's Tale* was not played by the Queen's Men, however. As in the case of *Gammer Gurton's Needle*, information supplied on a titlepage raises questions and opens channels of speculation which one feels obliged to pursue while suspecting that they may peter out. It is possible that Peele may have written the play for a boy's company, from whom the Queen's Men somehow, at some time, acquired it. The large number of female parts, the larger number

[64] I have made the obvious modernization in the play's title, a move resisted by editors to date: the 'tale' is the one told by Madge, 'the old wife', and the singular possessive of 'wife' is 'wife's'. The S.R. entry reads: 'a pleasant Conceipte called the owlde wifes tale'. But 'wives' is common for the singular possessive in Elizabethan English; see, e.g., W. Warner's translation of *Menaechmi* (1595): 'cloake of my wives' (I.ii); 'Hercules wives father' (V.i).

[65] *Henslowe's Diary*, ed. R. A. Foakes and R. T. Rickert (Cambridge, 1961), p. 7. On the Queen's Men, see Chambers, *ES*, II, 104–15.

[66] See notes to Dramatis Personae, l. 13, and ll. 778–80.

of minor characters including 'extras' who sing and dance, the songs, and the whole fantastical, lighthearted atmosphere of the play suggest children. Some doubling is possible; Antic and Clunch go out, doubtless to play other parts. But ten characters, including the three spectators, are present for the finale. Perhaps Peele, like Udall, wanted to provide parts for as many young performers as he could. Several characters appear very briefly indeed, speak few or no lines and are not, in some cases, seen or heard from again (e.g., Venelia, Lampriscus, the Friar, the Hostess). Several of the male characters are, or could be, children or young adolescents (the three pages, the two brothers, Booby, Corebus, Wiggen, Jack). Erestus and Eumenides are young men. It is possible that the text we have represents a scaled-down revision, for a company on tour in the provinces, of a play written originally for children and for a special occasion.[67]

The childlike quality of the play, its air of ethereal, long-ago-and-far-away romance or fairytale, combined with the unmistakably English rusticity of Madge and Clunch and the 'local colour' of the churchyard scene, the liberal use of folklore motifs, legends and proverbs, and the multiple frame (play-within-a-tale-within-a-play), make *The Old Wife's Tale* unique in English drama. Such variegation in so slight a fabric (1170 lines in Q) makes it difficult to know what sort of play it really is. As Harold Jenkins puts it, after listing half a dozen different verdicts by critics: 'the quality of its appeal is so intangible as to be very difficult to assess'.[68] Its very brevity and the presence of glaring inconsistencies and confusions in the text pose the further question of whether it is, as it stands, fragmentary or whole. Is what we have in Q the play, the whole play and nothing but the play that George Peele wrote?

Sir Walter Greg declared that 'the quarto almost certainly represents a mutilated text and the indications of staging are confused'.[69] There is strong evidence that the printer's copy was an authorial manuscript draft (foul papers), not yet revised to its final 'fair' form.[70] The language of stage directions and some other features suggest the author in the process of sketching out his action and characters, not yet thinking about the practicalities of staging or having yet sorted out all his characters' names and

[67] Patricia Binnie records the opinions of two producers of the play that it may have been written for children (p. 34, n. 84).

[68] 'Peele's *Old Wives' Tale*', *MLR*, 34 (1939), 177–85; repr. in Max Bluestone and Norman Rabkin, eds., *Shakespeare's Contemporaries* (Englewood Cliffs, N.J., 1961), pp. 22–30 (p. 23).

[69] Greg, *OWT*, p. vii.

[70] The evidence is adduced in considerable detail by Hook, pp. 341–56.

roles. Stage directions like 'Hear a dog bark' (50), "Strikes Booby blind' (549), 'Huanebango is deaf and cannot hear' (631), and 'Enter Jack, invisible' (788) are narrative or explanatory rather than directive. The prodigal number of speaking parts (24) augmented by mutes (Venelia, the Furies) and singing harvest-men and fiddlers, bespeaks the 'fine frenzy' of the poet-author rather than the practical economy of a theatrical reviser. The Booby-Corebus confusion, the multiplicity of names for the Churchwarden and, on the other hand, the casual introduction, late in the play, of the names of important characters also are not typical of the traces left in other Elizabethan dramatic texts by anyone concerned about or involved in the actual performance.[71]

Establishing the printer's copy as authorial foul papers does not, however, resolve Jenkins's worry: 'Is there not still something unsatisfactory about the play as we have it? Is it not *too* huddled, do not the figures come and go *too* abruptly, are not one or two of the themes *too* slightly handled?' (p. 23). Jenkins's 'general impression' of the play is that it is an abridgement, cut by a reviser for performance on tour by a smaller-than-usual company. In the longer, original version postulated by Jenkins, there would be more exposition, Venelia would speak, Lampriscus would re-appear, we would see the blinded Booby meeting his sweet but ugly wife Celanta, as we see the deafened Huanebango meeting his beautiful virago Zantippa. The finale would bring all the characters back, and all would be seen—and heard—to be released from the slain conjurer's spells. Scenes such as Sacra-pant's and Delia's interview with the Friar (362–80) would be longer, with more being made of the Friar's satirical set-piece on usurers. So too would the meeting of Eumenides and Delia (824–41), the climax of the hero's quest and the rescue of the main heroine, be more fully enacted. Without attempting to write the missing play as Jenkins wishes to do, I am inclined to agree with him that there must once have been more to the play than is preserved in the 1595 quarto. Arguments that the terseness, disjointedness and sketchiness of the play are appropriate to a tale told by a forgetful old woman are too facile. Would such a tale be muddled *like that*? And would that in any case explain the real problems, like missing entrances and exits and other stage directions, the Booby-Corebus confusion, inexplicable shifts from verse to prose and vice-versa, or the apparent doubling of the abduction-and-enchantment plots (Sacrapant-Erestus-Venelia and Sacrapant-Eumenides-Delia), with the former left in such an undeveloped state? Nothing that we know about Elizabethan

---

[71] See notes on Dramatis Personae, below.

dramaturgy accounts for a complete play of less than 1200 lines, with the plethora of bit parts and undeveloped plots that distinguish *The Old Wife's Tale*.

But can the quarto text both derive from authorial foul papers and be a revision for performance by a touring company? The only way that an affirmative answer can be accommodated is to argue that Peele himself provided a scaled-down version of his own play for the touring party of Queen's Men. This is not at all improbable, especially if the play had been performed originally at court or for some special occasion. If the play were written for boys, some boys might well have gone with some of the Queen's men on tour. The quarto text, with its undeveloped plot, abbreviated scenes and sketchily-drawn characters, allows for, even asks for, expansion and extemporization. Peele wrote out a basic script, with all the characters included, which the players could adapt, extemporizing *ad lib*. This is, of course, speculation, as all ideas about the play's original state must be. It cannot be proved that the text has been cut, however short and unsatisfactory it may appear to us. It *may* have been written by Peele exactly as we have it, bar a few printers' blunders. The only *Old Wife's Tale* that critic and producer have to deal with, in any case, is the one preserved in the 1595 quarto.[72]

Critical views of *The Old Wife's Tale* have, for the most part, divided between those which appreciate its folktale quality, its fairy-world, dream-like enchantment, and those which see it as parody, satire, burlesque, farce, 'a saucy challenge of romance', in F. B. Gummere's words.[73] The truth, as usual, lies somewhere between these exclusive extremes, or rather subsumes them. Herbert Goldstone identified the play's distinctive quality as one of interplay between contrasting, even seemingly incompatible, styles and genres. The fullest development of this synthesizing

[72] For other views of the text and its puzzles, see Hook's judicious discussion (pp. 341–56); Binnie, pp. 6–20; S. Musgrove, 'Peele's *Old Wives Tale*: An Afterpiece?', *AUMLA*, 23 (1965), 86–95.

[73] Among studies which take the first view are Gwenan Jones, 'The Intention of Peele's *Old Wives Tale*', *Aberystwyth Studies*, 7 (1925), 79–93; Thorlief Larson, '*The Old Wives Tale* by George Peele', *Transactions of the Royal Society of Canada*, 29 (1935), 157–70; and M. C. Bradbrook, 'Peele's *Old Wives' Tale*: A Play of Enchantment', *ES*, 43 (1962), 323–30. The other view was first put, in passing, by Gummere (Gayley, p. 346). More recent extensions of it are by Ashley, *George Peele*, esp. pp. 131–6; and John Doebler, 'The Tone of George Peele's *The Old Wives' Tale*', *ES*, 53 (1972), 412–21.

view is by Joan C. Marx in a recent essay.[74] She argues that the play is:

> a comedy composed of several genres: folktale, romance, folk ritual, and farce. Each of the genres appears in 'straight', unparodied form, and is juxtaposed with the others; no one of them rules the entire play (p. 118).

This eclecticism is what gives Peele's play its unique flavour. Whatever his intention may have been—and if the text we have is in any way incomplete, we cannot begin to guess at that —the effect is both laughter and delight, as Sir Philip Sidney distinguished them.[75] The ludicrous bumptiousness of the braggart Huanebango (cousin germane to Roister Doister), and the broad knockabout comedy of the churchyard scene as well as the rustic jocularity of the frame material, provoke laughter, derisive on the one hand, good-humoured on the other. The romance of Eumenides's and the brothers' quest for the spellbound maiden Delia, held captive by the sorcerer Sacrapant who has also turned a handsome young man into an old one (with the added indignity of being changed into a bear at night) while his beloved Venelia runs through the wood, maddened by grief, induces pleasure of a different kind.[76] At least it will if played sensitively, or read with an awareness of the genres and conventions that Peele brought together and played off against one another. The ancient folk motif of the Grateful Dead, in the person of Jack the helpful ghost, is a further strand in Peele's charming tapestry.[77]

It has been suggested that *The Old Wife's Tale* is 'essentially about' giving (Binnie, p. 14). This would seem to be more a distinguishing trait of the sympathetic characters in the play—the Old Man, Lampriscus, Booby, Eumenides, Jack, as well as Clunch and Madge who give shelter, food and entertainment—than something so studiedly didactic as 'essentially about' implies. The

---

[74] Goldstone, 'Interplay in Peele's *The Old Wives Tale*', *Boston University Studies in English*, 4 (1960), 202–13; Marx, ' "Soft, Who Have We Here?": The Dramatic Technique of *The Old Wives Tale*', *Renaissance Drama*, 12 (1981), 117–43. Marx's article is valuable and her reading sympathetic, though she makes overmuch of some points.

[75] *An Apology for Poetry*, ed. Geoffrey Shepherd (1965), pp. 136–7.

[76] Critics have noticed the parallel between Peele's Eumenides-brothers-Delia-Sacrapant plot and that of Milton's masque *Comus*, and have usually made gratuitous comparisons, to Peele's detriment.

[77] For full discussion of the folktale, fairytale and folk play sources of *OWT*, see esp. Hook, pp. 319–41; Sarah L. C. Clapp, 'Peele's Use of Folklore in *The Old Wives Tale*', *UTSE*, 6 (1926), 146–56; Charles A. Adams, 'The Tales in Peele's *Old Wives' Tale*', *Midwest Folklore*, 13 (1962), 13–20.

traditional moralities of chivalric romance, of folktale, of heroic legend, are presented in uncomplicated, black-and-white tones in Peele's play. Pairs of characters embody antithetical or at least alternative versions of valour, femininity, wisdom, loyalty, generosity and other virtues: Eumenides and Huanebango, the Old Man and Sacrapant, Zantippa and Celanta, Corebus and Wiggen versus the Churchwarden and Sexton. We are invited to note the contrasts between Sacrapant's forcible abduction of Delia and Eumenides's tireless search for her; between two pairs of siblings, the King of Thessaly's sons and Lampriscus's daughters; between the mute grief of the mad Venelia and the voluble flippancy of the shrew Zantippa. As well as obvious contrasts, we are shown pairs or groups of characters whose positions or predicaments parallel one another: two travelling companions Booby and Jack, Madge and the Hostess, the 'fairest flower' Delia and the 'foul wench' Celanta, both of whom find husbands in the end. Madge, Lampriscus and Booby offer simple fare of their own volition, while Sacrapant and the Friar, Jack and the Hostess appear magically to spread full tables. The wicked magician's flame is extinguished, his spell broken, Madge's tale ends; dawn breaks, the night's spell is broken, Peele's play ends. One could enumerate further such parallels, oppositions, contrasts, juxtapositions and reminiscences.

Indeed, this is the very fabric of the play, both its dazzling *mélange* and its enchanting simplicity. The vehicle is the tenor. For the entire play is, in the peculiarly obvious way that any framed or otherwise overtly self-conscious drama is, an extended metaphor of the dramatist's art. Peele makes his play of magic and romance a tale told by an old woman at night to entertain lost travellers, all of whom are themselves his own dramatic creatures; Shakespeare makes his play about an incredible shrew-taming a performance by travelling actors at night for a drunken tinker who has lost his identity, all of whom are themselves his own dramatic creatures. We watch as Madge's narrative shifts modes into the dramatic; characters who were being described, appear. Diegesis becomes mimesis.[78] But the narrative itself is told by a character in a play, and it contains a number of other mini-narratives, as characters introduce themselves and relate their

---

[78] The terms, corresponding approximately to 'narrative' and 'dramatic', were used thus by Plato, while Aristotle employed *mimesis* in a broader sense, that of poetic 'imitation' in general. A brief account is Gérard Genette's 'Frontières du Récit', in his *Figures II*, translated by Alan Sheridan as 'Frontiers of Narrative' in *Figures of Literary Discourse* (1982), pp. 128–33.

histories. Erestus sits down to 'tell a heavy tale' of his misfortune (173 ff.). Lampriscus tells of his vexed life with shrewish wives and daughters (207 ff.), Booby of his travels with Huanebango (309 ff.). Sacrapant recounts the story of his life up to the present (331 ff.), and then resumes it after an interruption (413 ff.). Eumenides tells Delia of his long travels in search of her (829 ff.). These pieces of inset narrative, whether spoken in dialogue, in monologue to the audience(s), or in soliloquy have the peculiar, ambiguous status of being both reported discourse in Madge's tale, mediated by her to her listeners and 'overheard' by the theatre audience at Peele's play, and direct discourse, immediately apprehended by Madge herself, her auditors and the theatre audience. With tales within a play, itself ostensibly a tale within a play, *The Old Wife's Tale* is a set of Chinese boxes all of which are visible simultaneously.

Madge's tale whiles away the night, she herself falls asleep while it enacts itself. Her waking and resuming of her story-teller's stance, but in a new tense (903–5 and note), dislocates all that we have seen and heard, as Puck's epilogue suddenly 'places' *A Midsummer Night's Dream*, all of it, as just that for the theatre audience: a dream-play. Shakespeare used frames and plays-within frequently in the earlier part of his career: *The Taming of the Shrew* (especially if we reclaim the Sly epilogue from *The Taming of A Shrew*), *The Comedy of Errors, Love's Labour's Lost, A Midsummer Night's Dream, As You Like It, The Merry Wives of Windsor,* 1 *Henry IV, Hamlet*; and prologues, presenters, choruses and epilogues appear also in 2 *Henry IV, Henry V, Troilus and Cressida* and *Romeo and Juliet.* Not until *Pericles* (c. 1608), however, did he use the more formally metadramatic device of setting his play in the narrative mode, with a teller. Gower, like Madge, begins to tell his tale, 'to sing a song that old was sung', but then hands over his story to 'the judgment of [our] eye'.

Madge and her listeners are surprised by the appearance of her characters ('God's me bones! Who comes here?'). Peele delibe-rately blurs the boundary between tale-within and play-within, and thereby makes the transition more startling. Madge the tale-teller, unlike Gower or the troupe of players who arrive at the Lord's house to perform *The Taming of the Shrew,* is herself entranced, like her auditors, by the magic of tale-telling. Madge's tale, with its abrupt changes from one genre to another and its 'huddle' of characters, incidents, motifs from different genres and different stories, both is and is about romance and fairytale, folktale and comedy, ritual and farce. Peele's play, with its shifts and juxtapositions, its singing and dancing and enchanting, its rich mixture and its delicate spider-web structure, both is and is about all those things too, but it is also and essentially about the mysteries of tale-telling, playmaking and dream-spinning.

STAGING

We do not know what sort of stage and scenery were erected, or where, in the great hall of Christ's College, Cambridge, in which we suppose *Gammer Gurton's Needle* to have been first performed in the 1550s or 1560s. We do not know that an entire theatre with an elaborate set was constructed within the great hall of Windsor Castle in 1552 when, as we imagine, Edward VI watched *Roister Doister*, but it is likely, in view of information about other royal performances in the period. Whether or not we take the word of the titlepage of *The Old Wife's Tale* that it was acted by the Queen's Men, we do not know whether it was played at court, in one of the London theatres, on village greens, in inn-yards or guild halls around the country, or in all of these venues at different times. Indeed, as Wickham observes: 'No acting company could have afforded to gear its repertory of plays so closely to the physical features of its own London public playhouses as to be unable to mount those plays at Court or in the provinces' (*EES*, II, pt. i, 174). Much less do we know how the different locations and dwellings, including Madge's house in the frame story, were represented on stage. The best that can be done is to note what design features and properties are evidently called for in the texts and then consider, in the light of what we do know about theatres in the sixteenth century, how particular scenes or smaller segments of the action might have been staged. Some such suggestions are made in the notes to the plays. All three plays raise particularly interesting questions for the student of staging.

Gammer Gurton's Needle, as we have noted, is the first English play to declare of itself that it was 'played on stage'. What did 'on stage' mean in the sixteenth century? It could mean no more than that it was played, acted, 'on stage' merely adding emphasis to that assertion. It would seem, though, that a special structure was meant. The word 'stage' is first recorded by *OED* in the sense of 'the platform in a theatre upon which spectacles, plays, etc. are exhibited', in 1551, and then, notably, in a translation from Latin. It is possible to push this usage back by several years, from the Cambridge college accounts of disbursements for plays. For example, at Trinity College in 1546–7, a carpenter and his helper were paid for five days' work 'about the stage'; the previous year 'A great Rownd Candlesticke for the stage in the hall' was provided. In the same year the Queen's College accounts contain

the macaronic entries 'pro confectione le stage' and 'pro apposi-
tione le scaffold et demolitione le stage.' The Queen's accounts
also speak of 'scena', 'scaffolde', 'tripodes', 'skrene', and 'theatrum'.[79] But the earliest use of 'stage' in an unequivocally
theatrical reference occurs, coincidentally, in the Christ's College
accounts for 1532–3: 'It [em] for settyng vp ye stage for ye play &
for naylles xij d'. (p. 205). It should be noted that 'stage' was in
use for a very long time before this, as meaning any 'raised floor,
platform, scaffold', specifically 'for the exhibition of something to
be viewed by spectators' (*OED*). Thus the use of 'stage' to denote
a platform for the acting of plays is a natural extention of a
common usage.

   In *The Staging of Plays before Shakespeare*, the fullest study yet
made of the techniques of staging plays indoors in the period,
Richard Southern argues that 'formerly at any rate, to present a
play before an audience did not necessarily imply putting it on
stage at all' (p. 15). With a wealth of drawings, and based on
implied actions and stage directions in the plays, Southern
illustrates how they might have been performed in the Tudor
great halls, using the floorspace at the lower, screens end of the
hall as the playing area, and the openings (usually two) in the
wooden screens which traversed the hall at its lower end to
provide a passage outside the room itself, as the entrances to the
playing area. Spectators, including perhaps servants of the
household, would be standing around the screens openings, which
led to the kitchen behind the hall; dialogue in a number of plays
indicates the proximity of the audience to the playing area, even
their encroachment upon it, as it seems not to have been precisely
circumscribed, and their inhibiting the free movement of the
actors in and out. In *Gammer Gurton's Needle*, for example,
Diccon cries, 'Make here a little roomth', presumably addressed to
members of the audience, to clear the way for Gammer's entrance.
Southern takes as his paradigm the use of the screens openings
and hall floor, and examines a large number of plays (some sixty
or so) to see what may be gathered about staging techniques.

   Gammer Gurton's Needle receives special attention from Southern (pp. 399–423). I shall not summarize the whole of his
discussion, but limit myself to those features of the play which he
singles out as being of particular interest. First, there is Hodge's
reference to the hall (II.i, 106); we are surely justified in assuming

[79] Reference are to G. C. Moore Smith, 'The Academic Drama at Cambridge' (see
n. 34); pp. 153–4, 185. Udall used the word metaphorically in his translation of
Erasmus's commentary on Matthew, published in 1548 (*OED*).

that this is the great hall of Christ's College, and that, therefore, the play was performed there. Then there are numerous references to doors and doorposts throughout the play; this suggests that there are houses with doors on the set. Houses for both Gammer Gurton and Dame Chat are called for (e.g., I.v, 10 and II.ii), and characters at various times come from and go into these houses. Furthermore, action that occurs out of the audience's sight inside one of the houses is reported. In I.iv, Cock enters from Gammer's house (1. 39), then goes back into the house (43). At 46, he replies to Hodge from within; Hodge then enters the house (49). At I.v, 9, Cock comes out and tells Gammer and Tib what Hodge is doing inside, including his chasing Gib the cat upstairs. Gammer calls to Hodge to come down (1. 31), and Hodge replies obviously from within and 'upstairs'.

Modern producers have usually provided the view of Hodge 'upstairs' in the house, looking with his candle for the runaway Gib. In an outdoor production at Shorter College (Rome, Georgia) in 1972, the director had a first-floor window at which Hodge could be seen; he stood on a platform reached by a ladder inside the house, and spoke his lines (I.v, 32–5, 37, 39) out of the window to the others standing below looking up. The Medieval Players, in 1982, used a booth stage and did not seek such verisimilitude. Hodge simply mounted a ladder which allowed him to be seen from about the chest upward, above the booth curtains; here too he spoke down, over the curtains, to the others. We cannot be sure whether the original set for *Gammer Gurton's Needle* at Christ's College provided for the first-floor effect or not, but as it is made so explicit in the text, my guess would be that it did.

If that is the case, a fairly solid structure, with as least a ladder, if not a raised platform, inside is required. Southern considers various ways in which the two houses might have been positioned at the screens end of the hall (see illustrations, pp. 415–21). A further factor, making *Gammer Gurton's Needle* more complicated than many other plays of the period, is the necessity of a third entrance, other than the doors of the two houses. Diccon at I.i; Hodge at I.ii, II.iii, III.i; Tib at I.iv and I.v; Diccon at II.i, II.v, IV.iv and V.ii; Cock at III.iii and iv; Dr Rat at IV.i, IV.iv and V.i, all enter or exit or both from and to places other than Gammer's and Chat's houses. On Southern's hall-and-screens model, this means that the two houses cannot be built directly over and abutting the two screens entrances (p. 410). T. W. Craik (p. 14) says that there was an additional doorway in a side wall near the lower end of the Christ's College Hall, before it was remodelled in the eighteenth century. This could have provided the third entrance. If so, *Gammer Gurton's Needle* would be an example of the dramatist's exploitation of physical features uniquely available to him.

Another special feature called for in *Gammer Gurton's Needle* is the hole in Dame Chat's house into which Dr Rat crawls in IV.ii. The most obvious way to represent this is by an opening in the side of Dame Chat's house, a three-dimensional structure projecting outward toward the audience. The hole would be in the side wall more or less perpendicular to the front of the stage or playing area, and Dr Rat could be seen disappearing into the hole, then reappearing, perhaps feet first, while sounds of beating and shouting emanate from within (see note to IV.iv, 29–44). In the Medieval Players' production, Rat's legs were visible, protruding from behind the booth curtain stage left and thrashing about as he was 'beaten'; the 'hole' was simply the side of the booth.

It is abundantly clear from the college accounts that the performing of plays occasioned a great deal of construction work in the halls and much expense. The Trinity payment to two carpenters for five days' work 'about the stage' is typical, but payments for eight or ten days' work are not uncommon. Payments are for both setting up and pulling down the stage, for underpinning the screen, for taking out and replacing glass in windows and, frequently, for repairing broken windows as well as wainscoting, forms and trestles. At Queen's in 1546–7, a Mr Meres was paid fifteen shillings and twopence for 350 boards 'ad le skrene et ad theatrum'. In 1584–5, Christ Church, Oxford, spent more than thirty-six pounds on just two plays.[80] Large quantities of candles and torches are frequently mentioned. The amounts of time, money and material expended in the staging of plays in the universities strongly suggest that more substantial and elaborate stages and sets were being built than Southern implies in his modified hall floor-and-screens designs. It would not take two or three men five days or more and several hundred boards to erect a low platform or footpace and two lath-and-canvas houses. Possibly a more elaborate set on a raised, fairly deep stage was built.[81]

It is possible even that the relative positions of audience and stage were reversed, with the stage at the upper, dais end of the hall and a tiered auditorium reaching from immediately in front of the stage back up to the screens end. We know that such

---

[80] R. E. Alton, ed., 'The Academic Drama in Oxford: Extracts from the Records of Four Colleges', MSC, V (1959), p. 39.

[81] On the 'classical' stage in the Renaissance, see below pp. liv—lv.

theatres were built in the hall of Christ Church, Oxford, in 1566, 1605 and 1636 for royal performances.[82] Presumably such a structure had been erected in the hall of King's College, Cambridge, for the queen's visit in 1564, but it was judged to be 'too little' (i.e., low?) and too close to the queen's seat, and so the performance (of Plautus's *Aulularia*) was moved to the chapel where a 40' × 40' stage was built.[83] These were clearly very special occasions, but we cannot assume that it was only for the rare royal visit that a stage was built at the upper end of the hall, with scaffold seating for spectators at the other. The Norwich Chamberlain's accounts record a payment in 1546–7 'for fechyng of tymber & makyng the skaffold at the [far] ende of the halle'. So, outside the university too, stages were being built at the upper, dais end of a hall.[84] The college accounts reveal that a great deal of labour and expense went into what was, most of the time, merely the entertainment of the college's own members, by and for themselves. Therefore, it is at least possible that *Gammer Gurton's Needle* was performed on a large, raised stage before an audience seated, not on their benches along the sides of the hall, but in a raked auditorium specially built for the purpose. At Oxford in 1566, balconies were built along the sides for spectators, and the drawings for the 1605 royal performances call for 'a rayle over the skreene' with scaffolds built up in the space behind the screen, 'to see conveniently' (Orrell, p. 140). So Diccon's 'Make here a little roomth' was not necessarily directed at spectators crowded about the screen door impeding the actor's entrance; maybe they were crowded about or on the stage itself.[85] Nor need the musicians upon whom he calls for music (II.v, 11–12) have been stationed in the gallery above the screen. In any case, it would be wrong to suppose that a primitive, floor-level set was the most that would be available to university dramatists. Roger Ascham in a letter from Flanders (c. 1550) implies considerably more: 'The city of Antwerp exceeds all other cities, as the refectory of St John's Hall, Cambridge, exceeds itself when furnished, at Christmas, with its theatrical apparatus for acting

[82] Boas, *UD*, pp. 98–107; John Orrell, 'The Theatre at Christ Church, Oxford, in 1605', *ShS*, 35 (1982), 129–40, and Plate II; Gerald Eades Bentley, *The Jacobean and Caroline Stage*, 7 vols (Oxford; 1941–68), V (1956), 1191. For a survey of these and other Christ Church dramatic events, see W. G. Hiscock, *A Christ Church Miscellany* (Oxford, 1946), pp. 165–86.

[83] Boas, *UD*, pp. 90–94; Wickham *EES*, I, 248–50.

[84] Reprinted in Wickham, *EES*, II, pt. i. p. 333; see also Wickham's discussion on pp. 251–7.

[85] This certainly happened in the Elizabethan public theatre. See Thomas Dekker's *The Gull's Hornbook* (1609), ch. vi; repr. in Chambers, *ES*, IV, 365–9.

plays'.[86] University dramatists, designers and carpenters were clearly capable, by mid-century, of very elaborate and impressive large-scale sets, even of erecting complete theatres in halls and chapels, and were not at all limited to the relatively simple designs and techniques of the interluders.[87].

One other distinctive feature of *Gammer Gurton's Needle* should be noted here, as it has to do with both dramatic representation and also the actual conditions in which the play was originally performed. There are frequent references in the play to the lack of light or the need for a candle, and to evening or night. A torch-lit hall at night was still very dimly lit by modern standards.[88] In a play in which seeking for a minuscule lost object, the proverbial needle, is a major part of the action, for the characters who are searching to speak of needing more light is scarcely surprising. They might merely be making a virtue of necessity, referring outside the play-world to the real dimness of the place in which they were acting, as Hodge certainly does at III.iii, 36. There is much to suggest though that the dimness is also being represented, that it is dusk, even night time, in the play-world too. Hodge might need a candle to search inside the house (I.iv, 37; v, 10ff.) even in daylight, but it is, according to Cock's account, so dark that Hodge can see nothing and mistakes Gib's eyes for glowing coals. Gammer calls off the search (I.v, 57) until 'another time, when we have more light'. Diccon, although he is fabricating, alleges that he has seen Chat sewing by candlelight with Gammer's needle. Hodge speaks of having eaten nothing 'this livelong day' (II.i, 18); Gammer vows to make Dame Chat 'curse this night' (III.iii, 22); Diccon convinces Chat that Hodge will rob her hen house 'this same night' (IV.iii, 34), and Chat speaks later of having been warned of the danger to her poultry 'this afternoon' (V.ii, 41). When the supposed Hodge (really Dr Rat) is bringing assault and battery charges against Chat, he states that it was 'within less than these two hours' that he was injured (V.ii, 29). That incident too occurred when it was too dark for Chat and her maids to recognize their intruder (V.i, 16; V.ii, 25–6). Gammer vows, at the end, not to 'rest this night' until

---

[86] Quoted by Lily B. Campbell, *Scenes and Machines on the English Stage during the Renaissance* (1923; repr. New York, 1960), pp. 87–8.

[87] Southern is sometimes overly meticulous in his culling of evidence from the plays, and too literal in his interpretation of it. His adoption *a priori* of the hall-and-screens model becomes too restrictive when he comes to consider a play like *GGN*. He admits that the evidence of the 1636 Christ Church stage being situated at the upper end 'is disturbing to any earnest reconstruction' (p. 402). Nevertheless, his detailed examination of the plays is invaluable.

[88] See Southern's impression of a torch-lit hall (facing p. 264).

she spends her last halfpenny in drinks for all (V.ii, 323).

There is thus substantial evidence that Mr S. set his play in the late afternoon and early evening, when mistaking and misprising, so essential to the comedy of errors, are all too easy. The significance of this nocturnal setting both in the early history of English drama and in the play's atmosphere is discussed at some length by Jean-Marie Maguin in a valuable recent study in French.[89] Maguin finds that Mr S. is the first English playwright to set scenes explicitly at night, or at least in the penumbral hours, and partially in notably dark places like Gammer's loft and Dame Chat's 'lead'. The shadowy Mr S. would seem to have been even more innovative than has hitherto been allowed.

Roister Doister was almost certainly written for a royal performance and would surely have been staged with all of the lavishness and sophistication that Nicholas Udall and his collaborators at Windsor were capable of. As an avowed imitation of Roman comedy, it may well have been staged on what Renaissance scholars understood to be the Roman scene, derived from Italian reconstructions of Roman practice. The source of Renaissance knowledge of the theatres of the ancients was *De Architectura* by Vitruvius, a first-century B.C. Roman engineer and town planner.[90] Vitruvius's treatise was first printed in Rome in 1486. In his study of Roman buildings Vitruvius had included the theatres, and Renaissance scholars were quick to mine this valuable document for information about the theatres in which their admired Terence, Plautus and the others were performed. Numerous editions followed that of 1486 and an Italian translation appeared as early as 1521. An Italian architect, Sebastiano Serlio (1475–1554), published his *Architettura* in several books between 1537 and 1551. Though conceived as a commentary and elaboration upon the work of Vitruvius, Serlio's book, with its practical, detailed treatment of stage architecture, scenery, perspective and machinery, is the earliest published account of Renaissance theatrical practice. It was tremendously influential. Curiously, no English translation appeared until 1611, and Inigo Jones is the first English designer known to have employed perspective in stage scenery. Serlio's scene designs, based on his study of Vitruvius and his own experience as a theatre architect, were incorporated in subsequent editions of Vitruvius's treatise.

---

[89] *La Nuit dans le Théâtre de Shakespeare et de ses Prédécesseurs*, 2 vols (Lille, 1980), I, 174–89.
[90] See Campbell (n. 86); Barnard Hewitt, ed., *The Renaissance Stage: Documents of Serlio, Sabbattini and Furttenbach* (Coral Gables, Fla., 1958); and Richard Leacroft, *The Development of the English Playhouse* (1973), esp. ch. i. The following summary is indebted to these three works.

Whether Udall was as familiar with contemporary Italian stage practice as he was with Roman drama and Donatan theory is doubtful.[91] He would probably have read Vitruvius at least. Serlio's designs, including that of the 'comical scene' appeared in a Paris edition of Vitruvius in 1547.[92] It is tempting to imagine that *Roister Doister* was performed on something like Serlio's 'comical scene', with houses on either side for Ralph and Christian Custance and a perspective street running up the middle between sets of wings, but it may have been too early for such a sophisticated perspective scene in England. The belated English reception of Serlio suggests that his work, at least, was not widely known here in the 1550s, though it is hard to believe that no one before Inigo Jones even experimented with perspective sets.

Southern assumes that *Roister Doister* 'could be played either on a booth stage or in front of hall-screens with equal facility' (p. 400). Craik too takes for granted a hall-and-screens theatre, but allows that a lath-and-canvas street scene might have been constructed (pp. 13–14). Chambers noted that *Roister Doister* requires only one house, Dame Custance's, while *Gammer Gurton's Needle* clearly requires two (*ES*, III, 27). But if anything like the Italian court set was used by Udall for his court comedy, Ralph's house too may have been present, facing Dame Custance's. (This may seem unlikely, as Dobinet says he is looking for a house that he does not know when he enters in II.i.) Even a hall-and-screens venue would not preclude provision of two houses plus a third, independent entrance, as Southern amply demonstrates in his discussion of *Gammer Gurton's Needle*.

The Old Wife's Tale requires rather more complicated scenery than either of the other two plays, or it does if any sort of representation of the several distinct locations specified in the text is to be made. Wickham's reminder that an Elizabethan company would have to be prepared to mount its plays in a variety of places is apposite. In some theatres it may have been possible to represent individually, by means of movable wings and machinery, each of the locations and all of the magical business indicated in the text. Elsewhere, the older methods of suggestion and implication of lieu practiced by the interluders would have had to be employed.

[91] Southern is sceptical too (pp. 413–14). For a fuller discussion, see Wickham, *EES*, II, pt. i. 245–75. Wickham sees evidence that some aspects of Italian practice were being imitated in England as early as the 1530s.

[92] *Architecture ou Art de bien bastir, de Marc Vitruve Pollion . . .* , translated by Jean Martin; facsimile reprint by The Gregg Press (Ridgewood, N.J., 1964). Serlio's 'comical scene' illustration is on p. 78; it is frequently reproduced, e.g., in Campbell, p. 36; Hewitt, p. 28; Chambers, *ES*, IV, 359.

In the frame action, both a wood in which the three pages are lost and encounter Clunch, and an interior, that of Madge's cottage, are called for. Then, while the three spectators remain ostensibly inside Madge's house, the inner play unfolds, with action occurring in at least four places: the Old Man's cross, Sacrapant's study, the magic well, and an inn. It would be easy to indicate all of these locations simultaneously, and it is more likely that this was done than that scenes were changed. The movement from place to place and the brevity of many scenes must render the latter procedure impracticable. In any case, the magic well and Sacrapant's cell are both 'present' at 1. 614 when the Furies issue forth from the cell and 'lay Huanebango by the well of life'. The mound with the magic light inside is also at or near the conjurer's cell. The 'inn' at which Jack and Eumenides dine (11. 717–49) need not be represented as a separate place; Jack re-enters with the hostess, 'setting meat on the table', only one line after he exits (see 716 s.d. and note). The 'inn' comes to Eumenides. Erestus's cross, with Sacrapant's flame and the magic well, is the other important symbolic landmark in the inner play. One might expect these three places to remain visible throughout the play, the emblematic foci of its supernatural forces—the old man's holiness, the sorcerer's fiendishness and the mundane folk magic of the head in the well.

It is not necessary to imagine a churchyard for the scene with Wiggen, Corebus, the Churchwarden and the Sexton. It, as well as other episodes of unspecified location, could be played down front. Madge, Frolic and Fantastic simply sit to one side, in front of the 'house', or *domus*, if there was one.[93] Sacrapant's cell has a curtain, which Jack pulls aside to reveal the sleeping Delia (822), and behind which she and Sacrapant presumably hide at 1. 383. The 'discovery space' of the public theatre stage, or the curtained booth of its simpler forebear, the outdoor booth-and-trestle stage, would serve that purpose. At court, the study or cell, as well as Madge's cottage might be constructed. Indeed the entire set would doubtless be more elaborate, with several houses, as in the masques.[94] A trap (and hence a raised stage) is called for when Jack 'leaps down in the ground' at the end. Since the head rises from a magic well, the latter could have been positioned over the trap and removed after the last scene in which it is used, leaving the trap for Jack.

[93] One solution, having characters in the inner play enter via Madge's fireplace, is described by Frank W. Cady in his performing text of the play for a production at Middlebury College, Vermont, in 1911.

[94] See illustrations and descriptions in Stephen Orgel and Roy Strong, *Inigo Jones: The Theatre of the Stuart Court*, 2 vols (1973).

The fact that printer's copy for *The Old Wife's Tale* was authorial, with no precise indications of staging, makes such a discussion as this speculative in the extreme. The masque-like qualities of the play, with music, dancing, monsters (Furies) and some use of spectacle and machinery, suggest that it was designed for a court or some other private occasion, whatever may have been its subsequent fortunes in the hands of the Queen's Men.[95]

THIS EDITION

THE TEXTS ARE based on the earliest editions of the three plays, freshly examined and collated with a number of later editions. Each play survives in a single sixteenth-century edition; thus the choice of copy text made itself: for *GGN*, the quarto of 1575, published by Thomas Colwell, of which eleven copies are extant; for *RD*, the quarto, lacking title page, published c. 1566 by Thomas Hackett, surviving in one copy, at Eton College; for *OWT* the quarto of 1595, printed by John Danter for Ralph Hancock and John Hardie, of which four copies survive.

I have seen nearly all of the eleven extant copies of *GGN*, which divide into some with uncorrected title page ('anp', 'Imprented') and some with those errors corrected. The first group includes the British Museum, Chapin and Huntington copies; the second, the Bodleian, Dyce (Victoria and Albert Museum), both Folger, and the New York Public Library copies. In copies of the latter group a few more misprints in the text are corrected (see Brett-Smith, p. xii), but a few others are introduced; the 'corrected' copies were 'discorrected' in one or two instances where the 'uncorrected' copies are correct. Both groups share a large number of misprints, incorrect speech prefixes and other evidence of careless printing: worn and broken letters, uneven inking, inverted founts, omitted words, etc. The edition of 1661 is apparently printed from a copy of Q (see Introduction, n. 33), as it preserves many of the latter's patent errors. Kirkman's copy (if it was his that provided the printer's copy for 1661), would seem to have belonged to the BM ('uncorrected') group; 1661 preserves its glaringly wrong 'what' for 'wyth' at I.ii, 16.

The unique copy of *RD* is reasonably well printed, and poses few problems for the editor. The occasional erroneous speech prefix can usually be emended by attending to the content of the dialogue. Several songs and a text of the 'Psalmody' for Ralph's

[95] See the discussion of staging by Hook, pp. 373–6.

mock-funeral in III.iii, which differs somewhat from that printed in the body of the play at that point, are appended to the play text in Q. I have interpolated four lines from this appended text; the additions are in square brackets and are recorded in the notes. As the two versions of the 'Psalmody' vary slightly even in some lines that they have in common, I have printed the second version at the end of the play. The songs, however, are simply inserted in the appropriate places in the text.

The problems posed by the text of *OWT* have been mentioned in the Introduction. Two of the four copies show an uncorrected inner forme E, while the other two are corrected. Among the 'corrections' in the latter, however, are substantive variants which are not accepted by all editors. The readings adopted in this edition and the reasons for them are given in the notes at the relevant passages. Q has no act and scene divisions.

The present edition is a freely modernized one; by that, I do not mean 'translated' into modern English. The words of the originals have been retained, except in cases of clear or probable error, and such emendations are indicated in the textual notes. Obsolete words are, of course, retained, in forms as near as possible to the original consistent with modern convention such as dropping final *e*, *i* for *j*, *u* for *v*, etc. Archaic forms of words still current have been modernized to conform to *OED*'s entry-forms. Spelling in the originals is wildly inconsistent, and forms have been regularized; that is, a word will always be spelt the same way in this edition, regardless of how many different spellings it may have in the quartos. Where modernization of an archaic form results in loss of rhyme, this is indicated in a note (e.g., *well/nee'le* where Q has *weele/neele*).

The dialect in *GGN* (and a few lines in *RD*) has, after consideration of the alternatives, been left largely as it is in the quartos. Rather than sprinkle the text with apostrophes, I have retained the elided forms (*cham* = 'ich am'; *chave* = 'ich have'), and glossed each form at its first occurrence and occasionally thereafter if there is a possibility of confusion. Sometimes I have regularized a Q dialect form to accord with its own normal practice. In the case of *ichold* and *ichould*, I have had to decide in each instance whether 'ich hold', 'ich could', 'ich would' or 'ich should' is meant, and have emended where it seemed necessary; for 'ich would', I give *chwould* in all instances, to distinguish it from *chould* ('ich could' or 'ich should'). All such emendations are noted and glossed. 'Needle' occurs as both *neele* and *nedle*; I use the modern spelling when the word is bisyllabic, 'nee'le' when it is monosyllabic.

I have tried to keep editorial stage directions to a minimum, preferring to make suggestions and comments about staging in the explanatory notes. It is not, I think, the job of an editor to 'stage' the play on the page. It is his job to comment and explain when staging questions arise in the dramatic text he is editing. In *GGN* and *RD*, a great deal of the action can be inferred from the dialogue and there are a few explanatory or descriptive directions in the quartos. As was customary in the mid-sixteenth century, the names of all characters who appear at any time in a scene are listed at the beginning of the scene; the editor must add entrances and exits at the appropriate places. The state of the *OWT* quarto text makes some interpolation of stage directions other than entrances and exits necessary. All editorial additions are in square brackets and are noted.

Punctuation is modernized, a measure that is particularly called for where *GGN* and *RD* are concerned. I have used exclamation marks rather liberally, especially in *GGN* where the name-calling, swearing and general furor are anything but matter-of-fact. Abbreviations in the originals, including tildes, initials in speech prefixes and abbreviated stage directions are silently expanded. Latin stage directions are translated.

FURTHER READING

Joel B. Altman, *The Tudor Play of Mind* (Berkeley, Cal., 1978)

L. R. N. Ashley, *George Peele*, Twayne's English Authors Series (New York, 1970)

T. W. Baldwin, *Shakspere's Five-Act Structure* (Urbana, Illinois, 1947)

J. E. Bernard, Jr., *Prosody of the Tudor Interlude* (New Haven, 1939; repr. New York, 1969)

David Bevington, *From 'Mankind' to Marlowe* (Cambridge, Mass., 1962)

F. S. Boas, *An Introduction to Tudor Drama* (Oxford, 1923)

F. S. Boas, *University Drama in the Tudor Age* (Oxford, 1914)

M. C. Bradbrook, *The Growth and Structure of Elizabethan Comedy* (1955)

E. K. Chambers, *The Elizabethan Stage*, 4 vols (Oxford, 1923)

E. K. Chambers, *The Medieval Stage*, 2 vols (1903)

T. W. Craik, *The Tudor Interlude* (Leicester, 1958)

W. L. Edgerton, *Nicholas Udall*, Twayne's English Authors Series (New York, 1965)

Michael Hattaway, *Elizabethan Popular Theatre* (1982)

William Hazlitt, *Lectures on the Dramatic Literature of the Age of Elizabeth* (1820). Esp. Lecture V (on *GGN*)

Marvin T. Herrick, *Comic Theory in the Sixteenth Century* (Urbana, Illinois, 1950; repr. 1964)

Sidney Lanier, 'The Domestic Life of Shakspere's Time—IV', *Peabody Lectures*, XXIII (1879), in *Shakspere and his Forerunners*, ed. Kemp Malone, The Centennial Edition of the Works of Sidney Lanier, III (Baltimore, 1945), 280–91. A fanciful flight in which the young Shakespeare is imagined by the American poet as seeing *RD* at the Blackfriars in 1582.

Richard Leacroft, *The Development of the English Playhouse* (1973). Esp. chapters 1 and 2

Jean-Marie Maguin, *La Nuit dans le Théâtre de Shakespeare et de ses Prédécesseurs*, 2 vols (Lille, 1980). Discusses nocturnal setting of *OWT* as well as *GGN*

John B. Moore, *The Comic and the Realistic in English Drama* (Chicago, 1925; repr. New York, 1965)

G. C. Moore Smith, *College Plays Performed in the University of Cambridge* (Cambridge, 1921). Supplements his Malone Society volume of records

A. P. Rossiter, *English Drama from Early Times to the Elizabethans* (1950)

Leo Salingar, *Shakespeare and the Traditions of Comedy* (Cambridge, 1974)

Norman Sanders, Richard Southern, T. W. Craik and Lois Potter, *The Revels History of Drama in English*, volume II: 1500–1576 (1980)

Michael Shapiro, *The Children of the Revels: The Boy Companies of Shakespeare's Time and their Plays* (New York, 1977)

Richard Southern, *The Staging of Plays before Shakespeare* (1973)

Bernard Spivack, *Shakespeare and the Allegory of Evil* (1958)

T. H. Vail Motter, *The School Drama in England* (1929)

Glynne Wickham, *Early English Stages 1300–1660*, 3 vols (1959–81; vol. IV forthcoming). Esp. vol. III, ch. viii, 'English Comedy from its Origins to 1576'

F. P. Wilson, *The English Drama 1485–1585*, Oxford History of English Literature, IV, pt. i (Oxford, 1969)

Steven C. Young, *The Frame Structure in Tudor and Stuart Drama*, Salzburg Studies in English Literature (Salzburg, 1974)

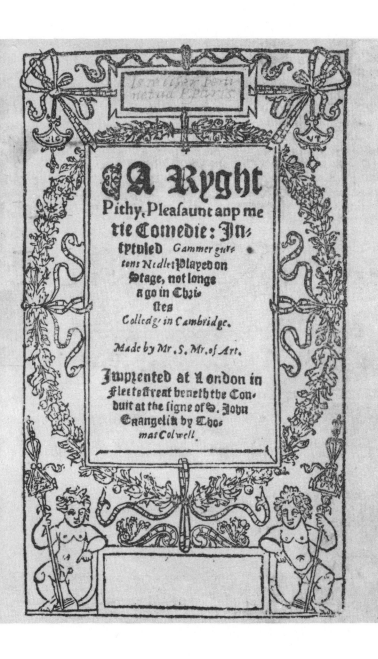

Is no liber post illi
nescia Expurio

A Ryght

Pithy, Pleaſaunt anp me
rie Comedie: In-
tytuled *Gammer gur-*
tons Nedle: Played on
Stage, not longe
a go in Chri-
ſtes
Colledg in Cambridge.

Made by Mr. S. Mr. of Art.

Imprented at London in
Fleetſtreat beneth the Con-
duit at the ſigne of S. John
Euangeliſt by Tho-
mas Colwell.

The names of the Speakers in this Comedy

DICCON, *the Bedlam*
HODGE, *Gammer Gurton's servant*
TIB, *Gammer Gurton's maid*
GAMMER GURTON
COCK, *Gammer Gurton's boy*
DAME CHAT
DOCTOR RAT, *the curate*
MASTER BAILEY
DOLL, *Dame Chat's maid*
SCAPETHRIFT, *Mast' Bailey's servant*
[GIB, *Gammer Gurton's cat*]
Mutes

God Save the Queen

6 COCK eds. (Docke Q)
  boy houseboy
11 *Mast'* ed. (mayst Q) master

---

2 *the Bedlam* (i.e., Bethlehem) Originally the Hospital of St Mary of Bethlehem in London, founded in the 13th century as a priory, and by the time of the play, a royal foundation for the care of the mentally ill. Inmates of the hospital, and by extension, any insane person, came to be called by its name. Partially-cured patients were often discharged, with a license to beg and a tin plate as an identifying badge. Hence, the term came to be loosely employed to refer to beggars and vagrants as well as madmen. See Introduction, p.xxx.

7 CHAT Both the English verb and the French for 'cat' (*chat*; feminine form, *chatte*).

8 *curate* Either the incumbent priest or parson of a parish, or a deputy, a clergyman licensed by the bishop to perform the incumbent's duties in his place. The latter usage is peculiar to the Church of England, and first occurs in the mid-16th century (*OED*); the incumbent is now usually called 'vicar'. Doctor Rat is obviously the parish priest (IV.i, 2) and is, in fact, called both 'parson' (III.iii, 59) and 'vicar' (IV.ii, 1; V.ii, 262).

9 BAILEY The bailiff (whence the proper name), a local sheriff's officer who executes writs, makes arrests, etc.

13 *Mutes* Presumably neighbours and townspeople who gather to watch scenes like the fight in III.iii and the finale (V.ii), though no reference is made in the text to persons other than the principals. In fact, Doll and Scapethrift, though named, are mutes; they are given no lines to speak.

14 *the Queen* Elizabeth I. This refers to the time of publication (1575) rather than to that of composition and performance. See Introduction, p.xxix.

The Prologue

As Gammer Gurton, with many a wide stitch
Sat piecing and patching of Hodge her man's breech,
By chance or misfortune as she her gear tossed,
In Hodge's leather breeches her needle she lost.
When Diccon the Bedlam had heard by report   5
That good Gammer Gurton was robbed in this sort,
He quietly persuaded with her in that stound
Dame Chat, her dear gossip, this needle had found;
Yet knew she no more of this matter, alas,
Than knoweth Tom, our clerk, what the priest saith at mass. 10
Hereof there ensued so fearful a fray,
Mas' Doctor was sent for, these gossips to stay,
Because he was curate and esteemed full wise;
Who found that he sought not, by Diccon's device.
When all things were tumbled and clean out of fashion,   15
Whether it were by fortune or some other constellation,
Suddenly the nee'le Hodge found by the pricking
And drew it out of his buttock where he felt it sticking,
Their hearts then at rest with perfect security,
With a pot of good nale they struck up their *plaudite*.   20

2 *piecing* mending
   breech (now used only in plural, *breeches*) trousers; also, specifically, the trousers
   seat
3 *her gear tossed* went about her work
7 *Persuaded with* convinced
   in that stound at that time
8 *gossip* familiar acquaintance
9 *she* (i.e., Dame Chat)
12 *Mas'* Master
   stay restrain or pacify
15 *tumbled . . . fashion* utterly chaotic
17 *nee'le* (neele Q)
20 *nale* ale
   plaudite (L., *applaud*) appeal for applause at the end of a play or other performance

10 *Than . . . mass* The clerk would have been a member of a 'minor order', i.e., inferior
   to deacons and priests, who assisted the priest in the various services. He would
   have had little or no formal theological training, hence might not have understood
   the Latin used by the priest. The reputed ignorance of the lower clergy, including
   parish priests, was notorous and from the later Middle Ages was a common theme
   in literature.
16 *constellation* In astrology, the positions of planets in relation to one another is
   supposed to exert influence on earthly events.

Act I, Scene i

[*Enter* DICCON]

DICCON

    Many a mile have I walked, divers and sundry ways,
    And many a good man's house have I been at in my days,
    Many a gossip's cup in my time have I tasted,
    And many a broach and spit have I both turned and basted.
    Many a piece of bacon have I had out of their balks,   5
    In running over the country with long and weary walks.
    Yet came my foot never within those door cheeks
    To seek flesh or fish, garlic, onions or leeks,
    That ever I saw a sort in such a plight
    As here within this house appeareth to my sight.   10
    There is howling and scowling, all cast in a dump,
    With whewling and puling as though they had lost a trump;
    Sighing and sobbing, they weep and they wail—
    I marvel in my mind what the devil they ail!
    The old trot sits groaning with 'Alas!' and 'Alas!'   15
    And Tib wrings her hands and takes on in worse case.
    With poor Cock, their boy, they be driven in such fits,
    I fear me the folks be not well in their wits.
    Ask them what they ail, or who brought them in this stay,
    They answer not at all but 'Alack and wellaway!'   20

---

  4 *broach* pointed instrument for roasting meat upon, a spit
  7 *cheeks* side-posts or uprights of a door
  9 *sort* group of people
11 *cast . . . dump* melancholy, depressed
12 *whewling and puling* moaning and whining
    lost a trump (i.e., in a card game)
15 *trot* hag
20 *Alack and wellaway* (exclamation of sorrow)

---

s.d. Diccon enters from somewhere other than the two houses, obviously, as does
    Hodge in the next scene. See the discussion of staging in the Introduction.
  5 *balks* Tie-beams of houses, stretching from wall to wall. In one-storey houses,
    boards would be laid across these, forming a loft, or balk, in which dried food and
    other articles were stored.

When I saw it booted not, out at doors I hied me
And caught a slip of bacon when I saw that none spied me,
Which I intend not far hence, unless my purpose fail,
Shall serve for a shoeing-horn to draw on two pots of ale.

Act I, Scene ii

[*Enter* HODGE]

HODGE
See, so cham arrayed with dabbling in the dirt—
She that set me to ditching, ich would she had the squirt!
Was never poor soul that such a life had
Gog's bones, this vilthy glay has dressed me too bad!
God's soul, see how this stuff tears—   5
Ich were better to be bearward and set to keep bears!
By the mass, here is a gash, a shameful hole indeed;
And one stitch tear further, a man may thrust in his head!

DICCON
By my father's soul, Hodge, if I should now be sworn,
I cannot choose but say thy breech is foul betorn.   10
But the next remedy in such a case and hap
Is to planch on a piece as broad as thy cap.

HODGE
Gog's soul, man, 'tis not yet two days fully ended
Since my dame Gurton, cham sure, these breeches
    amended;

---

21 *booted not* was to no avail
   hied me took mysel'
22 *slip* slice
 1 *cham* (dialect) I am
 2 *ich* (dialect) I
   squirt diarrhoea
 4 *Gog's bones* by God's bones
   vilthy glay (dialect) filthy clay
 8 *and* if
11 *next* nearest
12 *planch...piece* clap on a patch

1–2 Hodge is apparently a field labourer. Gammer Gurton is reasonably well-to-do:
   she maintains three servants, and has a cow and a sow at least (IV.i, 22).

But cham made such a drudge to trudge at every need,   15
Chwould rend it though it were stitched with sturdy
      packthread.

DICCON
Hodge, let thy breeches go, and speak and tell me soon,
What devil aileth Gammer Gurton and Tib her maid to
      frown.

HODGE
Tush, man th'art deceived, 'tis their daily look;
They cower so over the coals, their eyes be bleared with
      smoke.   20

DICCON
Nay, by the mass, I perfectly perceived as I came hither
That either Tib and her dame hath been by the ears
      together,
Or else as great a matter, as thou shalt shortly see.

HODGE
Now ich beseech our Lord they never better agree!

DICCON
By Gog's soul, there they sit as still as stones in the
      street,   25
As though they had been taken with fairies or else with
      some ill sprite.

HODGE
Gog's heart, I durst have laid my cap to a crown
Chwould learn of some prancome as soon as ich came to
      town.

16 *Chwould* ed. (chwold Q) I would
   packthread ed. (pacthreede Q)
22 *hath* have (the singular form for a plural verb is common)
   by the ears fighting
26 *taken with* possessed, bewitched by
   sprite spirit
28 *prancome* prank, strange thing

27 *durst...crown* Would dare to wager my cap against a crown (five shillings).

DICCON

    Why, Hodge, art thou inspired? Or didst thou thereof
        hear?

HODGE

    Nay, but ich saw such a wonder as ich saw not this seven
        year: 30
    Tom Tankard's cow, by Gog's bones, she set me up her
        sail,
    And flinging about his half-acre fisking with her tail
    As though there had been in her arse a swarm of bees—
    And chad not cried, 'Tphrowh, whore!', she 'ad leapt
        out of his leas!

DICCON

    Why, Hodge, lies the cunning in Tom Tankard's cow's
        tail?   35

HODGE

    Well, chave heard some say such tokens do not fail.
    But canst thou not tell, in faith, Diccon, why she frowns
        or whereat?
    Hath no man stolen her ducks or hens, or gelded Gib her
        cat?

DICCON

    What devil can I tell, man? I could not have one word!
    They gave no more heed to my talk than thou wouldst to
        a turd.   40

HODGE

    Ich can not still but muse what marvellous thing it is;
    Chill in and know myself what matters are amiss.

31 *set . . . sail* hoisted up her tail (like a sail)
32 *fisking* whisking
34 *And chad* If I had
   she 'ad ed. (shead Q)
   leas pastures
35 *cunning* intelligence
36 *chave* ed. (ich chave Q) I have
40 *turd* ed. (lorde Q)
42 *Chill* I'll

---

40 *turd* J. C. Maxwell's suggestion (*N&Q*, 190 [1953], 266). The same rhyme, with
word, occurs also at I.v, 52–3, where Hodge does give heed to a turd. It would be in
keeping with a prominent motif in the play, and no editor has satisfactorily
explained why Diccon should impute to the credulous Hodge, of all people, a
particular contempt for the nobility. Such usage of the word, connoting
worthlessness or triviality, is amply documented in *OED*.

DICCON
> Then farewell, Hodge, awhile, since thou dost inward
>   haste,
> For I will into the good wife Chat's, to feel how the ale
>   doth taste.   [*Exit*]

Act I, Scene iii

HODGE
> Cham aghast, by the mass, ich wot not what to do—
> Chad need bless me well before ich go them to!
> Perchance some felon sprite may haunt our house
>   indeed,
> And then chwere but a noddy to venture where cha' no
>   need.
>   [*Enter* TIB]

TIB [*Aside*]
> Cham worse than mad, by the mass, to be at this
>   stay!   5
> Cham chid, cham blamed and beaten all th' hours on the
>   day;

44 s.d. *Exit* eds.
 1 *wot* know
 2 *Chad* I had
 4 *chwere* I were
   noddy simpleton
 5 *at this stay* in this predicament
 6 *chid* chided, scolded

---

44 *Chat's . . . taste* Dame Chat's house is obviously an alehouse, where ale was both
   brewed and sold, and could be consumed on the premises. Originally, brewers sold
   their ale to customers who took it away. Consumption on the premises seems to
   have begun in the late Middle Ages.
44 s.d. Where does Diccon go? Chat's door is only a few feet away; Diccon's 'into'
   suggests its proximity. But he clearly does not go there until II.ii, 19. In the
   meantime, he is on hand to comment on the song which opens Act II and to
   perform the 'conjuring' scene (II.i) with Hodge. A director might resolve the
   problem by having Diccon stand aside only, and not exit here, so that he is 'on'
   during the song, but his presence onstage during scenes in which he does not take
   part (I.iii, I.iv, I.v) would establish a precedent which would then need to be
   maintained throughout. I follow other editors in providing an exit for Diccon; a
   director will decide how best to do it. See II.i headnote.

Lamed and hunger-starved, pricked up all in jags,
Having no patch to hide my back, save a few rotten rags.

HODGE

I say, Tib, if thou be Tib, as I trow sure thou be,
What devil make-ado is this between our dame and thee?   10

TIB

Gog's bread, Hodge, thou had a good turn thou wert not
    here this while!
It had been better for some of us to have been hence a
    mile.
My gammer is so out of course and frantic all at once,
That Cock, our boy, and I, poor wench, have felt it on
    our bones.

HODGE

What is the matter, say on, Tib, whereat she taketh so
    on?   15

TIB

She is undone, she saith, alas, her joy and life is gone.
If she hear not of some comfort, she is, faith, but dead;
Shall never come within her lips one inch of meat ne
    bread.

HODGE

By'r Lady, cham not very glad to see her in this dump—
Chold a noble her stool hath fallen and she hath broke
    her rump!   20

TIB

Nay, and that were the worst, we would not greatly care,
For bursting of her huckle-bone or breaking of her
    chair;
But greater, greater is her grief, as, Hodge, we shall all
    feel.

  7 *pricked up* dressed
    jags tatters
  9 *trow* believe
 10 *made-ado* uproar (?)
 13 *out of course* distracted
 18 *ne* nor
 20 *Chold* I hold, wager
    noble (gold coin worth six shillings and eight pence)
 22 *bursting* breaking
    huckle-bone hip-bone

HODGE

Gog's wounds, Tib, my gammer has never lost her
    nee'le?

TIB

Her nee'le!

HODGE   Her nee'le?   25

TIB

Her nee'le, by him that made me! It is true, Hodge, I
    tell thee!

HODGE

Gog's sacrament, I would she had lost th'heart out of her
    belly!
The devil or else his dam, they ought her sure a shame!
How a murrain came this chance, say, Tib, unto our
    dame?

TIB

My gammer sat her down on her pess and bad me reach
    thy breeches,   30
And by and by—a vengeance on it!—or she had take
    two stitches
To clap a clout upon thine arse, by chance aside she
    leers,
And Gib, our cat, in the milk pan she spied, over head
    and ears.
'Ah, whore! Out, thief!' she cried aloud, and swapped
    the breeches down;
Up went her staff and out leapt Gib at doors into the
    town,   35
And since that time was never wight could set their eyes
    upon it.

---

28 *dam* ed. (dame Q) mother
   ought owed
29 *murrain* ed. (murryon Q) plague *how a murrain* how the devil
30 *pess* hassock or cushion
31 *or* before
32 *clout* patch
   leers glances
34 *swapped* slapped
36 *wight* person

Gog's malison chave, Cock and I, bid twenty times light
 on it!

HODGE

And is not then my breeches sewed up, tomorrow that I
 should wear?

TIB

No, in faith, Hodge, thy breeches lie for all this never
 the near.

HODGE

Now a vengeance light on all the sort that better should
 have kept it—   40
The cat, the house, and Tib our maid that better should
 have swept it!
[Enter GAMMER GURTON]
See where she cometh crawling—come on, in twenty
 devils' way!
Ye have made a fair day's work, have you not! Pray you,
 say!

Act I, Scene iv

GAMMER GURTON

Alas, Hodge, alas! I may well curse and ban
This day that ever I saw it, with Gib and the milk pan;
For these and ill luck together, as knoweth Cock, my
 boy,
Have stack away my dear nee'le and robbed me of my
 joy,
My fair long straight nee'le that was mine only treasure. 5
The first day of my sorrow is, and last end of my
 pleasure.

39 *never the near* no nearer completion
42 *in twenty devils' way* (expression of impatience)
 1 *ban* curse
 4 *stack* struck

---

37 *Gog's . . . it* Cock and I have prayed twenty times that God's curse light upon the
 needle.
41 s.d. Q, as usual, simply lists Gammer Gurton's name with the others at the
 beginning of scene iv. But she is undoubtedly visible to the audience at 1.42.

HODGE

Might ha' kept it when ye had it, but fools will be fools
    still!

Lose that is vast in your hands ye need not, but ye will!

GAMMER GURTON

Go hie thee, Tib, and run, thou whore, to th'end here of
    the town;

Didst carry out dust in thy lap—seek where thou
    pouredst it down,   10

And as thou sawest me raking in the ashes where I
    mourned,

So see in all the heap of dust thou leave no straw
    unturned.

TIB

That chall, Gammer, swith and tite, and soon be here
    again!

GAMMER GURTON

Tib, stoop and look down to the ground—to it, and
    take some pain!

                                      [Exit TIB]

HODGE

Here is a pretty matter, to see this gear how it goes;   15

By Gog's soul, I think you would lose your arse and it
    were loose!

Your nee'le lost! It is pity you should lack care and
    endless sorrow!

Gog's death, how shall my breeches be sewed? Shall I go
    thus tomorrow?

GAMMER GURTON

Ah, Hodge, Hodge, if that ich could find my nee'le, by
    the reed,

Chwould sew thy breeches, ich promise thee, with full
    good double thread,   20

---

  7 *fools . . . still* Proverbial (Tilley F547).

  8 *vast* (dialect) fast

10 *pouredst* ed. (porest Q)

11 *raking* ed. (roking Q; rucking (i.e., crouching) eds.)

13 *chall* I shall

    swith and tite quickly, right away

14 *ground—to it* ed. (ground to it Q)

15 *gear* business

19 *reed* rood, cross

20 *Chwould* ed. (Chould Q) I would

And set a patch on either knee, should last these months
    twain.
Now God and good Saint Sithe I pray to send it home
    again!

HODGE

Whereto served your hands and eyes but this your nee'le
    to keep?
What devil had you else to do? Ye kept, ich wot, no
    sheep!
Cham fain abroad to dig and delve in water, mire and
    clay,   25
Sossing and possing in the dirt still from day to day.
A hundred things that be abroad, cham set to see them
    well,
And four of you sit idle at home and cannot keep a
    nee'le!

GAMMER GURTON

My nee'le, alas, ich lost it, Hodge, what time ich me up
    hasted
To save the milk set up for thee, which Gib our cat hath
    wasted.   30

HODGE

The devil he burst both Gib and Tib, with all the rest!
Cham always sure of the worst end, whoever have the
    best!
Where ha' you been fidging abroad since you your nee'le
    lost?

GAMMER GURTON

Within the house and at the door, sitting by this same
    post,

---

21 *months* eds. (monethes Q)
25 *fain* obliged
26 *sossing and possing* splashing and tramping
27 *well* ed. (weele Q)
28 *four of you* (i.e., Gammer, Tib, Cock, Gib the cat)
31 *The devil he* may the devil
33 *fidging* moving about restlessly

---

22 *Saint Sithe* Saint Osyth, a seventh-century East Saxon queen who founded a
    nunnery at Chich (now called Saint Osyth) in Essex, said to have been martyred
    by the Danes.

Where I was looking a long hour before these folks came
    here.   35
But wellaway, all was in vain, my nee'le is never the
    near!

HODGE
Set me a candle, let me seek and grope wherever it be.
Gog's heart, ye be so foolish, ich think, you know it not
    when you it see!

GAMMER GURTON
Come hither, Cock! What, Cock, I say!
            [Enter COCK]

COCK   How, Gammer?

GAMMER GURTON   Go hie thee soon
And grope behind the old brass pan, which thing when
    thou hast done,   40
There shalt thou find an old shoe, wherein if thou look
    well,
Thou shalt find lying an inch of a white tallow candle.
Light it and bring it tite away.

COCK   That shall be done anon.
                        [Exit]

GAMMER GURTON
Nay, tarry, Hodge, till thou hast light, and then we'll
    seek each one.

HODGE
Come away, ye whoreson boy! Are ye asleep? Ye must
    have a crier!   45

COCK [*Within*]
Ich cannot get the candle light—here is almost
    no fire.

HODGE
Chill hold thee a penny chill make ye come if that ich
    may catch thine ears!

36 *near* nearer
42 *candle* eds. (candell Q)
43 *anon* immediately

---

35 *these folks* Referring to the audience. Such frank acknowledgement of the
    audience's presence and proximity (as also at II.iv, 2 and III.iii, 36) is common in
    the interludes of the period.

Art deaf, thou whoreson boy? Cock, I say! Why, canst
    not hear's?

GAMMER GURTON
Beat him not, Hodge, but help the boy and come you
    two together.

                                          [*Exit* HODGE]

Act I, Scene v

[*Enter* TIB]

GAMMER GURTON
How now, Tib! Quick, let's hear what news thou hast
    brought hither.

TIB
Chave tossed and tumbled yonder heap over and over
    again,
And winnowed it through my fingers as men would
    winnow grain.
Not so much as a hen's turd but in pieces I tare it,
Or whatsoever clod or clay I found, I did not spare it.   5
Looking within and eke without to find your nee'le, alas,
But all in vain and without help: your nee'le is where it
    was.

GAMMER GURTON
Alas, my nee'le, we shall never meet—adieu, adieu for
    aye!

TIB
Not so, Gammer! We might it find if we know where it
    lay.

                        [*Enter* COCK]

COCK
Gog's cross, Gammer, if ye will laugh, look in but at the
    door,   10

3 *winnowed* sifted
4 *tare* tore
6 *eke* also
7 *without help* to no avail
8 *for aye* forever

---

3 *winnow grain* To expose it to a current of air, or sift it, so that the chaff blows away,
leaving the kernel.

And see how Hodge lieth tumbling and tossing amidst
    the floor,
Raking there some fire to find among the ashes dead
Where there is not one spark so big as a pin's head.
At last, in a dark corner, two sparks he thought he sees,
Which were indeed nought else but Gib our cat's two
    eyes!   15
'Puff!' quoth Hodge, thinking thereby to have fire
    without doubt;
With that Gib shut her two eyes and so the fire was out,
And by and by them opened even as they were before.
With that the sparks appeared even as they had done of
    yore;
And even as Hodge blew the fire, as he did think,   20
Gib, as she felt the blast, straightway began to wink,
Till Hodge fell of swearing, as came best to his turn,
The fire was sure bewitched and therefore would not
    burn.
At last Gib up the stairs, among the old posts and pins,
And Hodge, he hied him after till broke were both his
    shins,   25
Cursing and swearing oaths were never of his making,
That Gib would fire the house if that she were not taken!

GAMMER GURTON [*To the audience*]
See, here is all the thought that the foolish urchin
    taketh,
And Tib, methink, at his elbow almost as merry maketh.—
This is all the wit ye have when others make their moan! 30
Come down, Hodge! Where art thou? And let the cat
    alone!

HODGE [*Within*]
Gog's heart, help and come up! Gib in her tail
    hath fire,
And is like to burn all if she get a little higher!
'Come down', quoth you? Nay, then you might count
    me a patch—

---

11 *admidst* in the middle of
19 *of yore* before
22 *fell of* began
    as . . . turn such oaths as best served his purpose
26 *were . . . making* that he certainly did not invent
34 *patch* fool, dolt

The house cometh down on your heads if it take once
    the thatch!   35

GAMMER GURTON
It is the cat's eyes, fool, that shineth in the dark!

HODGE [*Within*]
Hath the cat, do you think, in every eye a spark?

GAMMER GURTON
No, but they shine as like fire as ever man see.

HODGE [*Within*]
By the mass, and she burn all, you sh' bear the
    blame for me!

GAMMER GURTON
Come down and help to seek here our nee'le that it were
    found.   40
Down, Tib, on thy knees, I say! Down, Cock, to the
    ground!
To God I make a vow, and so to good Saint Anne:
A candle shall they have apiece, get it where I can,
If I may my nee'le find in one place or in other.
               [*Enter* HODGE]

HODGE
Now a vengeance on Gib light, on Gib and Gib's mother, 45
And all the generation of cats both far and near!
Look on the ground, whoreson! Thinks thou the nee'le
    is here?

COCK
By my troth, Gammer, methought your nee'le here I
    saw,
But when my fingers touched it, I felt it was a straw.

---

39 *you sh'* ed. (yoush Q) you shall
   you . . . me it will be your fault, as far as I'm concerned
41 *thy* eds. (tho Q)
46 *generation* race

---

42 *Saint Anne* (or Hannah) Traditionally, the name of the Virgin Mary's mother. She
   is a character in several plays of the *Ludus Coventriae* mystery cycle (15th century).
47 This line is addressed to Cock. It and the following dialogue imply that Tib and
   Cock have picked objects from Hodge's clothing; he has been 'tumbling and
   tossing amidst the floor'.

TIB

  See, Hodge, what's this? May it not be within it?   50

HODGE

  Break it, fool, with thy hand, and see and thou canst
      find it.

TIB

  Nay, break it you, Hodge, according to your word.

HODGE

  Gog's sides! Fie, it stinks! It is a cat's turd!
  It were well done to make thee eat it, by the mass!

GAMMER GURTON

  This matter amendeth not; my nee'le is still where it
      was.   55
  Our candle is at an end. Let us all in quite,
  And come another time, when we have more light.

                               [*Exeunt*]

Act II

First a Song

    Back and side, go bare, go bare,
      Both foot and hand go cold;
    But Belly, God send thee good ale enough,
      Whether it be new or old.

    I can not eat but little meat,   5
      My stomach is not good;
    But sure I think that I can drink
      With him that wears a hood.
    Though I go bare take ye no care,
      I am nothing a-cold: 10
    I stuff my skin so full within
      Of jolly good ale and old.

First a Song There is nothing to indicate who sings the song, but it clearly was sung, as
    Diccon thanks the performers in i.1. A full version is given by Alexander Dyce in
    his edition of John Skelton's *Works* (1843), I, vii–ix, from a manuscript. It is
    reprinted as an appendix in Brett-Smith's edition of the play (pp. 71–4). Ralph
    Vaughan Williams set the song in Act I of his opera, *Sir John in Love* (1929), based
    on *The Merry Wives of Windsor*.
  8 *him that wears a hood* Probably a monk or friar, with satirical implication.

Back and side, go bare, go bare,
    Both foot and hand go cold;
But Belly, God send thee good ale enough,   15
    Whether it be new or old.

I love no roast but a nut-brown toast
    And a crab laid in the fire;
A little bread shall do me stead,
    Much bread I not desire.   20
No frost nor snow, no wind I trow,
    Can hurt me if I would;
I am so wrapped and throughly lapped
    Of jolly good ale and old.

Back and side go bare, etc.   25

And Tib my wife, that as her life
    Loveth well good ale to seek,
Full oft drinks she till ye may see
    The tears run down her cheeks.
Then doth she troll to me the bowl,   30
    Even as a malt-worm should;
And saith, 'Sweetheart, I took my part
    Of this jolly good ale and old'.

Back and side go bare, etc.

Now let them drink till they nod and wink   35
    Even as good fellows should do;
They shall not miss to have the bliss
    Good ale doth bring men to.
And all poor souls that have scoured bowls,
    Or have them lustily trolled,   40
God save the lives of them and their wives,
    Whether they be young or old.

Back and side go bare, etc.

18 *crab* crabapple
19 *do me stead* suffice me
23 *throughly lapped* thoroughly enfolded
30 *troll . . . bowl* pass it to me
31 *Malt-worm* (figuratively) lover of malt-liquor
39 *scoured* emptied by drinking

Act II, scene i

[*Enter* DICCON]

DICCON

Well done, by Gog's malt, well sung and well said!
Come on, Mother Chat, as thou art true maid,
One fresh pot of ale let's see, to make an end,
Against this cold weather my naked arms to defend.
This gear it warms the soul—now wind, blow on the
    worst,   5
And let us drink and swill till that our bellies burst!
Now were he a wise man by cunning could define
Which way my journey lieth or where Diccon will dine.
But one good turn I have, be it by night or day,
South, East, North or West, I am never out of my way.   10
                      [*Enter* HODGE]

HODGE

Cham goodly rewarded, am I not, do you think?
    Chad a goodly dinner for all my sweat and swink:
Neither butter, cheese, milk, onions, flesh nor fish,
Save this poor piece of barley bread—'tis a pleasant
    costly dish!

DICCON

Hail, fellow Hodge, and well to fare with thy meat, if
    thou have any;   15
But by thy words as I them smelled, thy daintrels be not
    many.

---

1 *by Gog's malt* (oath)
6 *swill* guzzle
11 *Cham* ed. (chym Q) *am* ed. (cham Q; here and occasionally elsewhere in Q the
    dialectic *ch-* form is used superfluously)
12 *swink* toil
16 *smelled* understood
    daintrels dainties

---

s.d. *Enter* DICCON. Some editors have Diccon enter with a pot of ale from Dame Chat's
    (Adams, Creeth). This would account for his absence since I.ii, especially since he
    has said that is where he was going (I.ii, 44) and seems appropriate in support of
    lines 1–6 here. But his greeting to Dame Chat and her reply in II.ii, 19–24 strongly
    suggest that their first meeting in the play occurs then. See I.ii, 44 n.

HODGE

Daintrels, Diccon? Gog's soul, man, save this piece of
    dry horse-bread,
Cha' bit no bit this livelong day, no crumb come in my
    head.
My guts they yawl, crawl and all my belly rumbleth,
The puddings cannot lie still, each one over other
    tumbleth.   20
By Gog's heart, cham so vexed, and in my belly penned,
Chwould one piece were at the spitalhouse, another at
    the castle's end!

DICCON

Why Hodge, was there none at home thy dinner for to
    set?

HODGE

Gog's bread, Diccon, ich came too late; was nothing
    there to get!
Gib—a foul fiend might on her light!—licked the milk
    pan so clean,   25
See, Diccon, 'twas not so well washed this seven year, as
    ich ween.
A pestilence light on all ill luck! Chad thought yet, for
    all this,
Of a morsel of bacon behind the door at worst should
    not miss;
But when ich sought a slip to cut, as ich was wont to do,
Gog's soul, Diccon, Gib our cat had eat the bacon too!   30
    Which bacon Diccon stole, as is declared before

DICCON

'Ill luck', quoth he! Marry, swear it, Hodge, this day,
    the truth to tell,
Thou rose not on thy right side, or else blessed thee not
    well.

---

19 *yawl, crawl* cry out and writhe in pain
20 *puddings* intestines
22 *spitalhouse* hospital
26 *ween* believe
30 *eat* eaten (pronounced 'et')
    s.d. *Which . . . before* (refers to I.i, 22)

---

17 *horse-bread* Coarse bread made of beans, bran, etc., as food for horses. Hodge's
    barley bread (l.14) would not really be of quite such poor quality.
31 *'Ill luck'* Diccon echoes Hodge (line 27).
31-2 *this day . . . side* Proverbial (Tilley S426). This just isn't your day.

Thy milk slopped up, thy bacon filched! That was too
    bad luck, Hodge!

HODGE

Nay, nay, there was a fouler fault: my gammer ga' me
    the dodge.

See'st not how cham rent and torn, my heels, my knees,
    and my breech?   35

Chad thought as ich sat by the fire, help here and there a
    stitch,

But there ich was pooped indeed.

DICCON   Why, Hodge?

HODGE   Boots

not, man, to tell.

Cham so dressed amongst a sort of fools, chad better be
    in hell!

My gammer, cham ashamed to say, by God, served me
    not well!

DICCON

How so, Hodge?

HODGE   Has she not gone, trowest now, and lost
    her nee'le?   40

DICCON

Her eel, Hodge? Who fished of late? That was a dainty
    dish!

HODGE

Tush, tush, her nee'le, her nee'le, her nee'le, man—'tis
    neither flesh nor fish!

A little thing with an hole in the end, as bright as any
    silver,

Small, long, sharp at the point, and straight as any
    pillar.

DICCON

I know not what a devil thou meanst! Thou bringst me
    more in doubt.   45

---

34 *ga' me the dodge* tricked me, let me down
37 *pooped* deceived, cheated
   Boots not it's no use
38 *Cham . . . sort* I am so badly served in such company
43 *silver* ed. (siller Q)

HODGE

> Knowest not with what Tom Tailor's man sits broaching
> through a clout?
> A nee'le, a nee'le, a nee'le! My gammer's nee'le is gone!

DICCON

> Her nee'le, Hodge, now I smell thee! That was a chance
> alone!
> By the mass, thou hadst a shameful loss, and it were but
> for thy breeches!

HODGE

> Gog's soul, man, chwould give a crown chad it but three
> stitches!   50

DICCON

> How sayest thou, Hodge! What should he have, again
> thy needle got?

HODGE

> By m' vather's soul, and chad it, chwould give him a
> new groat.

DICCON

> Canst thou keep counsel in this case?

HODGE   Else chwould my
> tongue were out!

DICCON

> Do thou but then by my advice and I will fetch it
> without doubt.

HODGE

> Chill run, chill ride, chill dig, chill delve, chill toil,
> chill trudge, shalt see.   55
> Chill hold, chill draw, chill pull, chill pinch, chill kneel
> on my bare knee.
> Chill scrape, chill scratch, chill sift, chill seek, chill bow,
> chill bend, chill sweat.
> Chill stoop, chill stir, chill cap, chill kneel, chill creep
> on hands and feet.
> Chill be thy bondman, Diccon, ich swear by sun and
> moon,

---

46 *broaching* making holes (i.e. sewing)
52 *vather's* (dialect) *father's*
    groat a coin worth four pence
58 *cap* take off my cap

And 'ch cannot somewhat to stop this gap, cham utterly
　　undone! 60
Pointing behind to his torn breeches

DICCON
　Why, is there any special cause thou takest hereat such
　　sorrow!

HODGE
　Kirstian Clack, Tom Simson's maid, by the mass, comes
　　hither tomorrow.
　Cham not able to say between us what may hap;
　She smiled on me the last Sunday, when ich put off my
　　cap.

DICCON
　Well, Hodge, this is a matter of weight, and must be
　　kept close; 65
　It might else turn to both our costs, as the world now
　　goes.
　Shalt swear to be no blab, Hodge?

HODGE　　　　　　　　　　　　　　　Chill, Diccon.

DICCON　　　　　　　　　　　　　　　Then go to.
　Lay thine hand here [*points to his buttocks*]; say after me
　　as thou shalt hear me do.
　Hast no book?

HODGE　　　　　　Cha' no book, I!

DICCON　　　　　　　　　　　Then needs must force us both
　Upon my breech to lay thine hand, and there to take
　　thine oath. 70

HODGE
　I, Hodge, breechless,
　Swear to Diccon, rechless,
　By the cross that I shall kiss,
　To keep his counsel close
　And always me to dispose 75
　To work that his pleasure is.
　　　　　　　Here he kisseth Diccon's breech

60 'ch cannot ed. (channot Q)
65 *close* secret
67 *go to* let's get on with it
72 *rechless* recklessly

71 From here to II.ii, 18, the verse shifts to short lined, tail-rhyme stanzas (*aabccb*).

DICCON
  Now, Hodge, see thou take heed,
  And do as I thee bid,
  For so I judge it meet;
  This needle again to win,   80
  There is no shift therein
  But conjure up a sprite.

HODGE
  What, the great devil, Diccon, I say?

DICCON
  Yea, in good faith, that is the way,
  Fet with some pretty charm.   85

HODGE
  Soft, Diccon, be not so hasty yet,
  By the mass, for ich begin to sweat—
  Cham afraid of some harm!

DICCON
  Come hither then, and stir thee not
  One inch out of this circle plat,   90
  But stand as I thee teach.

HODGE
  And shall ich be here safe from their claws?

DICCON
  The master devil with his long paws
  Here to thee cannot reach.
  Now will I settle me to this gear.   95

HODGE
  I say, Diccon, hear me, hear:
  Go softly to this matter.

DICCON
  What devil, man? Art afraid of nought?

HODGE
  Canst not tarry a little thought

---

79 *meet* proper
81 *shift* expedient
82 *sprite* ed. (spreete Q)
85 *fet* fetched
90 *plat* flat, horizontal

89–90 *stir . . . plat* Diccon presumably draws a circle on the ground.

Till ich make a curtsy of water?   100

DICCON
Stand still to it! Why shouldst thou fear him?

HODGE
Gog's sides, Diccon, methink ich hear him!
And tarry, chall mar all!

DICCON
The matter is no worse than I told it—

HODGE
By the mass, cham able no longer to hold it!   105
Too bad—ich must beray the hall!

DICCON
Stand to it, Hodge! Stir not, you whoreson!
What devil, be thine arse-strings bursten?
Thyself a while but stay!
The devil—I smell him—will be here anon!   110

HODGE
Hold him fast, Diccon! Cham gone, cham gone,
Chill not be at that fray!

                                        [*Exit*]

Act II, Scene ii

DICCON
Fie, shitten knave, and out upon thee!
Above all other louts, fie on thee!
Is not here a cleanly prank?
But thy matter was no better,
Nor thy presence here no sweeter;   5
To fly I can thee thank!

---

100 *make . . . water* urinate a small amount
103 *And tarry* if I stay here any longer
106 *beray* dirty, befoul

99–112 It is clear from the dialogue what effect Hodge's fear at the imminent
appearance of the devil is having on his system. The grossness is not entirely
gratuitous: it provides Hodge with a compelling reason for changing to his other
pair of trousers, the ones Gammer Gurton was mending when she lost the needle.
That he should be wearing those trousers is essential to the dénouement.
106 *the hall* Hodge refers to the hall (presumably of Christ's College, Cambridge)
where the play would have been performed.
4, 9, *thy matter; a foul . . . work* Sarcastic allusions to Hodge's soiling himself for fear of
the devil in the preceding scene.

Here is a matter worthy glozing
Of Gammer Gurton's needle losing,
And a foul piece of work.
A man, I think, might make a play   10
And need no word to this they say,
Being but half a clerk.
Soft, let me alone: I will take the charge
This matter further to enlarge
Within a time short.   15
If ye will mark my toys, and note,
I will give ye leave to cut my throat
If I make not good sport!
Dame Chat, I say, where be ye! Within?

DAME CHAT [*Within*]
Who have we there maketh such a din?   20

DICCON
Here is a good fellow, maketh no great danger.

DAME CHAT [*At her doorway*]
What, Diccon? Come near, ye be no stranger.

We be fast set at trump, man, hard by the fire;
Thou shalt set on the king if thou come a little higher.

DICCON
Nay, nay, there is no tarrying; I must be gone again.   25
But first for you in counsel I have a word or twain.

DAME CHAT
Come hither, Doll! Doll, sit down and play this game,
And as thou sawest me do, see thou do even the same.
There is five trumps beside the queen, the hindmost
     thou shalt find her.

---

7 *glozing* glossing, writing a scholarly commentary upon
16 *mark my toys* observe my devices
23 *trump* a card game, also known as ruff

10–12 *A man . . . clerk* Diccon, commenting on the frantic behaviour of others, for
     which he is in part responsible, says that even a half-educated man could make a
     play about it, without adding anything to what the characters themselves say.
19–31 Location of the action here is uncertain. Dame Chat is in her house and
     presumably invisible to the audience when Diccon calls to her (1. 19). He might
     then approach the doorway, looking into the house at 1. 21. Dame Chat's lines to
     Doll (27–30) could be spoken from within, or at the doorway. Certainly at 1. 31
     she 'enters', or comes out of her house.

Take heed of Sim Glover's wife—she hath an eye
    behind her! 30

[Enter DAME CHAT]

Now, Diccon, say your will.

DICCON   Nay, soft a little yet;
I would not tell it my sister, the matter is so great.
There I will have you swear by our dear Lady of
    Boulogne,
Saint Dunstan and Saint Donnick, with the three kings
    of Cologne,
That ye shall keep it secret.

DAME CHAT   Gog's bread, that will I do! 35
As secret as mine own thought, by God and the devil
    too!

DICCON

Here is Gammer Gurton your neighbour, a sad and
    heavy wight:
Her goodly, fair red cock at home was stole this last
    night.

DAME CHAT

Gog's soul! Her cock with the yellow legs that nightly
    crowed so just?

DICCON

That cock is stolen.

DAME CHAT   What, was he fet out of the hens'
    roost? 40

DICCON

I can not tell where the devil he was kept, under key or
    lock,
But Tib hath tickled in Gammer's ear that you should
    steal the cock.

---

34 *Donnick* ed. (Donnyke Q) Dominic
39 *just* regularly or accurately

33–4 *Lady of Boulogne . . . three kings of Cologne* Refers to a shrine to the Virgin Mary at
    Boulogne on the French Channel coast; St Dunstan (c. 909–988), Abbot of
    Glastonbury, then Archbishop of Canterbury, influential counsellor to King Edgar,
    and restorer of declining monastic life in England; St Dominic (1170–1221),
    Spanish founder of the Dominican order of preaching Friars; the three Magi, or
    Wise Men, whose supposed relics were taken to Germany in 1162 by Frederick
    Barbarossa and are enshrined in Cologne Cathedral.

Have I, strong whore? By bread and salt—

DICCON   Nay, soft, I say, be still!
Say not one word for all this gear.

DAME CHAT   By the mass, that I will!
I will have the young whore by the head and the old trot
    by the throat!   45

DICCON
Not one word, Dame Chat, I say, not one word, for my
    coat!

DAME CHAT
Shall such a beggar's brawl as that, thinkest thou, make
    me a thief?
The pox light on her whore's sides, a pestilence and a
    mischief!
Come out, thou hungry, needy bitch! O, that my nails
    be short!

DICCON
Gog's bread, woman, hold your peace! [*Aside*] This gear
    will else pass sport!   50
I would not for an hundred pound this matter should be
    known,
That I am author of this tale or have abroad it blown.—
Did ye not swear ye would be ruled, before the tale I
    told?
I said ye must all secret keep and ye said sure ye would!

DAME CHAT
Would you suffer yourself, Diccon, such a sort to revile
    you,   55
With slanderous words to blot your name and so to
    defile you?

DICCON
No, Goodwife Chat, I would be loath such drabs should
    blot my name,

---

44 *for . . . gear* in spite of this accusation
47 *brawl* offspring, brat
49 *O, that* how unfortunate that

50–2 *This gear . . . blown* These lines are surely spoken aside. Diccon is unlikely to let
    Chat know that he considers it all 'sport' or that he is the author of this tale.

But yet ye must so order all that Diccon bear no blame.

DAME CHAT

Go to then, what is your rede? Say on your mind; ye
    shall me rule herein.

DICCON

Godamercy to Dame Chat! In faith, thou must the gear
    begin.   60
It is twenty pound to a goose turd, my gammer will not
    tarry,
But hitherward she comes as fast as her legs can her
    carry,
To brawl with you about her cock, for well I heard Tib
    say
The cock was roasted in your house to breakfast
    yesterday,
And when ye had the carcass eaten, the feathers ye out
    flung,   65
And Doll, your maid, the legs she hid a foot deep in the
    dung.

DAME CHAT

O gracious God, my heart it bursts!

DICCON   Well, rule yourself a
    space,
And Gammer Gurton, when she cometh anon into this
    place,
Then to the quean, let's see! Tell her your mind and
    spare not;
So shall Diccon blameless be, and then, go to, I care not.   70

DAME CHAT

Then, whore, beware her throat! I can abide no longer!
In faith, old witch, it shall be seen, which of us two be
    stronger!
And, Diccon, but at your request, I would not stay one
    hour.

---

59 *rede* advice
60 *Godamercy to* God have mercy on
61 *It is . . . turd* the odds are . . .
69 *quean* harlot, strumpet

69–70 *Tell . . . care not* Say whatever you like to her, so long as you don't implicate me.

DICCON
  Well, keep it in till she be here, and then out let it pour;
  In the meanwhile get you in, and make no words of this. 75
  More of this matter within this hour to hear you shall
      not miss.
  Because I know you are my friend, hide it I could not,
      doubtless;
  Ye know your harm, see ye be wise about your own
      business.
  So fare ye well.

DAME CHAT   Nay, soft, Diccon, and drink. What,
      Doll, I say!
  Bring here a cup of the best ale! Let's see, come quickly
      away!   80
                             [*Exit*]

Act II, Scene iii

DICCON
  Ye see, masters, the one end tapped of this my short
      device;
  Now must we broach t'other too, before the smoke arise.
  And by the time they have awhile run, I trust ye need
      not crave it,
  But look, what lieth in both their hearts, ye are like,
      sure, to have it.

                [*Enter* HODGE]

HODGE
  Yea, Gog's soul, art alive yet! What, Diccon, dare ich
      come?   5

DICCON
  A man is well hied to trust to thee! I will say nothing,
      but mum.
  But and ye come any nearer, I pray you see all be sweet!

  1 *tapped* opened
  2 *before . . . arise* before someone gets suspicious
  3 *crave* beg to know
  6 *well hied* well sped, well served

---

  80 Although there is no stage direction, one assumes that Doll brings a cup of ale out
     to Diccon, who drinks it while he addresses the audience immediately afterwards.
  6 *I . . . mum* Proverbial (Tilley W767).

HODGE

    Tush, man, is Gammer's nee'le found? That chwould
       gladly weet.

DICCON

    She may thank thee it is not found, for if thou had kept
       thy standing,
    The devil he would have fet it out, even, Hodge, at thy
       commanding.   10

HODGE

    Gog's heart, and could he tell nothing where the nee'le
       might be found?

DICCON

    Ye foolish dolt, ye were to seek ere we had got our
       ground!
    Therefore his tale so doubtful was that I could not
       perceive it.

HODGE

    Then ich see well something was said; chope one day yet
       to have it.
    But Diccon, Diccon, did not the devil cry 'Ho, ho, ho'?   15

DICCON

    If thou hadst tarried where thou stoodst, thou wouldest
       have said so.

HODGE

    Durst swear of a book, a cheard him roar, straight after
       ich was gone!

---

  8 *weet* know
 12 *ye were . . . ground* you disappeared before we had stationed ourselves in the right
    place
 13 *doubtful* obscure
 14 *chope* I hope
 17 *Durst . . . book* I'd dare to swear on the Bible
    cheard ed. (chard Q) I heard

---

 15 *did . . . 'Ho, ho, ho'* Traditional cry of the devil, usually upon his entrance, in early
drama. See, for example, *The Conversion of St Paul* (in *English Moral Interludes*, ed.
Wickham), 1. 412 and preceding s.d.: '*Here to enter a devil with thunder and fire, and
to avaunt himself saying as foloweth* . . . : Belial. Ho! ho! Behold me, the mighty
prince of the parts infernal! Ho! Ho! infernal!'; saying "Oh, oh, oh!" '; compare the
s.d. '. . . Devil entereth saying "Oh, oh, oh!" ' in Thomas Garter's *Susanna* (c.
1569), 11. 1382–3. As Hodge's query implies, devils are expected to roar; Hodge,
despite having fled the scene, later asserts that the devil did roar (III.ii, 13).

But tell me, Diccon, what said the knave? Let me hear it
    anon.

DICCON

The whoreson talked to me, I know not well of what:
One while his tongue it ran and paltered of a cat,   20
Another while he stammered still upon a rat,
Last of all there was nothing but every word 'Chat,
    Chat'.
But this I well perceived before I would him rid:
Between Chat and the rat and the cat the needle is hid.
Now whether Gib our cat have eat it in her maw,   25
Or Doctor Rat our curate have found it in the straw,
Or this Dame Chat your neighbour have stolen it, God
    he knoweth.
But by the morrow at this time, we shall learn how the
    matter goeth.

HODGE

Canst not learn tonight, man? Seest not what is here?
                Pointing behind to his torn breeches

DICCON

'Tis not possible to make it sooner appear.   30

HODGE

Alas, Diccon, then chave no shift, but, lest ich tarry too
    long,
Hie me to Sim Glover's shop, there to seek for a thong,
Therewith this breech to tache and tie as ich may.

DICCON

Tomorrow, Hodge, if we chance to meet, shalt see what
    I will say.

                         [*Exit* HODGE]

20 *paltered* mumbled
23 *rid* dispatch
25 *maw* stomach
33 *tache* fasten, secure

29 s.d. *Pointing . . . breeches* Between his exit at the end of II.i and his entrance near the
    beginning of this scene, Hodge has changed his soiled trousers for the pair that
    Gammer Gurton had begun mending.

Act II, Scene iv

DICCON

    Now this gear must forward go, for here my gammer
        cometh.

    Be still awhile, and say nothing. Make here a little
        roomth.

             [*Enter* GAMMER GURTON]

GAMMER GURTON [*Aside*]

    Good Lord, shall never be my luck my nee'le again to
        spy?

    Alas the while, 'tis past my help; where 'tis still it must
        lie.

DICCON

    Now Jesus, Gammer Gurton, what driveth you to this
        sadness?   5

    I fear me, by my conscience, you will sure fall to
        madness!

GAMMER GURTON

    Who is that? What, Diccon? Cham lost, man—fie, fie!

DICCON

    Marry, fie on them that be worthy! But what should be
        your trouble?

GAMMER GURTON

    Alas, the more ich think on it, my sorrow it waxeth
        double.

    My goodly tossing spurrier's nee'le chave lost ich wot
        not where.   10

DICCON

    Your nee'le? When?

GAMMER GURTON   My nee'le, alas! Ich might full ill it spare,
As God himself he knoweth ne'er one beside chave.

---

  1 *Now . . . go* now my plot will advance

  2 *roomth* room

  8 *Marry* (interjection; originally 'Mary', i.e. the Virgin Mary)

10 *tossing* that moves to and fro quickly in sewing
    spurrier's spur-maker's

---

  2 *Make . . . roomth* Diccon instructs spectators to stand aside to let Gammer through.
See Introduction p. lii.

DICCON
    If this be all, good Gammer, I warrant you all is save.

GAMMER GURTON
    Why, know you any tidings which way my nee'le is gone?

DICCON
    Yea, that I do doubtless, as ye shall hear anon: 15
    A see a thing this matter toucheth within these twenty hours,
    Even at this gate before my face, by a neighbour of yours.
    She stooped me down and up she took a needle or a pin—
    I durst be sworn it was even yours, by all my mother's kin!

GAMMER GURTON
    It was my nee'le, Diccon, ich wot, for here, even by this
        post,   20
    Ich sat what time as ich up start, and so my nee'le it lost.
    Who was it, lief son? Speak, ich pray thee, and quickly
        tell me that.

DICCON
    A subtle quean as any in this town, your neighbour here,
        Dame Chat.

GAMMER GURTON
    Dame Chat, Diccon! Let me be gone, chill thither in
        post haste!

DICCON
    Take my counsel yet or ye go, for fear ye walk in waste.   25
    It is a murrain crafty drab and froward to be pleased;

13 *save* saved
16 *A see* I've seen
21 *Ich sat . . . up start* I was sitting at the time I started up
22 *lief* eds. (leive Q) dear
25 *or* before
26 *murrain* cursed
    drab slut, whore
    froward . . . pleased hard to please

15–23 Diccon's lie and false accusation of Dame Chat here complement his previous lie
    and the implicating of Tib and Gammer Gurton concerning the cock (II.ii).
17 *at this gate* Perhaps a small wicket gate opening on the street from Gammer
    Gurton's front yard; or simply the house door.

And ye take not the better way, your needle yet ye lose
    it,
For when she took it up, even here before your doors,
'What, soft, Dame Chat', quoth I 'that same is none of
    yours'.
'Avaunt', quoth she, 'Sir Knave. What pratest thou of
    that I find?   30
I would thou hadst kissed me I wot where!' (she meant,
    I know, behind).
And home she went as brag as it had been a body-louse,
And I after, as bold as it had been the goodman of the
    house.
But there, and ye had heard her, now she bagan to scold!
The tongue it went on pattens, by him that Judas sold!   35
Each other word I was a knave and you a whore of
    whores,
Because I spoke in your behalf and said the nee'le was
    yours.

GAMMER GURTON
Gog's bread, and thinks the callet thus to keep my nee'le
    me fro?

DICCON
Let her alone and she minds none other but even to
    dress you so.

GAMMER GURTON
By the mass, chill rather spend the coat that is on my
    back!   40
Thinks the false quean by such a slight that chill my
    nee'le lack?

27 *lose* Q (some eds. emend to *lese* to restore rhyme with *pleased*)
29 *soft* not so hasty
30 *Avaunt* begone
32 *brag* saucily
   as it as if she
33 *goodman* master
35 *went on pattens* made a great clatter
38 *callet* lewd woman, scold
   fro from
39 *Let . . . so* Leave her alone if she does not intend to do exactly that to you

DICCON

   Sleep not your gear, I counsel you, but of this take good
      heed:
   Let not be known I told you of it, how well soever ye
      speed.

GAMMER GURTON

   Chill in, Diccon, a clean apron to take and set before
      me;
   And ich may my nee'le once see, chill sure remember
      thee!　　　　　　　　　　　　　　　　　　　　　　　45

                             [Exit]

Act II, Scene v

DICCON

   Here will the sport begin, if these two once may meet;
   Their cheer, durst lay money, will prove scarcely sweet!
   My gammer, sure, intends to be upon her bones
   With staves or with clubs or else with cobblestones!
   Dame Chat, on the other side, if she be far behind　　　5
   I am right far deceived; she is given to it of kind.
   He that may tarry by it awhile, and that but short,
   I warrant him, trust to it, he shall see all the sport.
   Into the town will I, my friends to visit there,
   And hither straight again to see th' end of this gear.　　10
   [To the musicians] In the meantime, fellows, pipe up your
      fiddles; I say, take them,
   And let your friends hear such mirth as ye can make
      them.

                               [Exit]

---

42 *Sleep . . . gear* do not neglect this matter
6 *given . . . kind* naturally disposed to violent abuse
11 *pipe . . . fiddles* strike up the music

11–12 The musicians would most likely have been stationed in the gallery, above the
playing area, at the screens end of the college hall (see Introduction, pp. li–lii).

Act III, Scene i

[*Enter* HODGE]

HODGE

Sim Glover, yet gramercy! Cham meetly well sped now;
Th'art even as good a fellow as ever kissed a cow!
Here is a thong indeed, by the mass, though ich speak it—
Tom Tankard's great bald curtal, I think, could not
    break it!
And when he spied my need to be so straight and hard,   5
H'as lent me here his nawl to set the jib forward.
As for my gammer's nee'le, the flying fiend go weet,
Chill not now go to the door again with it to meet!
Chwould make shift good enough, and chad a candle's
    end;
The chief hole in my breech with these two chill amend.   10

Act III, Scene ii

[*Enter* GAMMER GURTON]

GAMMER GURTON

Now Hodge, mayst now be glad, cha' news to tell thee:
Ich know who has my nee'le; ich trust soon shalt it see.

HODGE

The devil thou does! Hast heard, Gammer, indeed, or
    dost but jest?

GAMMER GURTON

'Tis as true as steel, Hodge.

HODGE   Why, knowest well where didst lose it?

---

1 *gramercy* God grant you mercy
  meetly . . . sped well provided for
3 *thong* eds. (thynge Q)
4 *bald curtal* piebald horse with a docked tail
6 *H'as* ed. (Hays Q) He has
  nawl awl
  set . . . forward hasten matters on
  jib (gib Q) forward-most triangular sail in certain systems of ship's rigging
7 *the flying . . . weet* the devil take it
10 *these two* (i.e., the awl and thong)
4 *lose* ed. (leese Q)

GAMMER GURTON
  Ich know who found it and took it up. Shalt see, or it be
    long.   5

HODGE
  God's mother dear! If that be true, farewell both nawl
    and thong!
  But who has it, Gammer? Say on, chwould fain hear it
    disclosed.

GAMMER GURTON
  That false vixen, that same Dame Chat, that counts
    herself so honest!

HODGE
  Who told you so?

GAMMER GURTON   That same did Diccon the bedlam,
    which saw it done.

HODGE
  Diccon? It is a vengeable knave, Gammer, 'tis a bonable
    whoreson,   10
  Can do mo' things than that, else cham deceived evil.
  By the mass, ich saw him of late call up a great black
    devil!
  'O!' the knave cried, 'Ho, ho!' He roared and he
    thundered!
  And ye 'ad been here, cham sure you'ld murrainly ha'
    wondered!

GAMMER GURTON
  Was not thou afraid, Hodge, to see him in this place?   15

HODGE
  No, and he 'ad come to me, chwould have laid him on
    the face,
  Chwould have, promised him.

---

  5 *or* before
 10 *vengeable* vengeful (here, perhaps, simply 'very great')
    bonable abominable
 11 *mo'* ed. (mo Q) more
 14 *murrainly ha' wondered* been mightily astonished
 16 *he 'ad* ed. (chad Q)

10–11 *it is . . . evil* It would be a very great scoundrel indeed who could do more
    (villainous) things than Diccon, or I'm badly mistaken.
16 Hodge's bravery is after the fact; compare his behaviour at II.i, 86–112.

GAMMER GURTON But Hodge, had he no horns to push?

HODGE

As long as your two arms! Saw ye never Friar Rush
Painted on a cloth, with a sidelong cow's tale,
And crooked cloven feet and many a hooked nail?   20
For all the world, if I should judge, chwould reckon him
    his brother;
Look, even what face Friar Rush had, the devil had such
    another!

GAMMER GURTON

Now Jesus mercy, Hodge! Did Diccon in him bring?

HODGE

Nay, Gammer, hear me speak; chill tell you a greater
    thing.
The devil, when Diccon bad him (ich heard him
    wondrous well)   25
Said plainly here before us, that Dame Chat had your
    nee'le.

GAMMER GURTON

Then let us go and ask her wherefore she minds to keep it;
Seeing we know so much, 'twere a madness now to sleep it.

HODGE

Go to her, Gammer. See ye not where she stands in her
    doors?
Bid her give you the nee'le; 'tis none of hers, but yours.   30

25 *bad* commanded
28 *sleep it* ignore, neglect it

18–22 The Friar Rush legend was of Danish origin, popular in Germany, and
    obviously familiar in England by the mid-16th century, although the earliest extant
    English version dates from 1620. Rush was a devil, sent by Satan to create havoc
    among the friars. Later he became a mischievous spirit generally, like Puck or
    Robin Goodfellow. He is the main character in Thomas Dekker's play, *If it be not
    good, the Devil is in it* (c. 1611).

25–6 Hodge repeats what Diccon, not the devil, has said (II.iii, 19–27).

29 *See . . . doors* Dame Chat would have appeared at her door at some point during the
    scene, drawn (if explanation is needed) by the sound of Gammer's voice outside;
    she has been eagerly awaiting her since II.ii.

Act III, Scene iii

GAMMER GURTON

Dame Chat, chwould pray thee fair, let me have that is
    mine!
Chill not this twenty years take one fart that is thine;
Therefore give me mine own, and let me live beside
    thee.

DAME CHAT

Why art thou crept from home hither to mine own doors
    to chide me?
Hence, doting drab, avaunt, or I shall set thee further!   5
Intends thou and that knave me in my house to murder?

GAMMER GURTON

Tush, gape not so on me, woman! Shalt not yet eat me,
Nor all the friends thou hast in this shall not entreat me.
Mine own goods I will have, and ask thee no by-leave.
What, woman? Poor folks must have right, though the
    thing you agrieve.   10

DAME CHAT

Give thee thy right and hang thee up, with all thy
    beggar's brood!
What, wilt thou make me a thief, and say I stole thy
    good?

GAMMER GURTON

Chill say nothing, ich warrant thee, but that ich can
    prove it well:
Thou fet my good even from my door, cham able this to
    tell.

---

  1 *chwould* ed. (cholde Q)
  5 *doting* foolish
  6 *murder* ed. (murther Q)
  7 *on me, woman* eds. (no me Woman Q; no, woman 1661)
  9 *no by-leave* Boas (on beleve Q)
    and . . . by-leave without asking your permission
12 *good* goods, property

Throughout this scene, the play's centrepiece, neither woman names the object in
question, which Dame Chat thinks is the cock and Gammer, her needle. It is, of course,
Diccon's doing that they are at such utter cross-purposes.

DAME CHAT
> Did I, old witch, steal aught was thine? How should that
> thing be known?   15

GAMMER GURTON
> Ich cannot tell, but up thou tookst it as though it had
> been thine own.

DAME CHAT
> Marry, fie on thee, thou old gib, with all my very heart!

GAMMER GURTON
> Nay, fie on thee, thou ramp, thou rig, with all that take
> thy part!

DAME CHAT
> A vengeance on those lips that layeth such things to my
> charge!

GAMMER GURTON
> A vengeance on those callet's hips, whose conscience is so
> large!   20

DAME CHAT
> Come out, hog!

GAMMER GURTON   Come out, hog, and let me have right!

DAME CHAT
> Thou arrant witch!

GAMMER GURTON   Thou bawdy bitch, chill make thee
> curse this night!

---

15 *aught* ed. (oft Q) anything
17 *gib* cat (disparagingly, an old woman)
18 *ramp* vulgar woman
   rig wanton woman
20 *callet* lewd woman
21 *hog* eds. (Hogge . . . hogge Q; not 'Hodge' as a few eds. have it)
   let me have eds. (let have me Q)
22 *arrant* notorious

---

21 *Come out* It does not make sense for Chat, who is standing in the doorway of her
   house, literally to say 'Come out' to Gammer, who is outside already (11. 4,6). The
   sense is perhaps similar to that of 'calling someone out', i.e., challenging to a duel,
   or simply 'Come on'.

DAME CHAT
A bag and a wallet!

GAMMER GURTON   A cart for a callet!

DAME CHAT   Why, weenest thou thus to prevail?
I hold thee a groat, I shall patch thy coat!

GAMMER GURTON   Thou wert as good kiss my tail!
Thou slut, thou cut, thou rakes, thou jakes, will not
    shame make thee hide?   25

DAME CHAT
Thou scald, thou bald, thou rotten, thou glutton, I will
    no longer chide,
But I will teach thee to keep home!

GAMMER GURTON   Wilt thou, drunken beast?
        [*They fight*]

HODGE
Stick to her, Gammer, take her by the head! Chill
    warrant you this feast!
Smite, I say, Gammer! Bite, I say, Gammer! I trow ye
    will be keen!

24 *hold* wager
25 *cut* horse
    rakes vague term of abuse, used here merely for rhyme
    jakes privy
25–6 *hide/ . . . chide* Adams (hide/ . . . chide thee Q, 1661; some eds. supply 'thee' in
    1.25 and retain 'thee' in 1.26)
26 *scald* (term of abuse, from a scabby disease of the scalp)
28 *Chill . . . feast* I'll back you to win this event

23 *bag . . . wallet . . . cart* Dame Chat doubtless uses 'wallet' in the special sense of a
    beggar's bag, and Gammer Gurton alludes to the punishment of lewd women by
    tying them to the tailgate of a cart and whipping them through the town.
28–49 The main movements in the action of this scene can easily be inferred from the
    dialogue. Hodge obviously stands well away from the fray, urging Gammer on
    (11.28–31). She appears to be getting the worst of it, and he runs into the house to
    get a weapon (32–4), but despite his brave words (35–40), retreats quickly once
    again; the last part of 1.41 would be spoken from within the house. Between 11.39
    and 42, Doll has brought out a spit, with which Dame Chat threatens Hodge (42).
    Gammer takes advantage of this momentary diversion to grab Dame Chat from
    behind, but loses her hold and suffers a defiant parting blow (49).

Where be your nails? Claw her by the jaws, pull me out
    both her eyen!   30
Gog's bones, Gammer, hold up your head!

DAME CHAT   I trow, drab, I shall dress thee!
    [*To* HODGE] Tarry, thou knave! I hold thee a groat, I shall
    make these hands bless thee!
               [*Exit* HODGE *into* GAMMER GURTON'*s house*]
    Take thou this, old whore, for amends, and learn thy
    tongue well to tame,
    And say thou met at this bickering, not thy fellow but thy
    dame!

               [*Enter* HODGE *with a staff*]

HODGE
    Where is the strong-stewed whore? Chill gi'er a whore's
    mark!   35
    [*To the audience*] Stand out one's way, that ich kill none
    in the dark!
    Up, Gammer, and ye be alive! Chill fight now for us
    both!
    Come no near me, thou scald callet! To kill thee ich were
    loath!

DAME CHAT
    Art here again, thou hoddypeak? What, Doll, bring me
    out my spit!

HODGE
    Chill broach thee with this, by m' father's soul! Chill
    conjure that foul sprite!   40
          [COCK *appears at the door of* GAMMER'*s house*]
    Let door stand, Cock! [*To* DAME CHAT] Why, comes
    indeed?—Keep door, thou whoreson boy!

---

30 *eyen* eyes
34 *bickering* skirmish, altercation
   not . . . dame not your equal but your superior
35 *strong-stewed* belonging to the stews, or brothel
   gi'er ed. (geare Q) give her
38 *near* nearer
39 *hoddypeak* simpleton, blockhead

DAME CHAT
    Stand to it, thou dastard, for thine ears! I s' teach thee a
        sluttish toy!

HODGE
    Gog's wounds, whore, chill make thee avaunt! Take
        heed, Cock! Pull in the latch!

                                      [*Exit*]

DAME CHAT
    I'faith, Sir Loose-Breech, had ye tarried, ye should have
        found your match!

GAMMER GURTON
    Now 'ware thy throat, losel, thou s' pay for all!

HODGE [*From the doorway*]   Well said,
        Gammer, by my soul!   45
    Hoise her! Souse her! Bounce her! Trounce her! Pull out
        her throat-boll!

DAME CHAT
    Comst behind me, thou withered witch! And I get once
        on foot,
    Thou s' pay for all, thou old tarleather! I'll teach thee
        what 'longs to it!
    Take thou this to make up thy mouth, till time thou
        come by more!   [*Exit*]

HODGE [*Coming out*]
    Up, Gammer, stand on your feet! Where is
        the old whore   50
    Faith, would chad her by the face; chwould crack her
        callet crown!

42 *dastard* coward
    I s' ed. (Ise Q) I shall
    thee a Q (thee, a eds.)
    toy trick
45 *losel* worthless person
    thou s' ed. (thouse Q) thou shalt
    pay eds. (pray Q)
46 *hoise* 1661 (hoyse Q; house Boas) raise, hoist ('house' is a variant form of the same
    word)
    souse beat severely
    throat-boll Adam's apple
48 *tarleather* strip of sheepskin used to make thongs (here, a term of abuse)
    teach . . . it show you what's what

GAMMER GURTON

    Ah, Hodge, Hodge, where was thy help when vixen had
        me down?

HODGE

    By the mass, Gammer, but for my staff, Chat had gone
        nigh to spill you!
    Ich think the harlot had not cared, and chad not come,
        to kill you!
    But shall we lose our nee'le thus?

GAMMER GURTON   No, Hodge, chwere
    loath do so.   55
    Thinkest thou chill take that at her hand? No, Hodge,
        ich tell thee, no!

HODGE

    Chwould yet this fray were well take up and our own
        nee'le at home;
    'Twill be my chance else some to kill, wherever it be or
        whom!

GAMMER GURTON

    We have a parson, Hodge, thou knows, a man esteemed
        wise,
    Mast' Doctor Rat; chill for him send and let me hear his
        advice.   60
    He will her shrive for all this gear, and give her penance
        strait;
    We s' have our nee'le, else Dame Chat comes ne'er
        within heaven gate!

HODGE

    Yea, marry, Gammer, that ich think best. Will you now
        for him send?
    The sooner Doctor Rat be here, the sooner we s' ha' an
        end;
    And hear, Gammer! Diccon's devil, as ich remember
        well,   65

---

    53 *spill* kill
    55 *chwere* ed. (chwarde Q)
    57 *take up* concluded
    60 *Mast'* Master
    61 *shrive* hear confession and impose penance
       strait strict
    62 *We s'* ed. (Wese Q) we shall
    65 *hear* eds. (here Q)

Of Cat and Chat and Doctor Rat a felonious tale did tell;
Chold you forty pound that is the way your nee'le to get
　　again.

GAMMER GURTON
Chill ha' him straight! Call out the boy, we s' make him
　　take the pain.

HODGE
What, Cock, I say! Come out! What devil, canst not
　　hear?

COCK [*Within*]
How now, Hodge? How does Gammer! Is yet the weather
　　clear?　　　　　　　　　　　　　　　　　　　　　　　　　70
What would sh'ave me to do?

GAMMER GURTON　　　　　　　　Come hither, Cock, anon!
　　　　　　　　　　　[*Enter* COCK]
Hence swith to Doctor Rat! Hie thee that thou were
　　gone,
And pray him come speak with me; cham not well at
　　ease.
Shalt have him as his chamber, or else at Mother Bee's,
Else seek him at Hob Filcher's shop, for as cheard it
　　reported,　　　　　　　　　　　　　　　　　　　　　　75
There is the best ale in all the town, and now is most
　　resorted.

COCK
And shall ich bring him with me, Gammer?

GAMMER GURTON　　　　　　　　Yea, by and by, good Cock.

COCK
Shalt see that shall be here anon, else let me have on the
　　dock!
　　　　　　　　　　　　　　　　　　　　　　　　　　　　[*Exit*]

67 *Chold* I hold, wager
68 *straight* straightaway
70 s.p. COCK eds. (GAMMER Q)
71 *sh'ave* ed. (chave Q)
　　s.d. *Enter* COCK ed. (after l. 69 eds.)
72 *swith* quickly
75 *cheard* ed. (charde Q)
76 *resorted* frequented
78 *dock* buttocks

HODGE

    Now, Gammer, shall we two go in and tarry for his
        coming?

    What devil, woman! Pluck up your heart, and leave off
        all this glumming.   80

    Though she were stronger at the first, as ich think ye did
        find her,

    Yet there ye dressed the drunken sow, what time ye
        came behind her.

GAMMER GURTON

    Nay, nay, cham sure she lost not all, for set th' end to the
        beginning,

    And ich doubt not but she will make small boast of her
        winning.

Act III, Scene iv

[Enter TIB *with* GIB *the cat]*

TIB

    See, Gammer, Gammer! Gib, our cat, cham afraid what
        she aileth!

    She stands me gasping behind the door, as though her
        wind her faileth.

    Now let ich doubt what Gib should mean, that now she
        doth so dote.

HODGE

    Hold hither! Ich hold twenty pound your nee'le is in her
        throat!

    Grope her, ich say! Methinks ich feel it. Does not prick
        your hand?   5

---

80 *glumming* being glum or dejected

  2 *me* (used here as an expletive; the ethical dative)

  3 *doth so dote* appears out of her wits

  4 *Hold hither* hand her to me

    Ich hold ed. (ichould Q) I wager

83–4 Hodge has reminded Gammer of how she jumped upon Chat from behind, while
    Gammer recalls the parting blow she received from Chat afterwards (1. 49) and is
    sure Chat will claim victory; 'small' is ironic.

  3 *Now . . . doubt* 'Let' should perhaps be 'yet' (or 'mot' [=must] as Hazlitt
    conjectured); or 'ich' be amended to 'mich' or 'me'. But Q's version may be
    intentional, reflecting Tib's tenuous command of grammar.

GAMMER GURTON
   Ich can feel nothing.

HODGE   No, ich know there's not within this land
   A murrainer cat than Gib is, betwixt the Thames and
      Tyne;
   Sh'as as much wit in her head almost as chave in mine!

TIB
   Faith, sh'as eaten something that will not easily down;
   Whether she got it at home or abroad in the town,   10
   Ich cannot tell.

GAMMER GURTON Alas, ich fear it be some crooked pin!
   And then farewell, Gib! She is undone and lost all save
      the skin.

HODGE
   'Tis your nee'le, woman, I say! Gog's soul, give me a
      knife,
   And chill have it out of her maw, or else chall lose my
      life!

GAMMER GURTON
   What? Nay, Hodge, fie! Kill not our cat! 'Tis all the cats
      we ha' now!   15

HODGE
   By the mass, Dame Chat has me so moved, ich care not
      what I kill, ma' God a vow!
   Go to then, Tib, to this gear! Hold up her tail and take her!
   Chill see what devil is in her guts! Chill take the pains to
      rake her!

GAMMER GURTON
   Rake a cat, Hodge? What wouldst thou do?

---

  8 *Sh'as* ed. (Shase Q) she has
 12 *all save* except
 13 *'Tis* eds. (Tyb Q)
 16 *ma'* I make

---

 18 *rake* A term from farriery: 'to clean (a costive horse or its fundament) from ordure
   by scraping with the hand' (*OED*).

HODGE   What,
    thinkst that cham not able?
    Did not Tom Tankard rake his curtal t'other day,
      standing in the stable?   20

                [Enter COCK]

GAMMER GURTON
    Soft, be content. Let's hear what news Cock bringeth
      from Mast' Rat.

COCK
    Gammer, chave been there as you bad, you wot well
      about what;
    'Twill not be long before he come, ich durst swear of a
      book.
    He bids you see ye be at home, and there for him to
      look.

GAMMER GURTON
    Where didst thou find him, boy? Was he not where I
      told thee?   25

COCK
    Yes, yes, even at Hob Filcher's house, by him that
      bought and sold me!
    A cup of ale had in his hand, and a crab lay in the fire.
    Chad much ado to go and come, all was so full of mire.
    And Gammer, one thing I can tell; Hob Filcher's nawl
      was lost,
    And Doctor Rat found it again, hard beside the door
      post.   30
    Ich hold a penny can say something your nee'le again to
      fet.

GAMMER GURTON
    Cham glad to hear so much, Cock. Then trust he will
      not let
    To help us herein best he can; therefore till time he
      come,
    Let us go in. If there be aught to get thou shalt have
      some.

                    [Exeunt]

20 *t'other* ed. (toore Q)
23 *of a book* on the Bible
26 *him . . . me* Christ
31 *can* he can
32 *let* neglect, fail
34 *aught to get* any food to eat

Act [IV], Scene [i]

[*Enter* DOCTOR RAT]

DOCTOR RAT
A man were better twenty times be a bandog and bark,
Than here among such a sort be parish priest or clerk,
Where he shall never be at rest one pissing-while a day,
But he must trudge about the town, this way and that
    way;
Here to a drab, there to a thief, his shoes to tear and
    rent,   5
And that which is worst of all, at every knave's
    commandment!
I had not sit the space to drink two pots of ale
But Gammer Gurton's sorry boy was straightway at my
    tail,
And she was sick and I must come, to do I wot not what.
If once her finger's end but ache, 'Trudge! Call for
    Doctor Rat!'   10
And when I come not at their call, I only thereby lose,
For I am sure to lack therefore a tithe-pig or a goose.
I warrant you, when truth is known, and told they have
    their tale,
The matter whereabout I came is not worth a
    halfpennyworth of ale!
Yet must I talk so sage and smooth as though I were a
    glozer,   15

Act IV, Scene i eds. (The ii Acte. The iiii. Seane. Q, 1661)
  5 *his shoes* (the priest's not the thief's)
  7 *sit the space* been sitting long enough
 15 *glozer* ed. (glosier Q) flatterer

---

  1 *bandog* Originally, a dog kept chained because of its ferocity; here, simply a dog.
 12 *tithe-pig . . . goose* Donations from parishioners to the priest, upon which he
    depended to supplement his meagre salary. Specifically, the tithe was one-tenth of
    goods or wealth, to be given to the church for the maintenance of religion.
    Scriptural authority is found in the Old Testament (e.g., Leviticus 27:30,
    Deuteronomy 14:22, Malachi 3:10), and tithing was enforced by law in England as
    early as 900. As vicar, Dr Rat would have to collect the 'small' tithe (small animals,
    fruit, vegetables) himself, the 'large' tithe of the major crops going to the rector or
    incumbent, probably the bishop or a monastery (or, after the dissolution of
    monasteries in the 1530s, a lay rector). Thus his concern to remain on good terms
    with his parishioners.

Else or the year come at an end, I shall be, sure, the
    loser.
[*At* GAMMER GURTON*'s door*] What work ye, Gammer
    Gurton? Ho! Here is your friend, Master Rat.
                [*Enter* GAMMER GURTON]

GAMMER GURTON
    Ah, good master Doctor, cha' troubled, cha' troubled
    you, chwot well that!

DOCTOR RAT
    How do ye, woman? Be ye lusty, or be ye not well at
    ease?

GAMMER GURTON
    By gis, master, cham not sick, but yet chave a disease.   20
    Chad a foul turn now of late; chill tell it you, by gigs!

DOCTOR RAT
    Hath your brown cow cast her calf or your sandy sow
    her pigs?

GAMMER GURTON
    No, but chad been as good they had, as this, ich wot
    well.

DOCTOR RAT
    What is the matter?

GAMMER GURTON   Alas, alas, cha' lost my good nee'le!
    My nee'le, I say, and wot ye what? A drab came by and
    spied it,   25
    And when I asked her for the same, the filth flatly
    denied it!

DOCTOR RAT
    What was she that—

GAMMER GURTON   A dame, ich warrant you! She
    began to scold and brawl—
    Alas, Alas! [*Calling into the house*] Come hither, Hodge!
    [*To* DOCTOR RAT] This wretch can tell you all.

---

17 *What . . . ye* what are you doing
    Ho! ed. (hoow Q; How? eds.)
19 *lusty* in good health
20, 21 *gis; gigs* Jesus
22 *cast* given birth to prematurely

Act IV, Scene ii

[*Enter* HODGE]

HODGE
Good morrow, gaffer vicar!

DOCTOR RAT   Come on, fellow, let us hear.
Thy dame hath said to me thou knowest of all this gear;
Let's see what thou canst say.

HODGE   By m' fay, sir, that ye shall!
What matter soever here was done, ich can tell your
    ma'ship all.
My gammer Gurton here, see now,   5
    sat her down at this door, see now;
And as she began to stir her, see now,
    her nee'le fell in the floor, see now;
And while her staff she took, see now,
    at Gib her cat to fling, see now,   10
Her nee'le was lost in the floor, see now—
    Is not this a wondrous thing, see now?
Then came the quean, Dame Chat, see now,
    to ask for her black cup, see now,
And even here at this gate, see now,   15
    she took that nee'le up, see now.
My gammer then she yede, see now,
    her nee'le again to bring, see now,
And was caught by the head, see now—
    Is not this a wondrous thing, see now?   20
She tare my gammer's coat, see now,
    and scratched her by the face, see now;
Chad thought sh'ad stopped her throat, see now—
    Is not this a wondrous case, see now?

---

3 *fay* faith
4 *all* eds. (not in Q, 1661)
17 *yede* went
21 *tare* tore

---

1 *gaffer* Contraction of 'godfather' or 'grandfather'; the masculine form of 'gammer'.
    Apparently applied originally by country people to elderly persons or those entitled
    to respect. The earliest recorded occurrences of both forms are in this play.
14 *to . . . cup* This new detail is the product of Hodge's imagination, embroidering
    upon the original hint supplied by Diccon (II.iv, 16–37).

When ich saw this, ich was wroth, see now,   25
   and start between them twain, see now;
Else ich durst take a book oath, see now,
   my gammer had been slain, see now!

GAMMER GURTON
This is even the whole matter, as Hodge has plainly told,
And chwould fain be quiet for my part, that chwould.   30
But help us, good master, beseech ye that ye do,
Else shall we both be beaten and lose our nee'le too.

DOCTOR RAT
What would ye have me to do? Tell me that I were gone;
I will do the best that I can, to set you both at one.
But be ye sure Dame Chat hath this your nee'le found?   35
                [*Enter* DICCON]

GAMMER GURTON
Here comes the man that see her take it up off the
   ground;
Ask him yourself, Master Rat, if ye believe not me,
And help me to my nee'le, for God's sake and Saint
   Charity!

DOCTOR RAT
Come near, Diccon, and let us hear what thou can
   express.
Wilt thou be sworn thou seest Dame Chat this woman's
   nee'le have?   40

---

25 *wroth* angry
26 *start* went
33 *that . . . gone* so that I may go do it
34 *set . . . one* make peace between you
35 s.d. *Enter* DICCON Boas (after 1.39 eds.)
38 *Saint Charity* eds. (saint charitie Q)

---

38 *Saint Charity* Q's small letters may mean that no proper name is intended; 'saint'
would mean 'holy'. However, such usage, as proper names, was current until the
seventeenth century (e.g., Saint Cross, Saint Spirit, Saint Trinity; compare 'By Gis
and by Saint Charity', *Hamlet* IV.v, 56). There were said to be three sisters, Saints
Faith, Hope and Charity, martyred in Rome under the emperor Hadrian, but 'the
concatenation of names is itself suspicious' (Donald Attwater, *A Dictionary of
Saints* [1965], p. 127). The tradition was well established by the tenth century,
when the three (Fides, Spes, Caritas) figured as dramatic characters, the holy
daughters of Wisdom, in a Latin play, *Sapientia*, by a German nun, Hrotsvitha (or
Roswitha). See *The Plays of Roswitha*, trans. C. St John (1923), pp. 131–58; and
Young, I, 1–8.

DICCON
> Nay, by Saint Benit, will I not! Then might ye think me
> rave!

GAMMER GURTON
> Why, didst not thou tell me so even here? Canst thou for
> shame deny it?

DICCON
> Ay, marry, Gammer; but I said I would not abide by it.

DOCTOR RAT
> Will you say a thing and not stick to it to try it?

DICCON
> 'Stick to it', quoth you, Master Rat? Marry, sir, I defy
> it!   45
> Nay, there is many an honest man, when he such blasts
> hath blown
> In his friends' ears, he would be loath the same by him
> were known.
> If such a toy be used oft among the honesty.
> It may beseem a simple man, of your and my degree.

DOCTOR RAT
> Then we be never the nearer, for all that you can tell!   50

DICCON
> Yea, marry, sir, if ye will do by mine advice and
> counsel.
> If Mother Chat see all us here, she knoweth how the
> matter goes.
> Therefore I rede you three go hence, and within keep
> close,
> And I will into Dame Chat's house, and so the matter
> use,
> That or you could go twice to church, I warrant you hear
> news.   55

---

41 *think me rave* believe me to be mad
44 *try* prove
47 *the same . . . known* that it were known to come from him
48 *honesty* honourable people
49 *beseem* be fitting for
53 *rede* advise

---

41 *Saint Benit* St. Benedict, sixth-century founder of the monastic movement.
43 He did so at II.iv, 43.

She shall look well about her, but I durst lay a pledge,
Ye shall of Gammer's nee'le have shortly better
   knowledge.

GAMMER GURTON
Now, gentle Diccon, do so, and good sir, let us trudge.

DOCTOR RAT
By the mass, I may not tarry so long to be your judge!

DICCON
'Tis but a little while, man! What? Take so much pain!   60
If I hear no news of it, I will come sooner again.

HODGE
Tarry so much, good Master Doctor, of your gentleness.

DOCTOR RAT
Then let us hie us inward and, Diccon, speed thy
   business.

                            [Exeunt except DICCON]

[Act IV, Scene iii]

DICCON [*To the audience*]
Now, sirs, do you no more but keep my counsel just,
And Doctor Rat shall thus catch some good, I trust.
But Mother Chat, my gossip, talk first withal I must,
For she must be chief captain to lay the Rat in the dust.
                  [*Enter* DAME CHAT]
Good even, Dame Chat, in faith, and well met in
   this place.   5

DAME CHAT
Good even, my friend Diccon. Whither walk ye this
   pace?

---

60 *Take . . . pain* put yourself to this slight inconvenience
1 *do . . . just* if you will only keep my secret
4 s.d. *Enter* DAME CHAT eds.
5, 6 *Good even* Boas (God deven Q)
6 *this pace* at such a pace

Act IV, Scene iii There is no scene division here in Q, but based on its practice
  heretofore, a new scene should begin here, and most eds. introduce one. In Q, scene
  ii continues to the end of Act IV.
5–6 Q's 'God deven' probably represents a contraction of 'God give you good even',
  and some editors retain it.

DICCON
By my truth, even to you, to learn how the world goeth.
Heard ye no more of the other matter? Say me now, by
    your troth.

DAME CHAT
Oh yes, Diccon! Here the old whore and Hodge, that
    great knave—
But, in faith, I would thou hadst seen! O Lord, I dressed
    them brave!   10
She bare me two or three souses behind in the nape of
    the neck,
Till I made her old weasand to answer again, 'Keck!'
And Hodge, that dirty dastard, that at her elbow stands,
If one pair of legs had not been worth two pair of hands,
He had had his beard shaven, if my nails would have
    served,   15
And not without a cause, for the knave it well deserved!

DICCON
By the mass, I can thee thank, wench, thou didst so well
    acquit thee!

DAME CHAT
And th'adst seen him, Diccon, it would have made thee
    beshit thee
For laughter. The whoreson dolt at last caught up a
    club,
As though he would have slain the master devil
    Beelzebub;   20
But I set him soon inward.

DICCON   O Lord, there is the thing
That Hodge is so offended, that makes him start and
    fling!

DAME CHAT
Why? Makes the knave any moiling, as ye have seen or
    heard?

10 *dressed . . . brave* beat them soundly
11 *bare* bore, gave
    souses blows
12 *weasand* windpipe
13 *dastard* coward
14 *If . . . hands* if Hodge had not been so quick on his legs (in running away)
21 *thing* reason
23 *makes . . . moiling* is he raving

DICCON
> Even now I saw him last, like a madman he fared,
> And sware by heaven and hell he would awreak his
> sorrow, 25
> And leave you never a hen on live by eight of the clock
> tomorrow.
> Therefore mark what I say and my words see that ye
> trust:
> Your hens be as good as dead if you leave them on the
> roost.

DAME CHAT
> The knave dare as well go hang himself as go upon my
> ground!

DICCON
> Well, yet take heed, I say; I must tell you my tale round. 30
> Have you not about your house, behind your furnace or
> lead,
> A hole where a crafty knave may creep in for need?

DAME CHAT
> Yes, by the mass, a hole broke down, even within these
> two days.

DICCON
> Hodge, he intends this same night, to slip in there
> aways.

DAME CHAT
> O Christ, that I were sure of it! In faith, he should have
> his meed! 35

---

25 *sware* swore
  awreak be avenged for
26 *on live* alive
30 *tell . . . round* finish my story
31 *furnace* oven
35 *meed* reward

---

31 *lead* Most eds. describe as a large pot or cauldron, made of lead, often used for brewing. See, however, Southern, pp. 407–8 for the suggestion that the lead (rhymes with 'need') may have been a sort of smoke-conduit cut through the wall of the house from the back of the fireplace to the outside, a feature reportedly present in some Tudor cottages. But *OED* gives no examples of such a usage and Dame Chat's reply (1. 33) to Diccon's leading question may seem to imply that the hole was not a regular architectural feature of her house. On the whole, Southern's conjecture is persuasive. Dame Chat would, nevertheless, as an alewife, have a large brewing pot.

DICCON
> Watch well, for the knave will be there, as sure as is
>   your creed!
> I would spend myself a shilling to have him swinged
>   well.

DAME CHAT
> I am as glad as a woman can be, of this thing to hear tell!
> By Gog's bones, when he cometh, now that I know the
>   matter,
> He shall sure at the first skip to leap in scalding water,   40
> With a worse turn besides! When he will, let him come!

DICCON
> I tell you as my sister; you know what meaneth 'mum'!
>   [*Exit* DAME CHAT]

[Act IV, Scene iv]

DICCON
> Now lack I but my doctor to play his part again—
> And lo where he cometh towards, peradventure to his
>   pain!
>   [*Enter* DOCTOR RAT]

DOCTOR RAT
> What, good news, Diccon, fellow? Is Mother Chat at
>   home?

DICCON
> She is, sir, and she is not, but it please her to whom;
> Yet did I take her tardy, as subtle as she was.   5

36 *creed* religious faith
37 *swinged* thrashed
42 s.d. *Exit* DAME CHAT eds.
 2 *towards* this way
   s.d. Enter DOCTOR RAT eds.
 4 *She . . . whom* it depends on who wishes to see her
 5 *did . . . tardy* I caught her unawares

---

40 *He . . . water* Unless the meaning is only figurative, i.e., that Hodge will find himself
   in trouble ('in hot water'), this might be taken to support the identification of *lead*
   in l. 31 as a cauldron or large tub; but the cauldron of boiling water
   would be sitting in the fireplace where the thief would arrive after crawling
   through the smoke-lead from outside (see preceding note). Dame Chat plots a
   horrible reception for Hodge when he enters her house through the hole. The
   intruder's eventual fate is less grim, as befits a comedy.
Act IV, Scene iv See headnote to IV.iii.

DOCTOR RAT

The thing that thou wentst for, hast thou brought it to
pass?

DICCON

I have done that I have done, be it worse, be it better,
And Dame Chat at her wit's end I have almost set her.

DOCTOR RAT

Why, hast thou spied the nee'le? Quickly, I pray thee,
tell!

DICCON

I have spied it, in faith, sir, I handled myself so well,   10
And yet the crafty quean had almost take my trump.
But or all came to an end, I set her in a dump.

DOCTOR RAT

How so, I pray thee, Diccon?

DICCON   Marry, sir will ye hear?
She was clapped down on the backside, by Cock's
mother dear,
And there she sat sewing a halter or a band,   15
With no other thing save Gammer's needle in her hand.
As soon as any knock, if the filth be in doubt,
She needs but once puff, and her candle is out.
Now I, sir, knowing of every door the pin,
Came nicely, and said no word till time I was within;   20
And there I saw the nee'le, even with these two eyes.
Whoever say the contrary, I will swear he lies.

DOCTOR RAT

O Diccon, that I was not there then in thy stead!

DICCON

Well, if ye will be ordered and do by my rede,
I will bring you to a place, as the house stands,   25
Where ye shall take the drab with the nee'le in her
hands.

DOCTOR RAT

For God's sake, do so, Diccon, and I will gage my gown,
To give thee a full pot of the best ale in the town.

11 *had . . . trump* nearly found me out
12 *dump* gloomy mood
14 *Cock's* God's
20 *nicely* cautiously, quietly
27 *gage* pawn

DICCON
  Follow me but a little and mark what I will say.
  Lay down your gown beside you. Go to, come on your
      way!   30
  See ye not what is here? A hole wherein ye may creep
  Into the house, and suddenly unwares among them leap.
  There shall ye find the bitchfox and the nee'le together.
  Do as I bid you, man; come on your ways hither!

DOCTOR RAT
  Art thou sure, Diccon, the swill tub stands not
      hereabout?   35

DICCON
  I was within myself, man, even now; there is no doubt.
  Go softly, make no noise; give me your foot, Sir John.
  Here will I wait upon you till you come out anon.
                          [DOCTOR RAT *crawls into the hole*]

DOCTOR RAT [*Within*]
  Help, Diccon! Out alas, I shall be slain among
      them!

DICCON
  If they give you not the needle, tell them that ye will
      hang them.   40
  'Ware that!—How, my wenches, have ye caught the
      fox
  That used to make revel among your hens and cocks?
  Save his life yet, for his order, though he sustain some
      pain.—

32 *unwares* unexpectedly
33 *bitchfox* vixen
39 *Out alas* (exclamation of dismay)
41 *'Ware that* be sure not to forget that
43 *for . . . order* because he is a clergyman

29–44 Ways in which this episode might have been staged are discussed in the
  Introduction. Q provides no stage directions whatsoever. It is at least clear that Rat
  is 'within' during ll. 39–44, and that Diccon speaks first to him (40–41), then to
  Dame Chat and, presumably, Doll (41–3), perhaps through the door of Chat's
  house. It is also clear that Diccon disappears before Rat reappears vowing
  vengeance; Diccon is then absent until V.ii.
35 *swill tub* Tub for kitchen refuse, usually the slops (swill) fed to hogs.
37 *Sir John* A familiar name for priests, often contemptuous of their ignorance, as in
  'Sir John Lack-Latin'; compare 'Sir Oliver Martext' in *As You Like It*. 'Sir' in no
  way implies knighthood.

[*Aside*] Gog's bread! I am afraid they will beat out his
    brain!

                                    [*Exit*]

       [*Enter* DOCTOR RAT *from the hole*]

DOCTOR RAT
Woe worth the hour that I came here,   45
And woe worth him that wrought this gear!
A sort of drabs and queans have me blessed—
Was ever creature half so evil dressed?
Whoever it wrought and first did invent it,
He shall, I warrant him, ere long repent it.   50
I will spend all I have without my skin,
But he shall be brought to the plight I am in.
Master Bailey, I trow, and he be worth his ears,
Will snaffle these murderers and all that them bears.
I will surely neither bite nor sup   55
Till I fetch him hither, this matter to take up.

                                    [*Exit*]

Act V, Scene i

[*Enter* MASTER BAILEY, SCAPETHRIFT *his servant, and* DOCTOR RAT]

MASTER BAILEY
I can perceive none other, I speak it from my heart,
But either ye are in all the fault, or else in the greatest
    part.

DOCTOR RAT
If it be counted his fault, besides all his griefs,
When a poor man is spoiled and beaten among thieves,

---

45 *Woe worth* curse
47 *blessed* (ironic) beaten
48 *dressed* treated
54 *snaffle* restrain
    all . . . bears all who take their part
3 *griefs* ed. (grieves Q) injuries
4 *spoiled* seriously injured

At least a brief lapse of dramatic time must be assumed here, while Rat goes in search of,
finds and returns with Bailey, having told him his story meanwhile. A song or musical
interlude might have been performed, but there is no evidence for it in the text.

Then I confess my fault herein, at this season.   5
But I hope you will not judge so much against reason.

MASTER BAILEY
And, methinks, by your own tale, of all that ye name,
If any played the thief, you were the very same.
The women, they did nothing, as your words make
    probation,
But stoutly withstood your forcible invasion.   10
If that a thief at your window to enter should begin,
Would you hold forth your hand and help to pull him in,
Or you would keep him out? I pray you, answer me.

DOCTOR RAT
Marry, keep him out, and a good cause why!
But I am no thief, sir, but an honest learned clerk.   15

MASTER BAILEY
Yea, but who knoweth that when he meets you in the
    dark?
I am sure your learning shines not out at your nose!
Was it any marvel though the poor woman arose
And start up, being afraid of that was in her purse?
Methink you may be glad that your luck was no worse.   20

DOCTOR RAT
Is not this evil enough, I pray you, as you think?
                              Showing his broken head

MASTER BAILEY
Yea, but a man in the dark, if chances do wink,
As soon he smites his father as any other man,
Because for lack of light, discern him he ne can.
Might it not have been your luck with a spit to have
    been slain?   25

DOCTOR RAT
I think I am little better; my scalp is cloven to the brain!
If there be all the remedy, I know who bears the knocks.

5 *season* time
9 *make probation* prove
19 *of that* for that which
22 *if . . . wink* if he is unlucky
24 *ne can* cannot
27 *If . . . knocks* if that is all the comfort I can expect, I'm the one who has to suffer

MASTER BAILEY

By my troth, and well worthy, besides, to kiss the
    stocks!
To come in on the back side when ye might go about!
I know none such, unless they long to have their brains
    knocked out.   30

DOCTOR RAT

Well, will you be so good, sir, as talk with Dame Chat,
And know what she intended? I ask no more but that.

MASTER BAILEY [*To* SCAPETHRIFT]

Let her be called, fellow, because of Master Doctor.
                           [*Exit* SCAPETHRIFT]
I warrant in this case she will be her own proctor;
She will tell her own tale in metre or in prose,
And bid you seek your remedy and so go wipe your nose.

Act V, Scene ii

[*Enter* SCAPETHRIFT *and* DAME CHAT]

MASTER BAILEY

Dame Chat, Master Doctor upon you here complained,
That you and your maids should him much misorder,
And taketh many an oath that no word he feigned,
Laying to your charge how you thought him to murder;
And on his part again, that same man saith further,   5

---

33 s.d. *Exit* SCAPETHRIFT eds. (goes to Dame Chat's house Adams)
34 *proctor* attorney
s.d. *Enter . . .* CHAT eds.
  5 *further* ed. (furder Q)

---

29 *To . . . about* Alludes to Rat's sneaking into Chat's house through the hole when he
    might have used the front door.
33 s.d. As Adams realizes, since both women's houses are on stage, Scapethrift need do
    no more than leave Bailey and Rat and go over to Chat's door, knock, converse
    briefly with her, and bring her back with him to them. Scapethrift's name is
    omitted from the list of characters at the head of V.ii; he was forgotten because he
    has nothing to say, but he clearly has a function, that of going off in search of
    various characters as they are needed.
s.d. See above note to V.i, 33 s.d.
  2 Perhaps this line should be deleted. It disrupts the rhyme of ll.1 and 3 and is
    superfluous since ll. 4 and 5 rhyme correctly. But as it stands, Bailey's speech is a
    rhyme royal stanza (*ababbcc*) in hexameters.

He never offended you in word nor intent.
To hear you answer hereto, we have now for you sent.

DAME CHAT

That I would have murdered him? Fie on him, wretch,
And evil mought he thee for it, our Lord I beseech!
I will swear on all the books that opens and shuts　　　10
He feigneth this tale out of his own guts;
For this seven weeks with me I am sure he sat not down.
Nay, ye have other minions, in the other end of the
　　　town,
Where ye were liker to catch such a blow,
Than anywhere else, as far as I know.　　　　15

MASTER BAILEY

Belike then, Master Doctor, yon stripe there ye got not!

DOCTOR RAT

Think you I am so mad that where I was beat I wot not?
Will you believe this quean before she hath tried it?
It is not the first deed she hath done and afterward
　　　denied it.

DAME CHAT

What, man, will you say I broke your head?

DOCTOR RAT　　　　　　　　　　　　How canst
　　　thou prove the contrary?　　　　20

DAME CHAT

Nay, how provest thou that I did the deed?

DOCTOR RAT　　　　　　　　　Too plainly, by St. Mary!
This proof I trow may serve, though I no word spoke!
　　　　　　　　　　　　Showing his broken head

DAME CHAT

Because thy head is broken, was it I that it broke?

---

9 *evil . . . thee* ill may he thrive (Boas)
13 *minions* (contemptuous) creatures
16 *Belike* likely
18 *tried* proved

12–15 Dame Chat implies that Doctor Rat spends most of his time at the other, in her
　　opinion less respectable, end of town. He was found by Cock at Hob Filcher's
　　house (III.iv, 26); see gloss on *filching* (1. 53, below).

I saw thee, Rat, I tell thee, not once within this
    fortnight.

DOCTOR RAT

No, marry, thou sawest me not, for why thou hadst no
    light,   25
But I felt thee, for all the dark, beshrew thy smooth
    cheeks!
And thou groped me, this will declare, any day this six
    weeks.

Showing his head

MASTER BAILEY

Answer me to this, Master Rat: when caught you this
    harm of yours?

DOCTOR RAT

A while ago, sir, God he knoweth, within less than these
    two hours.

MASTER BAILEY

Dame Chat, was there none with you (confess i' faith)
    about that season?   30
What, woman, let it be what it will, 'tis neither felony
    nor treason.

DAME CHAT

Yes, by my faith, Master Bailey, there was a knave not
    far,
Who caught one good fillip on the brow with a door bar,
And well was he worthy, as it seemed to me.
But what is that to this man, since this was not he?   35

MASTER BAILEY

Who was it then? Let's hear.

DOCTOR RAT   Alas, sir, ask you that?
Is it not made plain enough by the own mouth of Dame
    Chat?

25 *for why* because
26 *beshrew* curse
27 *And* if
    groped grasped, seized
33 *fillip* blow

26 *beshrew . . . cheeks* A common oath. See note to *Roister Doister*, IV.ii, 14.

The time agreeth, my head is broken, her tongue cannot
    lie;
Only upon a bare 'nay' she saith it was not I.

DAME CHAT
No, marry, was it not, indeed, ye shall hear by this one
    thing: 40
This afternoon a friend of mine for good will gave me
    warning,
And bad me well look to my roost and all my capons'
    pens,
For if I took not better heed, a knave would have my
    hens.
Then I, to save my goods, took so much pains as him to
    watch,
And as good fortune served me, it was my chance him
    for to catch.   45
What strokes he bare away, or other what was his gains,
I wot not, but sure I am he had something for his pains.

MASTER BAILEY
Yet tells thou not who it was.

DAME CHAT   Who it was? A false thief,
That came like a false fox, my pullen to kill and
    mischief!

MASTER BAILEY
But knowest thou not his name?

DAME CHAT   I know it, but what
    then?   50
It was that crafty cullion Hodge, my Gammer Gurton's
    man.

MASTER BAILEY [*To* SCAPETHRIFT]
Call me the knave hither; he shall sure kiss the stocks.
I shall teach him a lesson for filching hens or cocks!
                                        [*Exit* SCAPETHRIFT]

---

49 *pullen* ed. (pullaine Q) poultry
50 *what then* what of it
51 *cullion* (Fr., *couillon* = testicle) rascal

---

53 s.d. Again Adams is aware of the set and the action. Bailey's impatience at l. 78 and
    the author's gloss on ll. 80–1 make sense only if we assume that Scapethrift is
    encountering resistance from Hodge in his efforts to bring him out for
    interrogation.

DOCTOR RAT
  I marvel, Master Bailey, so bleared be your eyes;
  An egg is not so full of meat as she is full of lies.   55
  When she hath played this prank, to excuse all this gear,
  She layeth the fault in such a one as I know was not
      there.

DAME CHAT
  Was he not there? Look on his pate, that shall be his
      witness!

DOCTOR RAT
  I would my head were half so whole; I would seek no
      redress!
                    [*Enter* GAMMER GURTON]

MASTER BAILEY
  God bless you, Gammer Gurton.

GAMMER GURTON   God dild you, master
      mine.   60

MASTER BAILEY
  Thou hast a knave within thy house, Hodge, a servant of
      thine;
  They tell me that busy knave is such a filching one,
  That hen, pig, goose or capon thy neighbour can have
      none.

GAMMER GURTON
  By God, cham much amoved to hear any such report;
  Hodge was not wont, ich trow, to b'ave him in that sort.   65

DAME CHAT
  A thievisher knave is not on live, more filching nor more
      false;
  Many a truer man than he has hanged up by the halse.

---

53 *filching* stealing
     s.d. *Exit* SCAPETHRIFT eds. (into Gammer's house Adams adds)
59 *half so whole* (i.e., as Hodge's)
     s.d. *Enter* GAMMER GURTON eds.
60 *dild* eds. (dylde Q; corrupt form of 'yield') reward
65 *wont* in the habit
     b'ave ed. (bave Q) behave
66 *on live* living
67 *halse* neck

And thou, his dame, of all his theft thou art the sole
    receiver—
For Hodge to catch and thou to keep, I never knew none
    better!

GAMMER GURTON [*To* MASTER BAILEY]
    Sir-reverence of your masterdom, and you were out a-door,   70
    Chwould be so bold, for all her brags, to call her arrant
      whore.
    [*To* DAME CHAT] And ich knew Hodge as bad as thou, ich
      wish me endless sorrow
    And chould not take the pains to hang him up before
      tomorrow!

DAME CHAT
    What have I stolen from thee or thine, thou ill-favoured
      old trot?

GAMMER GURTON
    A great deal more, by God's blessed, than chever by thee
      got!   75
    That thou knowest well; I need not say it.

MASTER BAILEY   Stop there, I
    say,
    And tell me here, I pray you, this matter by the way:
    How chance Hodge is not here? Him would I fain have
      had.

GAMMER GURTON
    Alas, sir, he'll be here anon; ha' be handled too bad.

DAME CHAT
    Master Bailey, sir, ye be not such a fool, well I know,   80

---

70 *Sir . . . a-door* with all respect to your worship, if you were not present
71 *Chwould* ed. (Chold Q)
72 *And . . . thou* if I knew that Hodge were as bad as you are
75 *chever* ich ever
79 *ha' be* ed. (ha be Q) he has been

But ye perceive by this lingering, there is a pad in the
    straw.
> *Thinking that Hodge's head was broke, and that*
> *Gammer would not let him come before them*

GAMMER GURTON
Chill show you his face, ich warrant thee. Lo now,
    where he is.
        [*Enter* SCAPETHRIFT *and* HODGE]

MASTER BAILEY
Come on, fellow. It is told me thou art a shrew, iwis:
Thy neighbour's hens thou takest, and plays the
    two-legged fox;
Their chickens and their capons too, and now and then
    their cocks.   85

HODGE
Ich defy them all that dare it say! Cham as true as the
    best!

MASTER BAILEY
Wert not thou take within this hour, in Dame Chat's
    hens' nest?

HODGE
Take there? No, master, chwould not do't, for a house
    full of gold!

DAME CHAT
Thou or the devil in thy coat, swear this I dare be bold!

DOCTOR RAT
Swear me no swearing, quean, the devil he give thee
    sorrow!   90
All is not worth a gnat thou canst swear till tomorrow.
Where is the harm he hath? Show it, by God's bread!

---

81 *But ye* that you do not
  lingering delaying
  pad toad
83 *shrew* rascal, villain
  iwis indeed
87, 88 *take* taken
88 chwould ed. (chold) Q)

---

81 *a pad . . . straw* Proverbial (Tilley P9). Usually a hidden danger; here, simply a
  cover-up.

Ye beat him, with a witness, but the stripes light on my
head!

HODGE

Beat me? Gog's blessed body, chould first, ich trow, have
burst thee!
Ich think, and chad my hands loose, callet, chwould have
crushed thee!   95

DAME CHAT

Thou shitten knave, I trow thou knowest the full weight
of my fist!
I am foully deceived unless thy head and my door bar
kissed.

HODGE

Hold thy chat, whore! Thou criest so loud can no man
else be heard.

DAME CHAT

Well, knave, and I had thee alone, I would surely rap
thy costard!

MASTER BAILEY

Sir, answer me to this: is thy head whole or broken?   100

DAME CHAT

Yea, Master Bailey, blessed be every good token!

HODGE

Is my head whole? Ich warrant you, 'tis neither scurvy
nor scald.
What, you foul beast, does think 'tis either pilled or
bald?
Nay, ich thank God! Chill not, for all that thou mayst
spend,

---

  93 *with a witness* (ironically) without a doubt
  94 *chould* ed. (chold Q) I should
  95 *chwould* ed. (chould Q)
     crushed ed. (crust Q)
  99 *costard* head
  102 *scald* scabby
  103 *pilled* shaven

---

  101 s.p. DAME CHAT Some editors give this line to Hodge, but the emendation is
      erroneous: Chat applauds Bailey's direct query to Hodge and 'blesses' the 'good
      tokens' (i.e., the marks of the beating) she expects to see on his head. Bailey refers
      to her blessing ('charm') in l. 107.

That chad one scab on my narse as broad as thy finger's
    end.   105

MASTER BAILEY
  Come nearer here.

HODGE   Yes, that ich dare.

MASTER BAILEY   By our lady, here
  is no harm!
  Hodge's head is whole enough, for all Dame Chat's
    charm.

DAME CHAT
  By Gog's blessed, however the thing he cloaks or
    smoulders,
  I know the blows he bare away, either with head or
    shoulders.
  Camest thou not, knave, within this hour, creeping into
    my pens,   110
  And there was caught within my house, groping among
    my hens?

HODGE
  A plague both on thy hens and thee! A cart, whore, a
    cart!
  Chwould I were hanged as high as a tree, and chwere as
    false as thou art!
  Give my gammer again her washical thou stole away in
    thy lap.

GAMMER GURTON
  Yea, Master Bailey, there is a thing you know not on,
    mayhap.   115
  This drab, she keeps away my good, the devil he might
    her snare!
  Ich pray you that ich might have a right action on her.

DAME CHAT
  Have I thy good, old filth, or any such old sow's?

105 *my narse* mine arse
108 *smoulders* smothers
114 *washical* what-do-you-call-it
117 *a . . . action* due process of law

I am as true, I would thou knew, as skin between thy
    brows!

GAMMER GURTON
Many a truer hath been hanged, though you escape the
    danger.   120

DAME CHAT
Thou shalt answer, by God's pity, for this thy foul
    slander!

MASTER BAILEY [*To* GAMMER GURTON]
Why, what can ye charge her withal? To say so
    ye do not well.

GAMMER GURTON
Marry, a vengeance to her heart! That whore has stolen
    my nee'le!

DAME CHAT
Thy needle, old witch! How so? It were alms thy skull
    to knock!
So didst thou say the other day that I had stolen thy
    cock   125
And roasted him to my breakfast, which shall not be
    forgotten.
The devil pull out thy lying tongue and teeth that be so
    rotten!

GAMMER GURTON
Give me my nee'le! As for my cock, chwould be very
    loath
That chould hear tell he should hang on thy false faith
    and troth.

MASTER BAILEY
Your talk is such, I can scarce learn who should be most
    in fault.   130

---

124 *were alms* would be a good deed
128 *chwould* ed. (chould Q)
129 *chould* ed. (chuld Q) I should

---

119 *as true . . . brows* Proverbial (Tilley S506). First recorded occurrence.
128–9 *As . . . troth* I would not like to be told that my cock's fate was dependent on your
    false oaths.

GAMMER GURTON
    Yet shall ye find no other wight save she, by bread and
        salt!

MASTER BAILEY
    Keep ye content awhile; see that your tongues ye hold.
    Methinks you should remember this is no place to scold.
    How knowest thou, Gammer Gurton, Dame Chat thy
        needle had?

GAMMER GURTON
    To name you, sir, the party, chould not be very glad.   135

MASTER BAILEY
    Yea, but we must needs hear it, and therefore say it
        boldly.

GAMMER GURTON
    Such one as told the tale, full soberly and coldly,
    Even he that looked on (will swear on a book)
    What time this drunken gossip my fair long nee'le up
        took:
    Diccon, master, the bedlam; cham very sure ye know
        him.   140

MASTER BAILEY
    A false knave, by God's pity! Ye were but a fool to trow
        him.
    I durst adventure well the price of my best cap
    That when the end is known, all will turn to a jape.
    [To GAMMER GURTON] Told he not you that, besides, she
        stole your cock that tide?

GAMMER GURTON
    No, master, no indeed, for then he should have lied;   145
    My cock is, I thank Christ, safe and well a-fine.

DAME CHAT
    Yea, but that ragged colt, that whore, that Tib of thine,
    Said plainly thy cock was stolen and in my house was
        eaten.

131 *wight* person
    by . . . salt (oath)
142 *adventure* wager
143 *jape* jest
144 *tide* time
146 *a-fine* in the end

That lying cut is lost, that she is not swinged and beaten;
And yet, for all my good name, it were a small amends.   150
I pick not this gear, hearst thou, out of my fingers' ends,
But he that heard it told me, who thou of late didst
    name:
Diccon, whom all men knows—it was the very same.

MASTER BAILEY [*To* GAMMER GURTON]
This is the case: you lost your needle about the doors,
And she answers again, she has no cock of yours.   155
Thus in your talk and action, from that you do intend,
She is whole five mile wide, from that she doth defend.
Will you say she hath your cock?

GAMMER GURTON   No marry, sir, that chill not.

MASTER BAILEY [*To* DAME CHAT]
Will you confess her needle?

DAME CHAT   Will I? No sir, will I not!

MASTER BAILEY
Then, there lieth all the matter.

GAMMER GURTON   Soft, master, by the way;   160
Ye know she could do little and she could not say nay!

MASTER BAILEY
Yea, but he that made one lie about your cock stealing
Will not stick to make another, what time lies be in
    dealing.
I ween the end will prove this brawl did first arise
Upon no other ground but only Diccon's lies.   165

DAME CHAT
Though some be lies, as you belike have espied them,

149 *lost* damned
    that . . . not if she is not
161 *Ye . . . nay* it's easy enough for her to say 'no'
163 *stick* hesitate
    what . . . dealing when lies are so current
166 *belike* in all likelihood

149–50 *That . . . amends* The slut deserves to be soundly thrashed, but even that would
    hardly compensate for my tarnished reputation.

Yet other some be true; by proof I have well tried them.

MASTER BAILEY
What other thing beside this, Dame Chat?

DAME CHAT   Marry sir,
even this:
The tale I told before, the selfsame tale it was his.
He gave me, like a friend, warning against my loss,   170
Else had my hens be stolen each one, by God's cross!
He told me Hodge would come, and in he came indeed,
But as the matter chanced, with greater haste than
speed.
This truth was said and true was found, as truly I report.

MASTER BAILEY
If Doctor Rat be not deceived, it was of another sort.   175

DOCTOR RAT [*To* DAME CHAT]
By God's mother, thou and he be a couple of subtle foxes!
Between you and Hodge, I bear away the boxes.
Did not Diccon appoint the place where thou shouldst
stand to meet him?

DAME CHAT
Yes, by the mass, and if he came, bad me not stick to
spit him.

DOCTOR RAT
God's sacrament! The villain knave hath dressed us
round about!   180
He is the cause of all this brawl, that dirty shitten lout!
When Gammer Gurton here complained, and made a
rueful moan,

---

167 *other some* some others
173 *speed* success
177 *boxes* blows
179 *spit* ed. (speet Q) stab
180 *dressed . . . about* played dirty tricks on all of us
182 *rueful* pitiful

---

173 *with . . . speed* Proverbial (Tilley H197): 'More haste than good speed'.

I heard him swear that you had gotten her needle that
    was gone.
And this to try, he further said he was full loath;
    howbeit,
He was content with small ado to bring me where to see
    it.   185
And where ye sat, he said full certain, if I would follow
    his rede,
Into your house a privy way he would me guide and
    lead,
And where ye had it in your hands, sewing about a clout
And set me in the black hole, thereby to find you out.
And whiles I sought a quietness, creeping upon my
    knees,   190
I found the weight of your door bar for my reward and
    fees!
Such is the luck that some men gets, while they begin to
    mell
In setting at one such as were out, minding to make all
    well.

HODGE
Was not well blessed, Gammer, to 'scape that scour?
    And chad been there,
Then chad been dressed, belike, as ill, by the mass, as
    gaffer vicar.   195

MASTER BAILEY
Marry, sir, here is a sport alone; I looked for such an
    end.
If Diccon had not played the knave, this had been soon
    amend.
My gammer here he made a fool, and dressed her as she
    was,

---

184 *try* prove
    loath; howbeit, eds. (loth how be it Q)
188 *clout* cloth
192 *mell* interfere
193 *in . . . out* trying to reconcile those who were at odds
194 *scour* attack
197 *amend* amended

183–9 Doctor Rat is recalling IV.iv, 10–34. Diccon had previously refused to swear
    (IV.ii, 39–49).

And goodwife Chat he set to school, till both parts cried
    'Alas!'
And Doctor Rat was not behind, while Chat his crown
    did pare;   200
I would the knave had been stark blind, if Hodge had
    not his share.

HODGE
  Cham meetly well sped already amongs, cham dressed like
    a colt!
  And chad not had the better wit, chad been made a dolt.

MASTER BAILEY [*To* SCAPETHRIFT]
  Sir knave, make haste Diccon were here! Fetch him
    wherever he be!

                  [*Exit* SCAPETHRIFT]

DAME CHAT
  Fie on the villain, fie, fie, that makes us thus agree!   205

GAMMER GURTON
  Fie on him, knave, with all my heart, now fie and fie
    again!

DOCTOR RAT
  'Now fie on him!' may I best say, whom he hath almost
    slain.

        [*Enter* SCAPETHRIFT *and* DICCON]

MASTER BAILEY
  Lo, where he cometh at hand! Belike he was not far.
  Diccon, here be two or three, thy company cannot spare.

DICCON
  God bless you, and you may be blessed, so many all at
    once.   210

DAME CHAT
  Come, knave, it were a good deed to geld thee, by
    Cock's bones!

199 *parts* parties
202 *amongs* all this while
    dressed served, treated
204 s.d. *Exit* SCAPETHRIFT eds.
205 *agree* disagree
210 *and* if
211 *geld* castrate
    Cock's God's

Seest not thy handiwork? Sir Rat, can ye forbear him?

[DOCTOR RAT *strikes* DICCON]

DICCON

A vengeance on those hands light, for my hands came
    not near him!
The whoreson priest hath lift the pot in some of these
    alewives' chairs,
That his head would not serve him, belike, to come
    down the stairs.   215

MASTER BAILEY

Nay, soft, thou mayst not play the knave and have this
    language too;
If thou thy tongue bridle awhile, the better mayst thou
    do.
Confess the truth as I shall ask and cease a while to
    fable,
And for thy fault I promise thee thy handling shall be
    reasonable.
Hast thou not made a lie or two, to set these two by the
    ears?   220

DICCON

What if I have? Five hundred such have I seen within
    these seven years.
I am sorry for nothing else but that I see not the sport
Which was between them when they met, as they
    themselves report.

---

212 *forbear him* restrain yourself from punishing him
    s.d. DOCTOR . . . DICCON Baskervill *et al.*
214 *lift* lifted
218 *fable* speak falsely
222 *see* saw

---

212 s.d. Baskervill et al. are surely right. Doctor Rat is egged on by Dame Chat, and
    Diccon's lines (213–5) make no sense if Rat has not done something; it is fairly
    obvious that he has done something with his hands, since Diccon curses them
    specifically.
214–5 *The whoreson . . . stairs* He was so drunk that he fell downstairs. This is Diccon's
    'explanation' for Rat's wounded head. He pretends to think he is being accused of
    actually beating Rat himself.
221 *within . . . years* Not intended as a precise length of time; vague, as is 'five hundred
    such'.

MASTER BAILEY

The greatest thing—Master Rat—ye see how he is
    dressed?

DICCON

What devil need he be groping so deep in Goodwife
    Chat's hens' nest?   225

MASTER BAILEY

Yea, but it was thy drift to bring him into the briars.

DICCON

God's bread! Hath not such an old fool wit to save his
    ears!
He showeth himself herein, ye see, so very a cox,
The cat was not so madly allured by the fox
To run into the snares was set for him, doubtless,   230
For he leapt in for mice, and this Sir John for madness!

DOCTOR RAT

Well, and ye shift no better, ye losel, lither and lazy,
I will go near for this to make ye leap at a daisy.
In the king's name, Master Bailey, I charge you set him
    fast.

226 *drift* plot, design
    briars trouble
228 *cox* eds. (coxe [=cokes] Q) fool, one easily 'taken in'
232 *lither* good-for-nothing
233 *will go near* am on the point of

---

226 *bring . . . briars* Proverbial (Tilley B673): 'To leave in the briars'.
228 *cox* To rhyme with 'fox', obviously. Compare the name 'Bartholomew Cokes', the
    ninny in Jonson's *Bartholomew Fair*.
229–31 *The cat . . . madness* Diccon refers to a story from the popular *History of Reynard
    the Fox* (and not Aesop's fables, in one of which it is the fox who is the victim of his
    own folly while the cat saves himself), translated by William Caxton in 1481 and
    reprinted several times before 1550 (ed. N. F. Blake, EETS, O.S.263 [1970], pp.
    19–23). The parallel to the Diccon-Rat episode of IV.iv is very close: Reynard leads
    Tybert the cat to a hole in a barn where he assures Tybert that he will find lots of
    mice. He knows that the priest whose barn it is has set a trap inside for Reynard
    himself, who had stolen a hen the night before. Tybert enters the hole, is caught in
    the snare and beaten by the priest and his son, while Reynard stands outside
    laughing and mocking. Ironically, Diccon had alluded to fox and hens at IV.iv,
    41–2, and then recalls the Reynard story explicitly here, when it is he himself who
    has played the fox's role. Dame Chat has made the same comparison at l. 49 and
    Bailey at 1.84.
233 *leap . . . daisy* Proverbial (Tilley D14). To be hanged. Occurs also in Udall's
    Respublica (1553).
234 *In . . . name* See Introduction, p.xxv.

DICCON
What, fast at cards or fast on sleep? It is the thing I did
    last.   235

DOCTOR RAT
Nay, fast in fetters, false varlet, according to thy deeds!

MASTER BAILEY
Master Doctor, there is no remedy, I must entreat you
    needs
Some other kind of punishment—

DOCTOR RAT   Nay, by all hallows!
His punishment, if I may judge, shall be naught else but
    the gallows!

MASTER BAILEY
That were too sore! A spiritual man to be so extreme!   240

DOCTOR RAT
Is he worthy any better, sir? How do ye judge and
    deem?

MASTER BAILEY
I grant him worthy punishment, but in no wise so great.

GAMMER GURTON
It is a shame, ich tell you plain, for such false knaves
    entreat!
He has almost undone us all—that is as true as steel—
And yet for all this great ado, cham never the near my
    nee'le!   245

MASTER BAILEY
Canst thou not say anything to that, Diccon, with least
    or most?

DICCON
Yea marry, sir, thus much I can say well: the needle is
    lost.

235 *on sleep* asleep
236 *varlet* knave
237 *needs* necessarily
238 *all hallows* all the saints
245 *never the near* no nearer
246 *with . . . most* at all

244 *as true as steel* Proverbial (Tilley S840).

MASTER BAILEY

Nay, canst not thou tell which way that needle may be
    found?

DICCON

No, by my fay, sir, though I might have an hundred
    pound.

HODGE

Thou liar, lickdish, didst not say the nee'le would be
    gitten?   250

DICCON

No, Hodge, by the same token, you were that time
    beshitten
For fear of Hobgobling—you wot well what I mean;
As long as it is since, I fear me yet ye be scarce clean.

MASTER BAILEY

Well, Master Rat, you must both learn and teach us to
    forgive.
Since Diccon hath confession made and is so clean
    shrive,   255
If you to me consent, to amend this heavy chance,
I will enjoin him here some open kind of penance.
Of this condition (where ye know my fee is twenty
    pence)
For the bloodshed, I am agreed with you here to
    dispense;

---

249 *fay* faith
250 *lickdish* parasite
    gitten gotten
259 *dispense* (legal term) to remit the penalty of the law in a particular case

---

252 *Hobgobling* Hobgoblin, another name for Puck or Robin Goodfellow, but also any
    mischievous or evil spirit, a bogeyman. Diccon refers to the devil he was conjuring
    in II.i.
255 *clean shrive* (past participle) Completely absolved, freed from the consequences of
    sin or crime. Technically, and as used here, the step between confession and
    penance, but often used as including confession as well.
254–61 The particulars of Bailey's proposition are not entirely clear, but he seems to be
    saying to Rat: since Diccon has confessed, I will impose a public penance on him, if
    you will drop your charges against him. In exchange for that, and in view of the
    injuries you have suffered, I am willing to cancel the charge against you (i.e., for
    illegally entering Dame Chat's house) though it will cost me the fee of twenty
    pence I would get for bringing you to justice. You may go free, if you agree to let
    the matter 'end with mirth'.

Ye shall go quit, so that ye grant the matter now to run, 260
To end with mirth among us all, even as it was begun.

DAME CHAT
Say 'yea', master vicar, and he shall sure confess to be
    your debtor,
And all we that be here present will love you much the
    better.

DOCTOR RAT
My part is the worst, but since you all hereon agree,
Go even to, Master Bailey! Let it be so for me.   265

MASTER BAILEY
How sayest thou, Diccon? Art content this shall on me
    depend?

DICCON
Go to, Master Bailey, say on your mind. I know ye are
    my friend.

MASTER BAILEY
Then mark ye well: to recompense this thy former
    action,
Because thou hast offended all, to make them
    satisfaction,
Before their faces here kneel down, and as I shall thee
    teach,   270
So thou shalt take an oath of Hodge's leather breech:
First, for Master Doctor, upon pain of his curse,
Where he will pay for all, thou never draw thy purse;
And when ye meet at one pot, he shall have the first
    pull,
And thou shalt never offer him the cup but it be full.   275
To Goodwife Chat thou shalt be sworn, even on the
    same wise,
If she refuse thy money once, never to offer it twice;
Thou shalt be bound by the same here, as thou dost take
    it,
When thou mayst drink of free cost, thou never forsake
    it.
For Gammer Gurton's sake, again sworn shalt thou be,   280

---

265 *Go even to* have done with you, be content
   for me for my part
270–1 *teach,/So thou* ed. (teach./For thou Q)

To help her to her needle again if it do lie in thee;
And likewise be bound, by the virtue of that,
To be of good abearing to Gib her great cat.
Last of all for Hodge, the oath to scan,
Thou shalt never take him for fine gentleman.   285

HODGE
Come on, fellow Diccon, chall be even with thee now!

MASTER BAILEY
Thou wilt not stick to do this, Diccon, I trow.

DICCON
No, by my father's skin! My hand, down I lay it,
Look, as I have promised; I will not denay it.
But Hodge, take good heed now thou do not beshite me! 290
                    And gave him a good blow on the buttock

HODGE
Gog's heart, thou false villain, dost thou bite me?

MASTER BAILEY
What, Hodge, doth he hurt thee or ever he begin?

HODGE
He thrust me into the buttock with a bodkin or a pin!
I say, Gammer! Gammer!

GAMMER GURTON   How now, Hodge, how now?

HODGE
God's malt, Gammer Gurton!

GAMMER GURTON   Thou art mad, ich trow!   295

HODGE
Will you see the devil, Gammer?

GAMMER GURTON   The devil, son? God bless us!

HODGE
Chwould ich were hanged, Gammer!

281 *do . . . thee* is in your power
282 *that* (i.e., that same oath)
283 *good abearing* (legal phrase which passed into popular usage) good behaviour
284 *scan* recite briefly, sum up
287 *denay* deny
292 *or ever* even before
293 *bodkin* dagger or hairpin

GAMMER GURTON   Marry, see, ye
     might dress us—

HODGE
  Chave it, by the mass, Gammer!

GAMMER GURTON   What? Not my ne'ele,
     Hodge!

HODGE
  Your ne'ele, Gammer, your ne'ele!

GAMMER GURTON   No, fie, dost but
     dodge!

HODGE
  Cha' found your ne'ele, Gammer—here in my hand be
     it!   300

GAMMER GURTON
  For all the loves on earth, Hodge, let me see it!

HODGE
  Soft, Gammer.

GAMMER GURTON Good Hodge—

HODGE   Soft, ich say, tarry a while.

GAMMER GURTON
  Nay, sweet Hodge, say truth, and do not me beguile.

HODGE
  Cham sure on it, ich warrant you; it goes no more astray.

GAMMER GURTON
  Hodge, when I speak so fair, wilt still say me nay?   305

HODGE
  Go near the light, Gammer. This—well, in faith, good
     luck!
  Chwas almost undone, 'twas so far in my buttock!

GAMMER GURTON
  'Tis mine own dear ne'ele, Hodge, sickerly I wot!

HODGE
  Am I not a good son, Gammer, am I not?

299 *dodge* prevaricate
308 *sickerly* without doubt
309 *Am I . . . am I* ed. (Cham I . . . cham I Q; the 'ch-' form is redundant here)

GAMMER GURTON
   Christ's blessing light on thee! Hast made me forever!   310

HODGE
   Ich knew that ich must find it, else chould a' had it
      never!

DAME CHAT
   By my troth, gossip Gurton, I am even as glad
   As though I mine own self as good a turn had!

MASTER BAILEY
   And I, by my conscience, to see it so come forth,
   Rejoice so much at it as three needles be worth!   315

DOCTOR RAT
   I am no whit sorry to see you so rejoice.

DICCON
   Nor I much the gladder for all this noise.
   Yet say 'Gramercy, Diccon', for springing of the game.

GAMMER GURTON
   Gramercy, Diccon, twenty times! O how glad cham!
   If that should do so much—your masterdom to come
      hither,   320
   Master Rat, Goodwife Chat and Diccon together—
   Cha' but one halfpenny, as far as ich know it,
   And chill not rest this night till ich bestow it.
   If ever ye love me, let us go in and drink.

MASTER BAILEY
   I am content, if the rest think as I think.   325
   Master Rat, it shall be best for you if we so do;
   Then shall you warm you and dress yourself too.

DICCON
   Soft, sirs, take us with you—the company shall be the
      more;

311 *chould* eds. (choud Q) I should
316 *no whit* not at all
318 *springing . . . game* (from hunting) flushing the quarry from its hiding place
320 *chould* I could
   your masterdom (i.e., Bailey)
327 *dress* take care of

328–9 The lines are addressed to Bailey and Rat, who perhaps set off together. In
   production, the characters might begin filing into Dame Chat's alehouse (1. 324:
   'let us go in and drink'), while Diccon speaks the last four lines to the audience.

As proud comes behind, they say, as any goes before.
[*To the audience*] But now, my good masters, since we
    must be gone,   330
And leave you behind us, here all alone,
Since at our last ending, thus merry we be,
For Gammer Gurton's needle's sake, let us have a
    plaudite!

                                      [*Exeunt*]
                  FINIS

329 *As . . . before* Proverbial (Tilley C536). Diccon acknowledges, somewhat
    sarcastically, the superior social status of the bailiff and the priest.
333 *let . . . plaudite* This appeal for applause echoes the last line of the Prologue.

ROISTER DOISTER

[Dramatis Personae

PROLOGUE

MATTHEW MERRYGREEK, *a mischievous flatterer and parasite,*
Roister Doister's agent
RALPH ROISTER DOISTER, *a foolish would-be soldier and lover*
DOBINET DOUGHTY ⎫
HARPAX   ⎬ *Roister Doister's servants*   5

DAME CHRISTIAN CUSTANCE, *a widow, betrothed to Gawin Goodluck*
MADGE (or MARGERY) MUMBLECRUST, *Dame Custance's old nurse*
TIBET TALKAPACE ⎫
ANNOT ALYFACE   ⎬ *Dame Custance's maids*
TOM TRUEPENNY *Dame Custance's servant*   10

---

2 MERRYGREEK Proverbial (Tilley M901). The supposed dissoluteness, wantonness, and perfidiousness of the Greeks was proverbial in the Renaissance; the prejudice was a legacy from the Romans. Plautus had given currency to the verbs *pergraecari* ('to spend the hours in mirth, luxurious drinking and eating, etc.') and *congraecare* ('to squander one's money in luxury and fast living'); *graecari* ('to play the Greek') meant 'to live luxuriously and effeminately'. 'Grecian faith' meant 'faithless' (Tilley F31; compare C822: 'Cretans are liars'; and G441). The Plautine verbs probably inspired Udall's invention of the name. See T. J. B. Spencer, ' "Greeks" and "Merrygreeks": A Background to *Timon of Athens* and *Troilus and Cressida'*, in Richard Hosley, ed., *Essays on Shakespeare and Elizabethan Drama in Honor of Hardin Craig* (1962), pp. 223–33.

3 ROISTER DOISTER Udall's coinage, from *roister* (i.e., *roisterer*), 'a swaggering or blustering bully; a riotous fellow' (*OED*). The earliest recorded occurrence of *roister* (or of any variant forms—*roistering, roisterous*, etc.) is in Thomas Wilson's *Rule of Reason* (1551), very shortly before Udall wrote his play (see Introduction, p. xxxii). There is a Ralph Roister in Ulpian Fulwell's *Like Will to Like* (c. 1568), and in George Gascoigne's *The Glass of Government* (1575), one of the characters, Dick Drum, is called 'a roister' in the Dramatis Personae.

4 DOUGHTY 'Valiant, brave, stout, formidable' (*OED*).

5 HARPAX The only Latin name in the play, borrowed from Plautus's *Pseudolus*, where Harpax is the servant of the soldier Polymachaeroplagides; the latter does not actually appear in the play (compare *OWT*, 1. 253). On its four occurrences in this play, the name is printed in Roman type, unlike the rest of the text, which is in blackletter for the most part.

6 CHRISTIAN CUSTANCE Suggests 'Christian Constance', or constancy, fidelity. Udall replaces the courtezan of Roman comedy with a pious, virtuous English gentlewoman and widow.

7 MUMBLECRUST From the verb *mumble*, meaning to chew ineffectively, as with toothless gums (see note at I.iii, 17). The name indicates Madge's old age. 'Madge' is a common first name for old women, as in *OWT*.

9 ALYFACE Perhaps 'Holyface', from the medieval form *hali*, or *alie* (see I.ii, 124n.) A more likely derivation is from *ale*.

90

SCRIVENER

GAWIN GOODLUCK, *a merchant, betrothed to Christian Custance*
SIM SURESBY, *Goodluck's servant*
TRISTRAM TRUSTY, *Goodluck's friend*

THE PARISH CLERK   15
Servants
Musicians   } *members of Roister Doister's household*]

---

11 SCRIVENER A professional penman, scribe or copyist, who wrote out letters and
   other documents from dictation or from drafts, making neat, presentable copies.

12 GAWIN GOODLUCK While alliteration may have been the sole consideration in
   Udall's choice of 'Gawin' (or 'Gavin'; Gawyn Q), he may have known that it was,
   as late as the fifteenth century, a Scottish form of *gain* (the noun), an apt
   cognomen for a successful merchant.

15 PARISH CLERK A non-speaking part. The clerk is called forth by Merrygreek in
   III.iii to toll the bell for Roister Doister. The clerk would have been a minor cleric
   or even a layman, who assisted the parish priest. See *GGN*, Prologue, 1.10n.

The Prologue

What creature is in health, either young or old,
But some mirth with modesty will be glad to use,
As we in this interlude shall now unfold?
Wherein all scurrility we utterly refuse,
Avoiding such mirth wherein is abuse;   5
Knowing nothing more commendable for a man's
   recreation
Than mirth which is used in an honest fashion.

For mirth prolongeth life and causeth health,
Mirth recreates our spirits and voideth pensiveness,
Mirth increaseth amity, not hindering our wealth,   10
Mirth is to be used both of more and less,
Being mixed with virtue in decent comeliness,
As we trust no good nature can gainsay the same;
Which mirth we intend to use, avoiding all blame.

The wise poets long time heretofore   15
Under merry comedies wise secrets did declare,
Wherein was contained very virtuous lore,
With mysteries and forewarnings very rare.
Such to write, neither Plautus nor Terence did spare,
Which among the learned at this day bears the bell;   20
These, with such other, therein did excel.

4 *scurrility* vulgarity
9 *voideth* drives away
10 *amity* friendliness
11 *of . . . less* by persons of high and low estate
13 *gainsay* deny
18 *rare* strange
20 *bears* (singular verb with plural noun)

---

19 *Plautus . . . Terence* The two greatest Roman comic dramatists, some of whose plays
were common school texts in the Middle Ages and the Renaissance. Of Plautus (c.
254–184 B.C.), twenty-one plays survive, including *Miles Gloriosus*. Terence (c.
195–c. 159 B.C.) left only six plays, but his tremendous reputation in Renaissance
Europe was due in part to widely-known commentaries on his work by the fourth-
century grammarian Donatus. See Introduction, pp. xxxiv–xxxvii.
20 *bears the bell* Proverbial (Tilley B275). Takes first place; refers to the bellwether,
the leading sheep of the flock.

Our comedy or interlude which we intend to play
Is named *Roister Doister* indeed,
Which against the vainglorious doth inveigh,
Whose humour the roisting sort continually doth feed. 25
Thus by your patience we intend to proceed
In this our interlude, by God's leave and grace;
And here I take my leave for a certain space.

24 *inveigh* speak vehemently
25 *roisting* roistering, blustering

28 *for ... space* This may suggest either that the Prologue was spoken by an actor who reappeared later in another part, or that the person who spoke it was acting as master of ceremonies for the occasion and would return later to present another part of the programme.

Act I, Scene i

Enter MATTHEW MERRYGREEK, *singing*

MERRYGREEK

As long liveth the merry man, they say,
As doth the sorry man, and longer by a day,
Yet the grasshopper, for all his summer piping,
Starveth in winter with hungry griping.
Therefore another said saw doth men advise   5
That they be together both merry and wise:
This lesson must I practise, or else ere long,
With me, Matthew Merrygreek, it will be wrong.
Indeed, men so call me, for by him that us bought,
Whatever chance betide, I can take no thought,   10
Yet wisdom would that I did myself bethink
Where to be provided this day of meat and drink;
For know ye, that for all this merry note of mine,
He might appose me now that should ask where I dine,
My living lieth here and there, of God's grace: 15
Sometimes with this good man, sometime in that place,
Sometime Lewis Loiterer biddeth me come near,
Sometime Watkin Waster maketh us good cheer,
Sometime Davy Diceplayer, when he hath well cast,

s.d. *Enter... singing* ed. (Mathewe Merygreeke. He entreth singing. Q)
   4 *griping* spasmodic pain in the bowels
   5 *said saw* oft-repeated proverb
   9 *him... bought* Jesus Christ
  10 *Whatever... thought* come what may, I don't care
  14 *appose* confront with hard questions
  17 *Loiterer* idler
  19 *well cast* won some money

1–2 *As long... sorry man* Proverbial (Tilley M71).
3–4 *grasshopper... griping* An allusion to the well-known fable of the grasshopper and the ant. See *Caxton's Aesop*, ed. R. T. Lenaghan (1967), pp. 133–4.
  6 *be... wise* Proverbial, as Merrygreek says (Tilley G324).
17–26 *Loiterer... Roister Doister* All of the names are 'types' of human foolishness or vice, as in the morality plays; most are self-explanatory. Roister Doister's name, occurring in this list with others, identifies him as one such type, the latest prey of the parasite Merrygreek.
18 *Waster* Specifically, one who squanders money and resources. Lavish entertainment is a characteristic of this type, as in the mid-fourteenth-century poem *Winner and Waster*.

Keepeth revel-rout as long as it will last.   20
Sometime Tom Titivile maketh us a feast,
Sometime with Sir Hugh Pye I am a bidden guest,
Sometime at Nichol Neverthrives I get a sop,
Sometime I am feasted with Brian Blinkinsop,
Sometime I hang on Hankin Hoddydoddy's sleeve—   25
But this day on Ralph Roister Doister's, by his leave.
For truly, of all men, he is my chief banker
Both for meat and money, and my chief sheet-anchor.
For, soothe Roister Doister in that he doth say,
And require what ye will, ye shall have no nay.   30
But now of Roister Doister somewhat to express,
That ye may esteem him after his worthiness:
In these twenty towns, and seek them throughout,
Is not the like stock, whereon to graft a lout.
All the day long is he facing and craking   35
Of his great acts in fighting and fray-making;
But when Roister Doister is put to his proof,

---

20 *revel-rout* boisterous merriment
   it his winnings
22 *Pye* (as in 'magpie') a chatterer
28 *sheet-anchor* eds. (shootanker Q) largest of a ship's anchors, used only in
   emergency; last resort
29 *soothe* ed. (sooth Q) declare to be true, uphold
   that whatever
30 *nay* refusal
31 *somewhat* something
32 *after* according to
35 *facing* boasting, swaggering
   craking (i.e., 'cracking') bragging
36 *fray-making* creating a disturbance
37 *put . . . proof* put to the test

---

21 *Titivile* Originally Titivillus or Tutivillus, a minor devil. He appears as a character
   in the Wakefield mystery play of the Last Judgement and in the morality play
   Mankind (c. 1470), where he is clearly identified: 'properly Titivillus signifieth the
   fiend of hell' (l.885; in Lester, ed., *Three Late Medieval Morality Plays*).
23 *sop* A piece of bread, either soaked in water or wine, or dipped in the grease of
   roasted meat; a scanty meal, as the host's name implies.
25 *Hoddydoddy* Fool or simpleton, but perhaps also a cuckold, from the horns of a kind
   of small snail called *hoddydoddy*.
34 *stock* In grafting, the stock is the stem into which the graft is inserted; but also a
   tree trunk or stump without branches, hence the type of what is lifeless, motionless,
   so a senseless or stupid person. The latter sense is confirmed by 'lout', an awkward
   fellow or bumpkin.

To keep the queen's peace is more for his behoof.
If any woman smile or cast on him an eye,
Up is he to the hard ears in love by and by,   40
And in all the hot haste must she be his wife,
Else farewell his good days and farewell his life!
Master Ralph Roister Doister is but dead and gone
Except she on him take some compassion;
Then chief of counsel must be Matthew Merrygreek: 45
'What if I for marriage to such an one seek?'
Then must I soothe it, whatever it is,
For what he saith or doth cannot be amiss.
Hold up his 'yea' and 'nay', be his nown white son;
Praise and rouse him well, and ye have his heart won,   50
For so well liketh he his own fond fashions,
That he taketh pride of false commendations.
But such sport have I with him as I would not lese,
Though I should be bound to live with bread and cheese.
For exalt him, and have him as ye lust, indeed,   55
Yea, to hold his finger in a hole for a need:
I can with a word make him fain or loath,

---

38 *behoof* advantage, benefit
40 *hard* very
   by and by immediately
49 *nown* own (from 'my nown' = 'mine own')
   white son darling boy (not 'son' in literal sense)
50 *rouse* stir up to action
53 *lese* lose
55 *lust* wish
57 *fain* eager
   loath reluctant

---

38 *queen's peace* If the play was written before mid-1553, as seems likely (see
   Introduction, p. xxxiii), this must reflect editorial (if not authorial) emendation at
   some time after Mary acceded to the throne in August, 1553, following the death of
   Edward VI in July and the short-lived attempt to install Lady Jane Grey. It would
   have continued to be appropriate after her death in 1558, of course, as she was
   succeeded by another queen, Elizabeth. The sense of these lines (35–8) is that,
   however much Roister Doister boasts of his prowess in combat, if he is pressed
   actually to do battle, he has a convenient excuse not to, in the laws against
   disturbing the peace.
43–4 Roister Doister is not only a boastful sham warrior, but also a parody of the
   courtly lover of medieval literature who swore he would die if his lady did not take
   pity on him. Udall's use of the Latinate 'compassion' recalls its occurrence in
   similar contexts in Chaucer and others; see, for example, *Troilus and Criseyde*,
   I.465–9.
56 *hold ... hole* Proverbial (Tilley F472): 'A fool often puts his finger in a hole'.

I can with as much make him pleased or wroth,
I can when I will make him merry and glad,
I can when me lust make him sorry and sad,   60
I can set him in hope and eke in despair,
I can make him speak rough and make him speak fair.
But I marvel I see him not all this same day;
I will seek him out—but, lo! he cometh this way.
I have yond espied him sadly coming,   65
And in love, for twenty pound, by his glumming.

Act I, Scene ii

[*Enter* RALPH ROISTER DOISTER]

ROISTER DOISTER
Come, death, when thou whilt, I am weary of my life!
MERRYGREEK [*Aside*]
I told you, I, that we should woo another wife.
ROISTER DOISTER
Why did God make me such a goodly person?
MERRYGREEK [*Aside*]
He is in by the neck—we shall have sport anon!
ROISTER DOISTER
And where is my trusty friend, Matthew Merrygreek?   5
MERRYGREEK [*Aside*]
I will make as I saw him not; he doth me seek.
ROISTER DOISTER
I have him espied, me thinketh: yond is he.
Ho, Matthew Merrygreek, my friend! A word with thee!
MERRYGREEK [*Aside*]
I will not hear him, but make as I had haste.—
Farewell, all my good friends, the time away doth waste,   10
And the tide, they say, tarrieth for no man.
ROISTER DOISTER
Thou must with thy good counsel help me if thou can.

61 *eke* also
65 *yond* yonder
66 *for twenty pound* I'll wager twenty pounds
   glumming looking glum
 4 *in* (i.e., in love)
   by up to
 6 *as* as if

11 *the tide...man* Proverbial (Tilley T323): 'The tide stays for no man'. A play by
   George Wapull, *The Tide Tarrieth No Man*, was published in 1576.

MERRYGREEK
    God keep thee, worshipful Master Roister Doister!
    And farewell, the lusty Master Roister Doister!
ROISTER DOISTER
    I must needs speak with thee a word or twain.   15
MERRYGREEK
    Within a month or two I will be here again;
    Negligence in great affairs, ye know, may mar all.
ROISTER DOISTER
    Attend upon me now, and well reward thee I shall.
MERRYGREEK
    I have take my leave, and the tide is well spent.
ROISTER DOISTER
    I die except thou help! I pray thee, be content;   20
    Do thy part well now, and ask what thou wilt,
    For without thy aid my matter is all spilt.
MERRYGREEK
    Then to serve your turn, I will some pains take,
    And let all mine own affairs alone for your sake.
ROISTER DOISTER
    My whole hope and trust resteth only in thee.   25
MERRYGREEK
    Then can ye not do amiss whatever it be.
ROISTER DOISTER
    Gramercies, Merrygreek, most bound to thee I am.
MERRYGREEK
    But up with that heart, and speak out like a ram!
    Ye speak like a capon that had the cough now;
    Be of good cheer! Anon ye shall do well enow.   30
ROISTER DOISTER
    Upon thy comfort, I will all things well handle.
    So, lo! That is a breast to blow out a candle!
    But what is this great matter? I would fain know;
    We shall find remedy therefore, I trow.
    Do ye lack money? Ye know mine old offers;   35
    Ye have always a key to my purse and coffers.

---

19 *take* taken
22 *spilt* ruined
27 *Gramercies* God grant you his mercies (i.e., thank you)
29 *capon* a castrated cock (also, the type of a dull-witted person)
30 *enow* eds. (ynow Q) enough

---

32 *So ... candle* Roister Doister presumably draws himself up and puffs out his chest,
upon which Merrygreek comments admiringly.

ROISTER DOISTER
  I thank thee. Had ever man such a friend?
MERRYGREEK
  Ye give unto me; I must needs to you lend.
ROISTER DOISTER
  Nay, I have money plenty all things to discharge.
MERRYGREEK [*Aside*]
  That knew I right well when I made offer so large.   40
ROISTER DOISTER
  But it is no such matter.
MERRYGREEK   What is it then?
  Are ye in danger of debt to any man?
  If ye be, take no thought nor be not afraid;
  Let them hardily take thought how they shall be paid.
ROISTER DOISTER
  Tut, I owe nought.
MERRYGREEK   What then? Fear ye imprisonment?   45
ROISTER DOISTER
  No.
MERRYGREEK   No, I wist ye offend not so to be shent.
  But if ye had, the Tower could not you so hold,
  But to break out at all times ye would be bold.
  What is it? Hath any man threatened you to beat?
ROISTER DOISTER
  What is he that durst have put me in that heat?   50
  He that beateth me, by his arms, shall well find
  That I will not be far from him nor run behind.
MERRYGREEK
  That thing know all men ever since ye overthrew

---

41 s.p. ROISTER DOISTER eds. (omitted in Q)
44 *hardily* ed. (hardly Q) indeed, surely
46 *offend not so* eds. (offend, not so Q; offend not, so other eds.)
47 *ye* eds. (he Q)
50 *durst have* would have dared
   put . . . heat rouse me to such fury
51 *by his arms* by Christ's arms

---

46 *I wist . . . shent* I know you have done nothing to deserve such disgrace.
47 *Tower* The Tower of London, long believed to have been built by Julius Caesar
   (see *Richard III*, III. i, 68–74). The White Tower, built by William the Conqueror,
   was used as a prison from the early twelfth century, and other parts were so used
   from time to time.
51–2 *He that . . . behind* In this ambiguous declaration, Roister Doister is made
   unwittingly to reveal his cowardice: he 'will not be far from' (but not very near
   either?) the antagonist who has (already) beaten him, nor 'run behind' him, i.e.
   not attack him from behind (but will run before him, in being chased away?).

The fellow of the lion which Hercules slew.
But what is it then?
ROISTER DOISTER　　　　Of love I make my moan.　　　　55
MERRYGREEK
　Ah, this foolish love! will't ne'er let us alone?
　But because ye were refused the last day,
　Ye said ye would ne'er more be entangled that way.
　I would meddle no more, since I find all so unkind.
ROISTER DOISTER
　Yea, but I cannot so put love out of my mind.　　　　60
MERRYGREEK
　But is your love—tell me first, in any wise—
　In the way of marriage or of merchandise?
　If it may otherwise than lawful be found,
　Ye get none of my help, for an hundred pound.
ROISTER DOISTER
　No, by my troth, I would have her to my wife.　　　　65
MERRYGREEK
　Then are ye a good man and God save your life.
　And what or who is she with whom ye are in love?
ROISTER DOISTER
　A woman, whom I know not by what means to move.
MERRYGREEK
　Who is it?
ROISTER DOISTER　　A woman, yond.
MERRYGREEK　　　　　　　　　　What is her name?
ROISTER DOISTER
　Her, yonder.
MERRYGREEK　　　Whom?
ROISTER DOISTER　　　　　　　　Mistress, ah . . .

---

55 *moan* complaint
56 *foolish love* ed. (foolish a love Q)
　　Will't ne'er ed. (Wilt neare Q)
57 *the last day* yesterday
59 *meddle no more* have no more to do (i.e., with women)
61 *in any wise* anyway
65 *to* as

---

54 *the lion . . . slew* The Nemean lion, an invulnerable beast, the slaying of which was the first of twelve labours imposed upon the legendary Greek hero Herakles (*Hercules*). Hercules killed the lion by strangling it, skinned it with its own claws and wore the skin as a trophy.
61–2 *But . . . merchandise* Do you wish to marry the lady or only to enjoy her as a prostitute? Merrygreek's scruple is further evidence of Udall's care to make the play unequivocally clean.

MERRYGREEK   Fie, fie, for shame!   70
    Love ye, and know not whom, but 'her, yond', 'a woman'?
    We shall then get you a wife I cannot tell when!
ROISTER DOISTER
    The fair woman that supped with us yesternight;
    And I heard her name twice or thrice, and had it right.
MERRYGREEK
    Yea, ye may see ye ne'er take me to good cheer with you; 75
    If ye had, I could have told you her name now.
ROISTER DOISTER
    I was to blame indeed, but the next time, perchance—
    And she dwelleth in this house.
MERRYGREEK   What, Christian
    Custance?
ROISTER DOISTER
    Except I have her to my wife, I shall run mad!
MERRYGREEK
    Nay, unwise perhaps, but I warrant you for mad.   80
ROISTER DOISTER
    I am utterly dead unless I have my desire.
MERRYGREEK
    Where be the bellows that blew this sudden fire?
ROISTER DOISTER
    I hear she is worth a thousand pound and more.
MERRYGREEK
    Yea, but learn this one lesson of me afore:
    An hundred pound of marriage money, doubtless,   85
    Is ever thirty pound sterling, or somewhat less,
    So that her thousand pound, if she be thrifty,
    Is much near about two hundred and fifty;
    Howbeit, wooers and widows are never poor.
ROISTER DOISTER
    Is she a widow? I love her better therefore.   90
MERRYGREEK
    But I hear she hath made promise to another.

---

75 *take . . . you* invite me to dinner
80 *warrant . . . mad* guarantee you will not go mad
88 *near* nearer

85–9 *An hundred . . . poor* The last line is proverbial; this is the first instance cited by
    Tilley (W342). The first two lines sound like a proverb, but if so, it is unrecorded.
    Merrygreek's point is that a bride's dowry always turns out to be worth much less
    in hard cash than it sounds beforehand.

ROISTER DOISTER
He shall go without her, and he were my brother.
MERRYGREEK
I have heard say, I am right well advised,
That she hath to Gawin Goodluck promised.
ROISTER DOISTER
What is that Gawin Goodluck?
MERRYGREEK   A merchant man.   95
ROISTER DOISTER
Shall he speed afore me? Nay, sir, by sweet Saint Anne!
Ah, sir, '*Backare!*' quod Mortimer to his sow;
I will have her mine own self, I make God a vow!
For I tell thee, she is worth a thousand pound!
MERRYGREEK
Yet a fitter wife for your ma'ship might be found.   100
Such a goodly man as you might get one with land,
Besides pounds of gold a thousand and a thousand,
And a thousand, and a thousand, and a thousand,
And so to the sum of twenty hundred thousand!
Your most goodly personage is worthy of no less.   105
ROISTER DOISTER
I am sorry God made me so comely, doubtless;
For that maketh me each where so highly favoured,
And all women on me so enamoured.
MERRYGREEK
'Enamoured', quod you? Have ye spied out that?
Ah sir, marry, now I see you know what is what.   110
'Enamoured', ka? Marry, sir, say that again!
But I thought not ye had marked it so plain.

92 *and* even if
96 *speed* succeed
97 *quod* quoth, said
100 *ma'ship* ed. (maship Q) mastership
110 *marry* (originally 'Mary') indeed
111 *ka* (abbreviated form) quotha, said he

---

96 *Saint Anne* Mother of the Virgin Mary (see note on *GGN*, I.v, 42).
97 *'Backare!'...sow* Proverbial (Tilley M1183). Actually, only the first line of a proverb, completed variously by: 'Went that sow back at that bidding, trow you?' or 'See, Mortimer's sow speaketh as good Latin as he' or ' "The Boar shall back first," quoth she, "I make a vow" '. (See John Heywood's *'Works' and Miscellaneous Short Poems*, ed. B. A. Milligan (Urbana, Illinois, 1956), p.191). 'Backare', apparently pseudo-Latin for 'Stand back', i.e., 'make way for your better', came to be used by itself, as in John Lyly's *Midas* (I.ii, 3) and *The Taming of the Shrew* (II.i, 73).
102–4 *a thousand...twenty hundred thousand* Such inflation is typical of the flattering servant or parasite; in *Miles Gloriosus*, Artotrogus, the parasite, does the 'sum' of Pyrgopolinices's victims: 100+100+30+60 = 7000 (I.42–6). See also I.iv, 52–8.

ROISTER DOISTER
Yes, each where they gaze all upon me and stare.
MERRYGREEK
Yea, Malkin, I warrant you, as much as they dare.
And ye will not believe what they say in the street,   115
When your ma'ship passeth by, all such as I meet,
That sometimes I can scarce find what answer to make.
'Who is this?' saith one; 'Sir Launcelot du Lake?'
'Who is this? Great Guy of Warwick?', saith another.
'No', say I, 'it is the thirteenth Hercules' brother.   120
'Who is this? Noble Hector of Troy?' saith the third.
'No, but of the same nest', say I, 'it is a bird.'
'Who is this? Great Goliah, Samson, or Colbrand?'

---

114 Boas suggested that this line should be spoken aside; 'Malkin' is a term of
contempt, meaning 'slut', and when addressed to a man, would imply effeminacy.
But Merrygreek would speak of people hardly daring to look upon Roister Doister
to him (more flattery), not in an aside. In this case, Roister Doister must be
supposed not to understand the insult. This is not entirely satisfactory, but the
sense of the line is obscure.

118 *Sir Launcelot du Lake* (Fr., *Lac*). One of the chief knights of the Round Table in
Arthurian legend, Arthur's dearest friend and secret lover of his queen, Guenevere.
In Sir Thomas Malory's collection of tales in prose (published by Caxton in 1485 as
Le Morte Darthur), Launcelot became the principal hero, supplanting Gawain,
Percival, Tristram, even Arthur himself.

119 *Guy of Warwick* Fictional hero of a very popular chivalric romance of the thirteenth
century, versions of which continued to be written (by Lydgate, among others)
and read for centuries. Set in the reign of Athelstan in the tenth century, it recounts
the deeds of Guy, performed in order to win the hand of Felice, daughter of the earl
of Warwick. These included slaying the Danish giant Colbrand near Winchester,
as well as a dragon and a gigantic cow. The legend was incorporated as history in
the chronicles, and the Beauchamp family, who became earls of Warwick c. 1268,
claimed descent from this famous 'ancestor'; the second Beauchamp earl
(1278–1315) bore his name, and built Guy's Tower at Warwick Castle.

120 *thirteenth Hercules' brother* Either (1) brother of the thirteenth Hercules, or (2)
thirteenth brother of Hercules, or perhaps even (3) thirteenth Hercules, 'brother'
being the imaginary interlocutor addressed by Merrygreek. In any case, it is
another instance of his hyperbolical flattery of Roister Doister, which cares little for
preciseness; a confusion with the Twelve Labours of Hercules may be implied.

121 *Hector of Troy* One of King Priam's many sons, brother of Paris, Troilus and
Aeneas. Leader of the Trojan forces in the war with the Greeks, until he was killed
by Achilles. Shakespeare treats the story in *Troilus and Cressida*.

123 *Goliah* Goliath, the Philistine giant slain by the shepherd boy David with a sling (I
Samuel 17).
Samson The Israelite hero and judge whose prodigious strength was given him by
God as long as his hair remained uncut. The story of his exploits, his betrayal by
the Philistine woman Delilah, his blinding, captivity and final revenge and death is
told in the Old Testament book of Judges (Chapters 13–16).
Colbrand (see note to line 119).

'No' say I, 'but it is a Brute of the Holy Land.'
'Who is this? Great Alexander, or Charlemagne?'   125
'No, it is the tenth Worthy', say I to them again.
I know not if I said well.
ROISTER DOISTER   Yes, for so I am.
MERRYGREEK
Yea, for there were but nine Worthies before ye came.
To some others, the third Cato I do you call;
And so as well as I can I answer them all.   130
'Sir, I pray you, what lord or great gentleman is this?'
'Master Ralph Roister Doister, dame', say I, 'iwis'.
'O Lord', saith she then, 'what a goodly man it is!
Would Christ I had such a husband as he is!'
'O Lord', say some, 'that the sight of his face we lack!'   135
'It is enough for you', say I, 'to see his back.

124 *Holy* ed. (Alie Q)
132 *iwis* indeed

---

124 *Brute . . . Holy Land* Brute, or Brutus, was the legendary great-grandson of Aeneas,
who discovered and gave his name (according to medieval etymology) to Britain.
Britons traced their ancestry through him to the Trojans. Titles of medieval
English chronicles (e.g., Layamon's *Brut*) reflect the strength of the legend.
Merrygreek is engaging in further reckless piling up of heroic epithets when he
relates Brutus to the Holy Land; the latter is suggested by mention of Goliath and
Samson in the preceding line. The quarto's 'Alie' (compare the medieval form *ali*,
hali) contributes to the long-ago-and-far-away tenor of Merrygreek's speech.
125 *Great Alexander* Alexander the Great (356–323 B.C.), King of Macedonia, pupil of
Aristotle. He extended his empire and with it Greek culture over most of the
known world. One of the Nine Worthies (see l. 126n.)
Charlemagne Charles the Great (c. 742–814), King of the Franks and Holy Roman
Emperor. A successful warrior and enlightened ruler, he patronised the church and
learning, while defending the Empire from enemies on all sides. Another 'Worthy'.
126 *tenth Worthy* The Nine Worthies—three pagan, three Hebrew, three Christian—
were Hector of Troy, Alexander the Great, Julius Caesar, Joshua, David, Judas
Maccabeus, Arthur, Charlemagne, and Godfrey of Bouillon (Boulogne) (c.
1060–1100), crusader and first Christian king of Jerusalem. There are numerous
references to them in medieval and Renaissance literature; the most expansive in
English is in the mid-fourteenth-century alliterative poem, *The Parliament of the
Three Ages*, ll. 300–583 (ed. M. Y. Offord, EETS, O.S. 246 (1959)). The tradition
seems to have begun with Jacques de Longuyon's *Les Voeux du Paon* (1312–13);
the fullest study is Horst Schroeder, *Der Topos der Nine Worthies in Literatur und
bildener Kunst* (Göttingen, 1971).
129 *third Cato* There were many Catos, but the two most famous were Cato the Censor
(the Elder) (234–139 B.C.), Roman soldier, lawyer, politician and moralist, and
his great-grandson, Cato of Utica (the Younger) (95–46 B.C.), also a politician, an
opponent of Julius Caesar, and father-in-law of the Brutus who conspired in the
assassination of Caesar (see *Julius Caesar*, II.i, 295). Merrygreek's 'third Cato' is
like his 'tenth Worthy'.

His face is for ladies of high and noble parages,
With whom he hardly 'scapeth great marriages.'
With much more than this and much otherwise.

ROISTER DOISTER

I can thee thank that thou such answers devise;   140
But I perceive thou dost me throughly know.

MERRYGREEK

I mark your manners for mine own learning, I trow.
But such is your beauty and such are your acts,
Such is your personage and such are your facts,
That all women, fair and foul, more and less,   145
They eye you, they lub you, they talk of you, doubtless.
Your pleasant look maketh them all merry,
Ye pass not by but they laugh till they be weary.
Yea, and money could I have, the truth to tell,
Of many, to bring you that way where they dwell.   150

ROISTER DOISTER

Merrygreek, for this thy reporting well of me—

MERRYGREEK

What should I else, sir? It is my duty, pardee!

ROISTER DOISTER

I promise thou shalt not lack while I have a groat.

MERRYGREEK

Faith, sir, and I ne'er had more need of a new coat.

ROISTER DOISTER

Thou shalt have one tomorrow, and gold for to spend.   155

MERRYGREEK

Then I trust to bring the day to a good end.
For as for mine own part, having money enow,
I could live only with the remembrance of you.
But now to your widow whom you love so hot.

ROISTER DOISTER

By Cock, thou sayest truth! I had almost forgot.   160

---

137 *parages* lineage
141 *throughly* thoroughly
144 *facts* deeds
146 *lub* (colloquial or childish) love
147 *pleasant* eds. (peasant Q)
152 *pardee* (Fr., *par dieu*) by God
153 *groat* (coin worth four pence)
160 *Cock* God

---

147 *pleasant* Q's 'peasant' could just be right, another of Merrygreek's sarcasms at the uncomprehending victim's expense.

MERRYGREEK
  What if Christian Custance will not have you? What?
ROISTER DOISTER
  Have me? Yes, I warrant you, never doubt of that.
  I know she loveth me, but she dare not speak.
MERRYGREEK
  Indeed, meet it were somebody should it break.
ROISTER DOISTER
  She looked on me twenty times yesternight,   165
  And laughed so—
MERRYGREEK   That she could not sit upright.
ROISTER DOISTER
  No, faith, could she not.
MERRYGREEK   No, even such a thing I cast.
ROISTER DOISTER
  But for wooing, thou knowest, women are shamefast.
  But and she knew my mind, I know she would be glad,
  And think it the best chance that ever she had.   170
MERRYGREEK
  To her then like a man and be bold forth to start!
  Wooers never speed well, that have a false heart.
ROISTER DOISTER
  What may I best do?
MERRYGREEK   Sir, remain ye awhile here;
  Ere long one or other of her house will appear.
  Ye know my mind.
ROISTER DOISTER   Yea, now hardly let me alone.   175
MERRYGREEK
  In the meantime, sir, if you please, I will home,
  And call your musicians, for in this your case
  It would set you forth, and all your wooing grace;
  Ye may not lack your instruments to play and sing.
ROISTER DOISTER
  Thou knowest I can do that.
MERRYGREEK   As well as anything.   180
  Shall I go call your folks, that ye may show a cast?

164 *meet* fitting
    break (i.e., break the news to Custance)
167 *cast* guessed
168 *shamefast* bashful, modest
169 *and* if
172 *speed well* succeed
173 *here* eds. (not in Q)
175 *hardly* boldly
178 *set you forth* further your cause
181 *show a cast* give a sample, demonstrate

ROISTER DOISTER
  Yea, run, I beseech thee, in all possible haste.
MERRYGREEK
  I go.   *Exit*
ROISTER DOISTER   Yea, for I love singing out of measure.
  It comforteth my spirits and doth me great pleasure.
  But who cometh forth yond from my sweetheart
      Custance?   185
  My matter frameth well; this is a lucky chance.

Act I, Scene iii

[*Enter*] MADGE MUMBLECRUST, *spinning on the distaff, and*
                TIBET TALKAPACE, *sewing*

MADGE
  If this distaff were spun, Margery Mumblecrust—
TIBET
  Where good stale ale is, will drink no water, I trust.
MADGE
  Dame Custance hath promised us good ale and white
      bread.
TIBET
  If she keep not promise, I will beshrew her head;
  But it will be stark night before I shall have done.   5

---

183 *out of measure* excessively
186 *frameth* is taking shape
  4 *beshrew* curse

---

183 Roister Doister may be punning unwittingly at his own expense: singing 'out of
     measure' would be a fault.
s.d. *spinning on the distaff* Although the spinning wheel was known in Europe from the
     fourteenth century, hand-spinning continued to be the most common method for
     some time. The *distaff*, a cleft stick about three feet long, was held under the left
     arm. Upon it were wound the fibres, either flax or wool, to be spun. They were fed
     into the right hand and twisted between thumb and index finger. The end of the
     twisted fibre was attached to the notched end of the *spindle*, a thin stick tapered at
     both ends, with a *whorl*, a disk of stone or wood, slipped on to it near the lower end
     like a collar. The weight of the whorl gave momentum to the rotating spindle
     which was suspended by the thread. The spun thread was wound onto the spindle
     until it was full.
  2 *stale ale* Ale that has stood long enough to clear, hence old and strong.
  3 *white bread* Bread made from wheaten flour, thus of finer quality than brown bread.

ROISTER DOISTER [*Aside*]
  I will stand here a while, and talk with them anon.
  I hear them speak of Custance, which doth my heart good;
  To hear her name spoken doth even comfort my blood.

MADGE
  Sit down to your work, Tibet, like a good girl.

TIBET
  Nurse, meddle you with your spindle and your whorl!   10
  No haste but good, Madge Mumblecrust, for whip and
      whirr,
  The old proverb doth say, never made good fur.

MADGE
  Well, ye will sit down to your work anon, I trust.

TIBET
  Soft fire maketh sweet malt, good Madge Mumblecrust.

MADGE
  And sweet malt maketh jolly good ale, for the nonce.   15

TIBET
  Which will slide down the lane without any bones.
  [*Sings*] 'Old brown bread crusts must have much
      good mumbling,
  But good ale down your throat hath good easy tumbling'.

ROISTER DOISTER [*Aside*]
  The jolliest wench that e'er I heard! Little mouse!
  May I not rejoice that she shall dwell in my house?   20

TIBET
  So, sirrah, now this gear beginneth for to frame.

10 *whorl* ed. (whirle Q)
11 *whirr* ed. (whurre Q) rush, hurry
12 *fur* (furre Q) furrow
13 *anon* immediately
15 *nonce* ed. (nones Q) present
16 *lane* throat
17 s.d. *Sings* eds. (Cantet Q)
    must ... mumbling need a lot of chewing
21 *sirrah* (term of address implying contempt or authority on the speaker's part, thus
    often to servants)
    gear ... frame we are beginning to make progress in our work

11 *No ... good* Proverbial (Tilley H199): 'No haste but good speed'.
11–12 *whip ... fur* Proverbial (Tilley W304, citing only this example). Apparently
    from ploughing.
14 *Soft ... malt* Proverbial (Tilley F280). From brewing.

MADGE
    Thanks to God, though your work stand still, your
        tongue is not lame.

TIBET
    And though your teeth be gone, both so sharp and so
        fine,
    Yet your tongue can run on pattens as well as mine.

MADGE
    Ye were not for nought named Tib Talkapace!   25

TIBET
    Doth my talk grieve you? Alack, God save your grace!

MADGE
    I hold a groat ye will drink anon for this gear.

TIBET
    And I will not pray you the stripes for me to bear.

MADGE
    I hold a penny ye will drink without a cup.

TIBET
    Wherein soe'er ye drink, I wot ye drink all up.   30

                  [*Enter* ANNOT ALYFACE, *knitting*]

ANNOT
    By Cock, and well sewed, my good Tibet Talkapace!

TIBET
    And e'en as well knit, my nown Annot Alyface.

ROISTER DOISTER [*Aside*]
    See what a sort she keepeth that must be my wife!
    Shall not I, when I have her, lead a merry life?

TIBET
    Welcome, my good wench, and sit here by me just.   35

   24 *run . . . pattens* make a great clatter
      pattens wooden shoes
   28 *the stripes . . . bear* (ironic) to take my punishment (i.e., the drink) for me
   30 s.d. *Enter . . . knitting* eds.
   33 *sort* company of people
   35 *by me just* close to me

   30 s.d. This seems the obvious place for Annot to enter, as she does not speak earlier,
      and l. 80 implies that she has entered and found the other two already there. In Q,
      she is simply listed, 'knitting', at the beginning of the scene with the others.

ANNOT
>And how doth our old beldame here, Madge
>>Mumblecrust?

TIBET
>Chide and find faults and threaten to complain.

ANNOT
>To make us poor girls shent to her is small gain.

MADGE
>I did neither chide nor complain nor threaten.

ROISTER DOISTER [*Aside*]
>It would grieve my heart to see one of them beaten.   40

MADGE
>I did nothing but bid her work and hold her peace.

TIBET
>So would I, if you could your clattering cease,
>But the devil cannot make old trot hold her tongue.

ANNOT
>Let all these matters pass, and we three sing a song.
>So shall we pleasantly both the time beguile now,   45
>And eke dispatch all our works ere we can tell how.

TIBET
>I shrew them that say nay, and that shall not be I.

MADGE
>And I am well content.

TIBET   Sing on then, by and by.

ROISTER DOISTER [*Aside*]
>And I will not away, but listen to their song;
>Yet Merrygreek and my folks tarry very long.   50

36 *beldame* aged woman
38 *shent* be punished
46 *eke* also
47 *shrew* beshrew, curse

TIB, ANN and MARGERY do sing here

Pipe, merry Annot, etc.

Trilla, trilla, trillarie.
Work, Tibet, work, Annot, work Margery,
Sew, Tibet, knit, Annot, spin Margery;
Let us see who shall win the victory.   55

TIBET

This sleeve is not willing to be sewed, I trow;
A small thing might make me all in the ground to throw!

Then they sing again

Pipe, merry Annot, etc.

Trilla, trilla, trillarie.
What, Tibet! What, Annot! What Margery!   60
Ye sleep but we do not—that shall we try:
Your fingers be numbed, our work will not lie.

TIBET

If ye do so again, well, I would advise you nay;
In good sooth, one stop more, and I make holiday.

They sing the third time

Pipe, merry Annot, etc.   65

Trilla, trilla, trillarie.
Now Tibet, now Annot, now Margery
Now whippet apace for the mastery;
But it will not be, our mouth is so dry.

61 *try* prove
62 *lie* (i.e., lie still)
68 *whippet* whip it, move briskly

---

51 *Pipe . . . etc.* Presumably a popular song. As the refrain is not printed in the quarto,
it must have been assumed that it would be familiar to readers from this one line.
63–4 These lines are unclear. If 'do so again' in l. 63 means 'say that again' we must
assume that only Annot and Madge sing ll. 59–62 and Tib replies. Or she may
mean 'If you sing again', or 'If you go on'. Nor is it certain what she means by 'one
stop more' in l. 64: perhaps a stanza to the song (though they in fact sing two
more), or a unit of measure in sewing; neither meaning for *stop* is given in *OED*. In
either case, she is saying that she will give up her sewing after one more.

TIBET

Ah, each finger is a thumb today, methink;   70
I care not to let all alone, choose it swim or sink.

They sing the fourth time

Pipe, merry Annot, etc.

Trilla, trilla, trillarie.
When, Tibet? When, Annot? When, Margerie?
I will not, I cannot, no more can I,   75
Then give we all over, and there let it lie.

Let her cast down her work

TIBET

There it lieth! The worst is but a curried coat;
Tut, I am used thereto, I care not a groat!

ANNOT

Have we done singing since? then will I in again;
Here I found you and here I leave both twain.   80

                                               Exit

MADGE

And I will not be long after. Tib Talkapace—

TIBET

What is the matter?

MADGE   Yond stood a man all this space,
And hath heard all that ever we spake together.

TIBET

Marry, the more lout he, for his coming hither,
And the less good he can, to listen maidens talk!   85
I care not and I go bid him hence for to walk;
It were well done to know what he maketh
    here away.

71 *to* if I
    choose it let it choose to
77 *The worst . . . coat* The worst I can get is a beating
79 *since* already
85 *can* is capable of
    listen listen to
87 *what . . . away* what he is doing hereabouts

76 s.d. *Let . . . work*. In Q, this is printed in Roman type in the margin opposite the last
    stanza of the song. 'Her' is Tibet, as l. 77 indicates, though the last line of the song
    implies that all three women abandon their work.

ROISTER DOISTER [*Aside*]
Now might I speak to them, if I wist what to say!

MADGE
Nay, we will go both off and see what he is.

ROISTER DOISTER
One that hath heard all your talk and singing, iwis.   90

TIBET
The more to blame you! A good thrifty husband
Would elsewhere have had some better matters in hand.

ROISTER DOISTER
I did it for no harm, but for good love I bear
To your dame Mistress Custance, I did your talk hear.
And, mistress nurse, I will kiss you for acquaintance.   95

MADGE
I come anon, sir!

TIBET   Faith, I would our dame Custance
Saw this gear!

MADGE   I must first wipe all clean, yea, I must.

TIBET
Ill 'chieve it, doting fool, but it must be cust!

[ROISTER DOISTER *kisses* MADGE]

MADGE
God yield you, sir! Chad not so much, ichot not when,
Ne'er since chwas bore, chwine, of such a gay
          gentleman!   100

---

88 *wist* knew
90 *iwis* indeed
91 *husband* husbandman, householder
98 *Ill 'chieve it* may it be unsuccessful (it = Madge)
   cust kissed
   s.d. ROISTER . . . MADGE eds.
99 *yield* reward
   Chad (stage dialect, as in *GGN*) I had
   ichot (ich wot) I know
100 *chwas* I was
   bore born
   chwine (I ween) I believe

ROISTER DOISTER
   I will kiss you too, maiden, for the good will I
      bear you.

TIBET
   No, forsooth, by your leave, ye shall not kiss me!

ROISTER DOISTER
   Yes, be not afeared; I do not disdain you a whit.

TIBET
   Why should I fear you? I have not so little wit.
   Ye are but a man, I know very well.

ROISTER DOISTER   Why then?   105

TIBET
   Forsooth, for I will not! I use not to kiss men.

ROISTER DOISTER
   I would fain kiss you too, good maiden, if I might.

TIBET
   What should that need?

ROISTER DOISTER   But to honour you, by this light.
   I use to kiss all them that I love, to God I vow.

TIBET
   Yea, sir? I pray you, when did ye last kiss your cow?   110

ROISTER DOISTER
   Ye might be proud to kiss me, if ye were wise.

TIBET
   What promotion were therein?

ROISTER DOISTER   Nurse is not so nice.

TIBET
   Well, I have not been taught to kissing and licking.

103 *a whit* whatsoever
106 *for* because
    use not am not in the habit
107 *fain* gladly
112 *nice* particular

109–10 *I use . . . cow* Tibet takes up Roister Doister's boast with an allusion to the
    proverb 'Every man as he loves, quoth the good man when he kissed his cow'
    (Tilley M103).

ROISTER DOISTER [*To* MADGE]
  Yet I thank you, mistress nurse, ye made no sticking.

MADGE
  I will not stick for a kiss with such a man as you!   115

TIBET
  They that lust! I will again to my sewing now.

                    [*Enter* ANNOT ALYFACE]

ANNOT
  Tidings, ho, tidings! Dame Custance greeteth you well.

ROISTER DOISTER
  Whom? Me?

ANNOT   You, sir? No, sir! I do no such tale tell.

ROISTER DOISTER
  But and she knew me here—

ANNOT   Tibet Talkapace,
  Your mistress Custance and mine must speak with your
          grace.   120

TIBET
  With me?

ANNOT   Ye must come in to her, out of all doubts.

TIBET
  And my work not half done? A mischief on all louts!
                    [*Exeunt* TIBET *and* ANNOT]

ROISTER DOISTER
  Ah, good sweet nurse!

MADGE [*Aside*]   A good sweet gentleman!

ROISTER DOISTER
  What?

MADGE
           Nay, I cannot tell, sir. But what thing would you?

ROISTER DOISTER
  How doth sweet Custance, my heart of gold, tell me,
          how?   125

114 *made . . . sticking* did not hesitate
116 s.d. *Enter* ANNOT ALYFACE eds.
122 s.d. *Exeunt . . .* ANNOT ed. (Ex|eunt| am |bae| Q)

---

116 *They that lust* (lust = list) Colloquial: 'Each to his own taste'.

MADGE
  She doth very well, sir, and commends me to you.

ROISTER DOISTER
  To me?

MADGE   Yea, to you, sir.

ROISTER DOISTER   To me? Nurse, tell me plain!
  To me?

MADGE   Yea.

ROISTER DOISTER   That word maketh me alive again!

MADGE
  She commended me to one last day, whoe'er it was.

ROISTER DOISTER
  That was e'en to me and none other, by the mass!   130

MADGE
  I cannot tell you, surely, but one it was.

ROISTER DOISTER
  It was I and none other! This cometh to good pass.
  I promise thee, nurse, I favour her.

MADGE   E'en so, sir.

ROISTER DOISTER
  Bid her sue to me for marriage.

MADGE   E'en so, sir.

ROISTER DOISTER
  And surely for thy sake she shall speed.

MADGE   E'en so, sir.   135

ROISTER DOISTER
  I shall be contented to take her.

MADGE   E'en so, sir.

---

126 *commends* eds. (commaunde Q)
129 *commended* eds. (commaunde Q)
132 *cometh . . . pass* is turning out well

---

126 *commends . . . you* Madge means 'commends herself to you', i.e., 'sends you her
    compliments'. The blunder was apparently a popular comic gag; see, for instance,
    Medwall's *Fulgens and Lucrece* (c. 1497), part ii, ll. 317–24 (ed. G Wickham, in
    English Moral Interludes (1976), p. 86.

ROISTER DOISTER
But at thy request and for thy sake.

MADGE   E'en so, sir.

ROISTER DOISTER
And come hark in thine ear what to say.

MADGE   E'en so, sir.

Here let him tell her a great long tale in her ear

Act I, Scene iv

[*Enter* MATTHEW MERRYGREEK, DOBINET DOUGHTY *and*
HARPAX, *and another musician*]

MERRYGREEK
Come on, sirs, apace, and quit yourselves like men;
Your pains shall be rewarded.

DOUGHTY   But I wot not when.

MERRYGREEK
Do your master worship as ye have done in time past.

DOUGHTY
Speak to them. Of mine office he shall have a cast.

MERRYGREEK
Harpax, look that thou do well too, and thy fellow.   5

HARPAX
I warrant, if he will mine example follow.

MERRYGREEK
Curtsy, whoresons! Duck you and crouch at every
        word.

DOUGHTY
Yes, whether our master speak earnest or bourd.

138 s.d. *Here . . . ear* (in Q, printed in the margin)
  1 *quit* acquit
  3 *worship* honour
  4 *office* service, duty
  8 *bourd* ed. (borde Q) jest

s.d. *and . . . musician* The presence of at least one other besides Doughty and Harpax is
    indicated in ll. 4–5.

MERRYGREEK
For this lieth upon his preferment indeed.

DOUGHTY
Oft is he a wooer, but never doth he speed.   10

MERRYGREEK
But with whom is he now so sadly rounding yond?

DOUGHTY
With *Nobs nicebecetur miserere* fond.

MERRYGREEK [*To* ROISTER DOISTER]
God be at your wedding! Be ye sped already?
I did not suppose that your love was so greedy.
I perceive now ye have chose of devotion;   15
And joy have ye, lady, of your promotion.

ROISTER DOISTER
Tush, fool, thou art deceived—this is not she.

MERRYGREEK
Well, mock much of her and keep her well, I 'vise ye.
I will take no charge of such a fair piece keeping.

MADGE
What aileth this fellow? He driveth me to weeping.   20

MERRYGREEK
What, weep on the wedding day? Be merry, woman!
Though I say it, ye have chose a good gentleman.

ROISTER DOISTER
Cock's nowns, what meanest thou, man? Tut, a whistle!

---

9 *lieth ... preferment* has a bearing upon his chance of success (with Dame Custance)
10 *speed* succeed
11 *sadly rounding* earnestly whispering
15 *chose ... devotion* made your choice out of pure love
18 *mock* eds. (mocke Q) (more of Merrygreek's workplay)
19 *charge ... keeping* responsibility for keeping such a handsome woman safe
23 *Cock's nowns* God's wounds
   whistle trifle, worthless thing

---

12 *Nobs nicebecetur miserere* (pseudo-Latin) *Nobs* is a familiar form of endearment applied to a woman. *Nicebecetur* is an obscure sixteenth-century term for a fine or dainty woman; Udall uses it elsewhere, and see John Heywood's *The Play of the Weather*, 1. 898 (ed. P. Happé, *Tudor Interludes*, 1972, p.169). *Miserere* is the imperative form of the Latin verb *misereor*, and means 'have pity'. Doughty's mockingly precious elaboration of Merrygreek's question might be freely translated: 'Saying such foolish stuff as "Sweetest, dearest, dainty duck, O pity me and change my luck!" '

MERRYGREEK
Ah sir, be good to her, she is but a gristle.
Ah, sweet lamb and cony!

ROISTER DOISTER   Tut, thou art deceived!   25

MERRYGREEK
Weep no more, lady; ye shall be well received.—
Up with some merry noise, sirs, to bring home the
    bride!

ROISTER DOISTER
Gog's arms, knave, art thou mad! I tell thee thou art
    wide!

MERRYGREEK
Then ye intend by night to have her home brought?

ROISTER DOISTER
I tell thee, no!

MERRYGREEK   How then?

ROISTER DOISTER   'Tis neither meant ne thought.   30

MERRYGREEK
What shall we then do with her?

ROISTER DOISTER   Ah, foolish harebrain,
This is not she!

MERRYGREEK   No is? Why then, unsaid again!
And what young girl is this with your ma'ship so bold?

ROISTER DOISTER
A girl?

MERRYGREEK   Yea. I daresay scarce yet threescore year old.

ROISTER DOISTER
This same is the fair widow's nurse, of whom ye wot.   35

MERRYGREEK
Is she but a nurse of a house? Hence home, old trot!
Hence at once!

---

24   s.p. MERRYGREEK eds. (R. Royster Q)
       gristle delicate person
25   *cony* (term of endearment for a woman; literally, 'rabbit')
28   *wide* (i.e., of the mark) mistaken
30   *ne* nor
32   *No is* is it not

ROISTER DOISTER   No, no!

MERRYGREEK   What, an' please your ma'ship,
  A nurse talk so homely with one of your worship?

ROISTER DOISTER
  I will have it so: it is my pleasure and will.

MERRYGREEK
  Then I am content. Nurse, come again, tarry still.   40

ROISTER DOISTER
  What, she will help forward this my suit, for her part.

MERRYGREEK
  Then is't mine own pigsnye, and blessing on my heart!

ROISTER DOISTER
  This is our best friend, man!

MERRYGREEK   Then teach her what to say.

MADGE
  I am taught already.

MERRYGREEK   Then go, make no delay!

ROISTER DOISTER [*To* MADGE]
  Yet hark one word in thine ear.

MERRYGREEK [*To the musicians*]   Back, sirs, from his tail!   45

ROISTER DOISTER
  Back, villains! Will ye be privy of my counsel?

MERRYGREEK
  Back, sirs! So! I told you afore ye would be shent!

ROISTER DOISTER [*To* MADGE]
  She shall have the first day a whole peck of argent.

MADGE
  A peck? *Nomine patris*! Have ye so much spare?

ROISTER DOISTER
  Yea, and a cartload thereto, or else were it bare,   50
  Besides other movables, household stuff and land.

37 *an'* if it
38 *homely* familiarly
42 *pigsnye* ed. (pygs nie Q; i.e., 'pig's eye', colloquial term of endearment)
47 *shent* shamed, reproached
48 *peck* (in dry measure, two gallons or one quarter of a bushel)
    argent silver, money
49 *Nomine patris* in the name of the Father
50 *thereto* in addition

MADGE
Have ye lands, too?

ROISTER DOISTER   An hundred marks.

MERRYGREEK   Yea, a thousand.

MADGE
And have ye cattle too? And sheep too?

ROISTER DOISTER   Yea, a few.

MERRYGREEK
He is ashamed the number of them to show.
E'en round about him, as many thousand sheep goes   55
As he and thou and I too have fingers and toes.

MADGE
And how many years old be you?

ROISTER DOISTER   Forty at least.

MERRYGREEK
Yea, and thrice forty to them.

ROISTER DOISTER   Nay, now thou dost jest!
I am not so old; thou misreckonest my years.

MERRYGREEK
I know that; but my mind was on bullocks and steers.   60

MADGE
And what shall I show her your mastership's name is?

ROISTER DOISTER
Nay, she shall make suit ere she know that, iwis.

MADGE
Yet let me somewhat know.

MERRYGREEK   This is he, understand,
That killed the Blue Spider in Blanchpowder Land.

---

52 *an hundred marks* (a mark = thirteen shillings)

---

64 *Blue Spider . . . Blanchpowder Land* This may refer to a specific story; some editors
cite Tom Thumb, but there is no blue spider in either of the earliest extant printed
versions, a prose *History of Tom Thumb, the Little*, by Richard Johnson (1621), and
a verse chapbook (1630). In the latter, it is Tom who is killed by a spider in the
kitchen. Blanchpowder, or *pouldre blanche*, is composed of cinnamon and nutmeg,
and was sprinked on roasted fruit. Merrygreek, in effect, is boasting that Roister
Doister killed a spider in the kitchen. Plautus's Pyrgopolinices fought at 'Weevil
Field'. Compare the hero's fight with a snail in the interlude *Thersites* (1537),
which may be by Udall.

MADGE
    Yea? Jesus! William! Zee law! Did he zo? Law!   65

MERRYGREEK
    Yea, and the last elephant that ever he saw,
    As the beast passed by, he start out of a busk,
    And e'en with pure strength of arms plucked out his great
        tusk!

MADGE
    Jesus! *Nomine patris*! What a thing was that!

ROISTER DOISTER
    Yea but, Merrygreek, one thing thou hast forgot.

MERRYGREEK   What?   70

ROISTER DOISTER
    Of th' other elephant.

MERRYGREEK   Oh, him that fled away.

ROISTER DOISTER
    Yea.

MERRYGREEK   Yea, he knew that his match was in place that day.
    Tut, he beat the King of Crickets on Christmas Day,
    That he crept in a hole and not a word to say.

MADGE
    A sore man, by zembletee!

---

65 *Zee law ... zo ... Law* (stage dialect) the Lord ... so ... Lord
67 *start* leapt
    busk bush
75 *sore* fierce
    by zembletee as it seems

---

65 *William* No specific reference may be intended; Madge is blurting out oaths and
    exclamations in her astonishment. There are various saints named William, notably
    William of Norwich (d.1144), a twelve year old boy said to have been murdered by
    Jews.
66-8 *elephant ... tusk* This fictitious feat is borrowed from *Miles Gloriosus* (I. 25–30)
    where it is recounted by Artotrogus, Merrygreek's counterpart, of his master, the
    braggart Pyrgopolynices; the latter allegedly broke an elephant's foreleg with a
    blow of his fist.
73 *beat ... Day* Another absurd 'conquest' like that over the Blue Spider. Crickets are
    traditionally associated with Christmas and the fireside.

MERRYGREEK   Why, he wrung a club   75
Once in a fray out of the hand of Beelzebub!

ROISTER DOISTER
And how when Mumfision—

MERRYGREEK   Oh, your custreling
Bore the lantern afield so before the gosling—
Nay, that is too long a matter now to be told.
Never ask his name, nurse; I warrant thee, be bold.   80
He conquered in one day, from Rome to Naples,
And won towns, nurse, as fast as thou canst make
    apples.

MADGE
Oh Lord! My heart quaketh for fear! He is too sore!

ROISTER DOISTER
Thou makest her too much afeared, Merrygreek. No
    more!
This tale would fear my sweetheart Custance right evil.   85

MERRYGREEK
Nay, let her take him, nurse, and fear not the devil.
But thus is our song dashed.—Sirs, ye may home again.

ROISTER DOISTER
No, shall they not! I charge you all here to remain!
The villain slaves! A whole day ere they can be found!

MERRYGREEK
Couch on your marrowbones, whoresons, down to the
    ground!   90
Was it meet he should tarry so long in one place
Without harmony of music, or some solace?

77 *custreling* groom or squire
80 *be bold* you may be sure
90 *couch* bow, kneel
    marrowbones eds. (marybones Q) knees
92 *solace* entertainment

---

76 *Beelzebub* A devil, sometimes represented as the chief, sometimes as a subordinate
    to Lucifer. He is called 'prince' and 'chief' of the devils in Matthew 12:24 and Luke
    11:15; in *Paradise Lost* Milton makes him one of the original fallen angels and
    Satan's second-in-command (I. 79–81; II. 299–300). Roister Doister's tally of
    'victims' thus ranges from spiders and crickets through a gosling (l. 78) and
    elephants to the devil himself.
77 *Mumfision* I have not succeeded in tracing this name. Perhaps a character from
    folklore or children's tales, or Udall's fantastical invention; compare Plautus's
    Bumbomachides Clutomistaridysarchides (*Miles Gloriosus*, I. 14).

Whoso hath such bees as your master in his head
Had need to have his spirits with music to be fed.—
By your mastership's license!

ROISTER DOISTER   What is that? A mote?   95

MERRYGREEK
No, it was a fool's feather had light on your coat.

ROISTER DOISTER
I was nigh no feathers since I came from my bed.

MERRYGREEK
No, sir, it was a hair that was fall from your head.

ROISTER DOISTER
My men come when it please them—

MERRYGREEK   By your leave!

ROISTER DOISTER   What is that?

MERRYGREEK
Your gown was foul spotted with the foot of a gnat.   100

ROISTER DOISTER
Their master to offend they are nothing afeared—
What now?

MERRYGREEK   A lousy hair from your mastership's beard.

ALL THE SERVANTS
And sir, for nurse's sake, pardon this one offence.
We shall not after this show the like negligence.

ROISTER DOISTER
I pardon you this once; and come sing ne'er the worse.   105

MERRYGREEK
How like you the goodness of this gentleman, nurse?

---

95 *mote* particle of dust
103 s.p. *All the servants* eds. (*O[mn]es famulae* |*sic*| Q; i.e., Doughty, Harpax and the
    other musician (the Latin should read *famuli*))

95–102 While these lines are spoken, Merrygreek is officiously and ostentatiously
    flicking specks of dust or plucking hairs from Roister Doister's clothing.
96 *fool's feather* The quarto spelling is *fooles*; Merrygreek puns on 'fowl/fool', at
    Roister Doister's expense. Court fools apparently sometimes wore feathers on their
    caps (see Francis Douce, *Illustrations of Shakespeare and of Ancient Manners*
    (1839), plate IV, facing p. 498. Semi-proverbial (*ODEP*, p.273).
100 *foot* Perhaps with a pun on *feute*, the trace or track of an animal.

MADGE
  God save his mastership that so can his men forgive!
  And I will hear them sing ere I go, by his leave.

ROISTER DOISTER
  Marry, and thou shalt, wench. Come, we two will
      dance.

MADGE
  Nay, I will by mine own self foot the song perchance.   110

ROISTER DOISTER
  Go to it, sirs, lustily!

MADGE   Pipe up a merry note!
  Let me hear it played, I will foot it, for a groat!

They sing

  [Whoso to marry a minion wife
  Hath had good chance and hap,
  Must love her and cherish her all his life,   115
  And dandle her in his lap.

  If she will fare well, if she will go gay,
  A good husband ever still,
  Whatever she lust to do or to say,
  Must let her have her own will.   120

  About what affairs soever he go,
  He must show her all his mind;
  None of his counsel she may be kept fro,
  Else is he a man unkind.]

ROISTER DOISTER
  Now, nurse, take this same letter here to thy mistress.   125
  And as my trust is in thee, ply my business.

113–24 *Whoso . . . unkind* eds. (not in Q; see note below)
113 *minion* darling
123 *fro* eds. (free Q) from

---

112 s.d.–124 *They sing . . . unkind* In the quarto, only the stage direction (*Cantent*) is
given. The song which was sung here is presumably the one labelled 'The Second
Song' among those printed under the heading 'Certain songs to be sung by those
which shall use this comedy or interlude' at the end of the play (see Introduction,
pp. lvii-lviii).

MADGE
    It shall be done.

MERRYGREEK   Who made it?

ROISTER DOISTER   I wrote it each whit.

MERRYGREEK
    Then needs it no mending.

ROISTER DOISTER   No, no.

MERRYGREEK   No, I know your wit.

ROISTER DOISTER
    I warrant it well.

MADGE   It shall be delivered.
    But if ye speed, shall I be considered?   130

MERRYGREEK
    Whough! Dost thou doubt of that?

MADGE   What shall I have?

MERRYGREEK
    An hundred times more than thou canst devise to crave.

MADGE
    Shall I have some new gear? For my old is all spent.

MERRYGREEK
    The worst kitchen wench shall go in lady's raiment.

MADGE
    Yea?

MERRYGREEK   And the worst drudge in the house
        shall go better   135
    Than your mistress doth now.

MADGE   Then I trudge with your letter.
                                                [*Exit*]

ROISTER DOISTER
    Now may I repose me—Custance is mine own!
    Let us sing and play homeward, that it may be known.

127 *each whit* the whole thing
133 *gear* clothes
    spent worn
134 *lady's* ed. (ladies Q; ladies' eds.)

---

129 *I . . . well* Most eds. reassign this line to Merrygreek, without explanation; Q clearly
    gives it to Roister Doister.

MERRYGREEK
But are you sure that your letter is well enough?

ROISTER DOISTER
I wrote it myself!

MERRYGREEK   Then sing we to dinner!   140
                   Here they sing, and go out singing

Act I, Scene V

[*Enter* CHRISTIAN CUSTANCE *and* MADGE MUMBLECRUST]

DAME CUSTANCE
Who took thee this letter, Margery Mumblecrust?

MADGE
A lusty gay bachelor took it me of trust,
And if ye seek to him, he will 'low your doing.

DAME CUSTANCE
Yea, but where learned he that manner of wooing?

MADGE
If to sue to him you will any pains take,   5
He will have you to his wife, he saith, for my sake.

DAME CUSTANCE
Some wise gentleman, belike! I am bespoken,
And I thought verily this had been some token
From my dear spouse, Gawin Goodluck, whom
          when Him please,
God luckily send home to both our hearts' ease.   10

MADGE
A jolly man it is, I wot well by report,
And would have you to him for marriage resort.
Best open the writing and see what it doth speak.

2 *took ... trust* entrusted it to me
3 *'low* allow
7 *bespoken* engaged to be married
9 *spouse* fiancé

139–40 *enough ... dinner* One of the few places in the play where rhyme is not kept.
140 s.d. *Here ... singing* No song is provided in Q, either here in the text or at the end of
    the play.

DAME CUSTANCE
At this time, nurse, I will neither read ne break.

MADGE
He promised to give you a whole peck of gold!   15

DAME CUSTANCE
Perchance lack of a pint when it shall be all told.

MADGE
I would take a gay rich husband, and I were you.

DAME CUSTANCE
In good sooth, Madge, e'en so would I, if I were thou.
But no more of this fond talk now. Let us go in,
And see thou no more move me folly to begin,   20
Nor bring me no mo' letters for no man's pleasure,
But thou know from whom.

MADGE   I warrant ye shall be sure.

[*Exeunt*]

Act II, Scene i

[*Enter* DOBINET DOUGHTY]

DOUGHTY
Where is the house I go to, before or behind?
I know not where nor when nor how I shall it find.
If I had ten men's bodies and legs and strength,
This trotting that I have must needs lame me at length.
And now that my master is new set on wooing,   5
I trust there shall none of us find lack of doing.
Two pair of shoes a day will now be too little
To serve me, I must trot to and fro so mickle.
'Go bear me this token!' 'Carry me this letter!'
'Now this is the best way, now that way is better!'   10
'Up before day, sirs, I charge you, an hour or twain!'
'Trudge! Do me this message, and bring word quick
          again!'
If one miss but a minute, then: 'His arms and wounds!

---

14 *break* (i.e., the seal of the letter)
16 *lack...told* a pint less than a peck when it is counted
19 *fond* foolish
21 *mo'* ed. (mo Q) more
 8 *mickle* much
13 *His* Christ's

I would not have slacked for ten thousand pounds!
Nay, see, I beseech you, if my most trusty page   15
Go not now about to hinder my marriage!'
So fervent hot wooing, and so far from wiving,
I trow never was any creature living.
With every woman is he in some love's pang;
Then up to our lute at midnight, 'Twangledum twang!'   20
Then 'Twang!' with our sonnets and 'Twang!' with our
         dumps,
And 'Heigh-ho!' from our hearts, as heavy as lead lumps.
Then to our recorder with 'Toodleloodle poop!',
As the howlet out of an ivy bush should whoop.
Anon to our gittern, 'Thrumpledum, thrumpledum,
         thrum!   25
Thrumpledum, thrumpledum, thrumpledum,
         thrumpledum, thrum!'
Of songs and ballads also he is a maker,
And that can he as finely do as Jack Raker.
Yea, and *extempore* will he ditties compose;
Foolish Marsias ne'er made the like, I suppose.   30
Yet must we sing them; as good stuff, I undertake,
As for such a penman is well fitting to make.
'Ah, for these long nights! Heigh-ho, when will it be day!
I fear, ere I come, she will be wooed away.'
Then when answer is made that it may not be: 35
'O death, why comest thou not by and by?' saith he.

---

16 *Go . . . about* is not now trying
21 *dumps* mournful or plaintive tunes (first *OED* occurrence)
24 *howlet* owl
   whoop eds. (hoope Q; hop some eds.)
25 *gittern* stringed instrument (like a guitar)
29 *extempore* extemporarily, without preparation
   ditties lyrics
36 *by and by* immediately

---

28 *Jack Raker* The type of a poetaster, one who 'rakes' together bits of bad verse, and probably not an historical person. The name may be proverbial; it occurs several times in the poems of John Skelton, where it is usually paired for rhyme, as here, with 'maker', in its medieval sense of 'poet'.

30 *Foolish Marsias* A somewhat inaccurate allusion to the legend of a peasant who found a flute lost by Athena, which produced beautiful music of its own accord. Marsias rashly challenged Apollo to a musical contest, lost, and was flayed alive by the god for his presumption. He did not actually compose 'ditties' as Roister Doister does.

31–2 *as good . . . make* His compositions are as good as one would expect, considering who the author is.

But then, from his heart to put away sorrow,
He is as far in with some new love next morrow.
But in the mean season, we trudge and we trot;
From dayspring to midnight, I sit not nor rest not.   40
And now am I sent to Dame Christian Custance;
But I fear it will end with a mock for pastance.
I bring her a ring, with a token in a clout;
And by all guess, this same is her house, out of doubt.
I know it now, perfect; I am in my right way.   45
And lo, yond the old nurse that was with us last day.

Act II, Scene ii

[*Enter* MADGE MUMBLECRUST]

MADGE [*Aside*]
I was ne'er so shook up afore since I was born!
That our mistress could not have chid I would have
     sworn,
And I pray God I die if I meant any harm.
But for my lifetime this shall be to me a charm.

DOUGHTY
God you save and see, nurse! And how is it with you?   5

MADGE
Marry, a great deal the worse it is, for such as thou.

DOUGHTY
For me? Why so?

MADGE   Why, were not thou one of them, say,
That sang and played here with the gentleman last day?

40 *dayspring* daybreak
42 *pastance* pastime
43 *token* keepsake, present
    clout cloth
 2 *chid* scolded
 4 *this . . . charm* this scolding will keep me from doing it again
 5 *save . . . see* bless and watch over
 6 *for* because of

46 *last day* This reference, and that at II.ii, 8, indicate that a night has passed since
    the end of Act I.

DOUGHTY

Yes, and he would know if you have for him spoken,
And prays you to deliver this ring and token.   10

MADGE

Now by the token that God tokened, brother,
I will deliver no token, one nor other.
I have once been so shent for your master's pleasure,
As I will not be again for all his treasure.

DOUGHTY

He will thank you, woman.

                    I will none of his thank!   15

MADGE

                               [*Exit*]

DOUGHTY

I ween I am a prophet: this gear will prove blank.
But what, should I home again without answer go?
It were better go to Rome on my head than so!
I will tarry here this month, but some of the house
Shall take it of me, and then I care not a louse!   20
But yonder cometh forth a wench, or a lad—
If he have not one Lombard's touch, my luck is bad!

---

11 *token . . . tokened* the gift that God gave (i.e., Jesus Christ)
16 *ween* think
   gear business

---

18 *go . . . head* Probably a variant of the proverb 'To go (hop) to Rome with a mortar
   on one's head' (Tilley R164). Compare 'I will ride to Rome on my thumb'
   (*Hickscorner*, in *Two Tudor Interludes*, ed. Ian Lancashire (Manchester, 1980), 1.
   445).
19–20 *I . . . me* I will wait here until someone from the house takes the ring from me,
   even if it takes a month.
22 *one Lombard's touch* Lombards (from Lombardy in Italy) were famous as bankers.
   Doughty hopes that the person who is arriving will have their 'touch' for gold and
   will relieve him of the ring he has been charged to deliver to Dame Custance.
   Lombard Street is in London's banking quarter. Compare *Mundus et Infans* (*Three
   Late Medieval Morality Plays*, ed. Lester), l. 672 and n.

Act II, Scene iii

[*Enter* TOM TRUEPENNY]

TRUEPENNY [*Aside*]
I am clean lost for lack of merry company!
We 'gree not half well within, our wenches and I.
They will command like mistresses, they will forbid;
If they be not served, Truepenny must be chid.
Let them be as merry now as ye can desire,   5
With turning of a hand our mirth lieth in the mire.
I cannot skill of such changeable mettle;
There is nothing with them but 'In dock, out nettle'!

DOUGHTY [*Aside*]
Whether is it better, that I speak to him first,
Or he first to me? It is good to cast the worst.   10
If I begin first, he will smell all my purpose;
Otherwise, I shall not need anything to disclose.

TRUEPENNY [*Aside*]
What boy have we yonder? I will see what he is.

DOUGHTY [*Aside*]
He cometh to me—it is hereabout, iwis.

TRUEPENNY
Wouldest thou aught, friend, that thou lookest so about? 15

DOUGHTY
Yea, but whether ye can help me or no, I doubt.
I seek to one Mistress Custance's house, here dwelling.

TRUEPENNY
It is my mistress ye seek to, by your telling.

DOUGHTY
Is there any of that name here but she?

---

6 *With ... hand* the next instant
7 *skill of* understand
  mettle disposition (antedates *OED*'s first occurrence)
10 *cast* anticipate
14 *it is hereabout* this is it
15 *aught* eds. (ought Q) anything
18 *to* eds. (too Q)

---

8 *In ... nettle* Proverbial (Tilley D421). Originally a charm uttered to cure nettle
stings while rubbing them with dock leaves, the expression had come, as early as
the fourteenth century, to signify changeableness.

TRUEPENNY

Not one in all the whole town that I know, pardee.   20

DOUGHTY

A widow she is, I trow.

TRUEPENNY   And what and she be?

DOUGHTY

But ensured to an husband.

TRUEPENNY   Yea, so think we.

DOUGHTY

And I dwell with her husband that trusteth to be.

TRUEPENNY

In faith, then must thou needs be welcome to me
Let us for acquaintance' sake shake hands together.   25
And whate'er thou be, heartily welcome hither.

          [*Enter* TIBET TALKAPACE *and* ANNOT ALYFACE]

TIBET

Well, Truepenny, never but flinging—

ANNOT   And frisking?

TRUEPENNY

Well, Tibet and Annot, still swinging and whisking?

TIBET

But ye roil abroad—

ANNOT   In the street, everywhere!

TRUEPENNY

Where are ye twain—in chambers?—when ye meet me
    there?   30
But come hither, fools, I have one now by the hand,

---

22 *ensured* engaged
23 *her... be* the one who expects to be her husband
27 *flinging* dashing about
28 *whisking* frolicking
29 *roil* roam, gad
30 *there* (i.e., 'in the street, everywhere')

---

31 *fools... hand* From the proverb 'You have not a fool in hand' (Tilley F514). Here
    Truepenny is not calling Doughty a fool, but making a joke which assumes
    familiarity with the proverb, from the juxtaposition of 'fools' (the girls) and 'having
    one (someone else) by the hand'. Compare *Twelfth Night*, I.iii, 61: 'Fair lady, do
    you think you have fools in hand?—Sir, I have not you by th' hand'.

Servant to him that must be our mistress' husband.
Bid him welcome.

ANNOT   To me truly is he welcome!

TIBET
Forsooth, and as I may say, heartily welcome!

DOUGHTY
I thank you, mistress maids.

ANNOT   I hope we shall better know.   35

TIBET
And when will our new master come?

DOUGHTY   Shortly, I trow.

TIBET
I would it were tomorrow: for till he resort,
Our mistress, being a widow, hath small comfort.
And I heard our nurse speak of an husband today,
Ready for our mistress, a rich man and a gay;   40
And we shall go in our French hoods every day,
In our silk cassocks, I warrant you, fresh and gay,
In our trick ferdegews and biliments of gold,
Brave in our suits of change, seven doublefold.
Then shall ye see Tibet, sirs, tread the moss so trim—   45
Nay, why said I 'tread'? Ye shall see her glide and
      swim,
Not 'lumperdee, clumperdee' like our spaniel, Rig.

TRUEPENNY
Marry then, prick-me-dainty, come toast me a fig!
Who shall then know our Tib Talkapace, trow ye?

35 *better know* know each other better
37 *resort* come back
42 *cassocks* long loose gowns
43 *trick* smart
   ferdegews farthingales, hooped petticoats
   biliments women's head or neck ornaments
44 *Brave . . . doublefold* handsome in our fourteen different sets of clothes (?)
45 *tread the moss* walk
48 *prick-me-dainty* one who is finical or affected in dress or manner

48 *toast . . . fig* Precise meaning unknown. Perhaps the type of the exaggeratedly
   fastidious command given by one playing at ostentatious wealth and elegance, like
   'Peel me a grape'. But compare proverbial connotations of *fig* as something
   worthless (Tilley F210, F211) or poisonous (F213).

ANNOT
  And why not Annot Alyface as fine as she? 50

TRUEPENNY
  And what, had Tom Truepenny a father or none?

ANNOT
  Then our pretty new-come man will look to be one.

TRUEPENNY
  We four, I Trust, shall be a jolly merry knot!
  Shall we sing a fit to welcome our friend, Annot?

ANNOT
  Perchance he cannot sing.

DOUGHTY   I am at all assays. 55

TIBET
  By Cock, and the better welcome to us always!

Here they sing

          A thing very fit
          For them that have wit,
          And are fellows knit,
          Servants in one house to be; 60
          Is fast for to sit,
          And not oft to flit,
          Nor vary a whit,
          But lovingly to agree.

          No man complaining, 65
          Nor other disdaining,
          For loss or for gaining,
          But fellows or friends to be;
          No grudge remaining,
          No work refraining, 70
          Nor help restraining,
          But lovingly to agree.

          No man for despite,
          By word or by write,
          His fellow to twite, 75

58 *had . . . none* don't I count as much as you
54 *fit* musical number
55 *am . . . assays* ready to try anything
56 *Cock* God
61 *fast* eds. (fast fast Q)
74 *by write* in writing
75 *twite* blame or taunt

But further in honesty;
No good turns entwite,
Nor old sores recite,
But let all go quite,
And lovingly to agree.   80

After drudgery,
When they be weary,
Then to be merry,
To laugh and sing they be free;
With chip and cherry,   85
Heigh derry derry,
Trill on the berry,
And lovingly to agree.

Finis

TIBET
Will you now in with us unto our mistress go?

DOUGHTY
I have first for my master an errand or two.   90
But I have here from him a token and a ring;
They shall have most thank of her that first doth it
    bring.

TIBET
Marry, that will I!

TRUEPENNY   See and Tib snatch not now!

TIBET
And why may not I, sir, get thanks as well as you?

[Takes the gifts from DOUGHTY]

---

77 *entwite* make the subject of reproach
79 *go quite* be forgiven
85 *chip . . . cherry* (perhaps for bird-sounds 'cheep' and 'chirree')
86 *Heigh . . . derry* (common song refrain)
87 *Trill . . . berry* (apparently a song refrain) sing on the hillside
    berry hillock, barrow
93 *and* if

---

94 s.d. *Takes . . .* DOUGHTY It must be Tibet who snatches the ring and token here; see
    sc. iv, 8–9.

ANNOT

    Yet get ye not all! We will go with you, both,   95
    And have part of your thanks, be ye never so loath.
           Exeunt [TIBET, ANNOT *and* TRUEPENNY]

DOUGHTY

    So my hands are rid of it, I care for no more!
    I may now return home; so durst I not afore.

                                 Exit

Act II, Scene iv

[*Enter* CHRISTIAN CUSTANCE, TIBET TALKAPACE, ANNOT
ALYFACE *and* TOM TRUEPENNY]

DAME CUSTANCE

    Nay, come forth all three! And come hither, pretty maid!
    Will not so many forewarnings make you afraid?

TIBET

    Yes, forsooth.

DAME CUSTANCE   But still be a runner up and down,
    Still be a bringer of tidings and tokens to town?

TIBET

    No, forsooth, mistress.

DAME CUSTANCE   Is all your delight and joy   5
    In whisking and ramping abroad like a tomboy?

TIBET

    Forsooth, these were there too, Annot and Truepenny.

TRUEPENNY

    Yea, but ye alone took it, ye cannot deny.

ANNOT

    Yea, that ye did.

TIBET   But if I had not, ye twain would.

DAME CUSTANCE

    You great calf, ye should have more wit, so ye should!   10
    But why should any of you take such things in hand?

---

  95 *both* (i.e., both of us)
  96 s.d. *Exeunt* . . . TRUEPENNY ed. (Exeant omnes Q; Exeat [TIBET] at l. 94 Q)
   6 *ramping* going about in a loose or immodest way

TIBET
Because it came from him that must be your husband.

DAME CUSTANCE
How do ye know that?

TIBET   Forsooth, the boy did say so.

DAME CUSTANCE
What was his name?

ANNOT   We asked not.

DAME CUSTANCE   Did ye no?

ANNOT
He is not far gone, of likelihood.

TRUEPENNY   I will see.   15

DAME CUSTANCE
If thou canst find him in the street, bring him to me.

TRUEPENNY
Yes.   *Exit*

DAME CUSTANCE   Well ye naughty girls, if ever I perceive
That henceforth you do letters or tokens receive,
To bring unto me from any person or place,
Except ye first show me the party face to face,   20
Either thou or thou, full truly aby thou shalt.

TIBET
Pardon this, and the next time powder me in salt!

DAME CUSTANCE
I shall make all girls by you twain to beware.

TIBET
If I ever offend again, do not me spare.
But if ever I see that false boy any more,   25

---

14 *Did ye no?* ed. (No did? Q)
21 *aby* pay the penalty
22 *powder . . . salt* (colloquial) pickle me; tan my hide

---

14 *Did ye no? Q's No did?* is clearly wrong, as a rhyme for *so* is required. *No* (= *not*)
was current as an adverb in the sixteenth century. Editors emend variously, e.g.
'Did ye? No?' (Boas). A word or two are probably missing: the verse line as it
stands has only ten syllables, even with *asked* sounded as a bisyllable.
22 *powder . . . salt* Sprinkling meat with salt was the only method of preserving it
before the days of refrigeration.

By your mistresship's license, I tell you afore,
I will rather have my coat twenty times swinged
Than on the naughty wag not to be avenged!

DAME CUSTANCE
Good wenches would not so ramp abroad idly,
But keep within doors and ply their work earnestly.   30
If one would speak with me that is a man likely,
Ye shall have right good thank to bring me word
     quickly.
But otherwise with messages to come in post
From henceforth, I promise you, shall be to your cost.
Get you in to your work.

TIBET *and* ANNOT   Yes, forsooth!

DAME CUSTANCE   Hence, both twain,   35
And let me see you play me such a part again!
                              [*Exeunt* TIBET *and* ANNOT]

                    [*Enter* TRUEPENNY]

TRUEPENNY
Mistress, I have run past the far end of the street,
Yet can I not yonder crafty boy see nor meet.

DAME CUSTANCE
No?

TRUEPENNY   Yet I looked as far beyond the people
As one may see out of the top of Paul's steeple.   40

DAME CUSTANCE
Hence, in at doors, and let me no more be vexed!

TRUEPENNY
Forgive me this one fault, and lay on for the next.
                                        [*Exit*]

DAME CUSTANCE
Now will I in too, for I think, so God me mend,
This will prove some foolish matter in the end.   *Exit*

27 *swinged* beaten
42 *lay on* beat me severely

---

37 *past . . . street* This may indicate that a perspective set, with a street running up the
middle and appearing to recede in the distance, was used. See Introduction, pp.
liv–lv.

40 *top . . . steeple* The steeple of St Paul's Cathedral in London was a popular sight-
seeing spot. It dominated the city's skyline and from the tower one had a panoramic
view of the city and surrounding countryside. The medieval church burned in the
Great Fire of 1666 and was replaced by the present structure, designed by Sir
Christopher Wren.

Act III, Scene i

[*Enter* MATTHEW MERRYGREEK]

MERRYGREEK
Now say this again: he hath somewhat to doing
Which followeth the trace of one that is wooing,
Specially that hath no more wit in his head
Than my cousin Roister Doister withal is led.
I am sent in all haste to espy and to mark   5
How our letters and tokens are likely to work.
Master Roister Doister must have answer in haste,
For he loveth not to spend much labour in waste.
Now as for Christian Custance, by this light,
Though she had not her troth in Gawin Goodluck plight, 10
Yet rather than with such a loutish dolt to marry,
I daresay would live a poor life solitary.
But fain would I speak with Custance, if I wist how,
To laugh at the matter.—Yond cometh one forth now.

Act III, Scene ii

[*Enter* TIBET TALKAPACE]

TIBET
Ah, that I might but once in my life have sight
Of him that made us all so ill shent, by this light!
He should never escape if I had him by the ear,
But even from his head I would it bite or tear.
Yea, and if one of them were not enow,   5
I would bite them both off, I make God avow!

MERRYGREEK [*Aside*]
What is he whom this little mouse doth so threaten?

TIBET
I would teach him, I trow, to make girls shent or beaten!

MERRYGREEK [*Aside*]
I will call her.—Maid, with whom are ye so hasty?

1 *somewhat . . . doing* a lot to do
4 *cousin* (term of familiarity, often used patronizingly)
6 *work* ed. (warke Q)
9 *by . . . light* (oath)
6 *avow* vow, solemn promise

TIBET
    Not with you, sir, but with a little wagpasty,   10
    A deceiver of folks by subtle craft and guile.

MERRYGREEK [*Aside*]
    I know where she is: Dobinet hath wrought some wile.

TIBET
    He brought a ring and token which he said was sent
    From our dame's husband, but I wot well I was shent,
    For it liked her as well, to tell you no lies,   15
    As water in her ship or salt cast in her eyes;
    And yet whence it came neither we nor she can tell.

MERRYGREEK [*Aside*]
    We shall have sport anon; I like this very well.—
    And dwell ye here with Mistress Custance, fair maid?

TIBET
    Yea, marry, do I, sir. What would ye have said?   20

MERRYGREEK
    A little message unto her by word of mouth.

TIBET
    No messages, by your leave, nor tokens forsooth!

MERRYGREEK
    Then help me to speak to her.

TIBET   With a good will, that.

[*Enter* CHRISTIAN CUSTANCE]

    Here she cometh forth. Now speak; ye know best what.

DAME CUSTANCE
    None other life with you, maid, but abroad to skip?   25

TIBET
    Forsooth, here is one would speak with your mistresship.

DAME CUSTANCE
    Ah, have ye been learning of mo' messages now?

10 *wagpasty* mischievous rogue
12 *where ... is* what she's talking about
    wile ruse, trick

15–16 *it ... eyes* Proverbial (Tilley W89): 'As welcome as water into a ship'; and
    compare D650: 'To cast dust in a man's eyes'.
18 *We ... anon* In promising 'sport', Merrygreek is playing the same role as Diccon;
    compare, e.g., *GGN*, II.v, 1.

TIBET
I would not hear his mind, but bad him show it to you.

DAME CUSTANCE
In at doors.

TIBET   I am gone.   *Exit*

MERRYGREEK   Dame Custance, God ye save.

DAME CUSTANCE
Welcome, friend Merrygreek. And what thing would ye
    have?   30

MERRYGREEK
I am come to you a little matter to break.

DAME CUSTANCE
But see it be honest, else better not to speak.

MERRYGREEK
How feel ye yourself affected here of late?

DAME CUSTANCE
I feel no manner change, but after the old rate.
But whereby do ye mean?

MERRYGREEK   Concerning marriage.   35
Doth not love lade you?

DAME CUSTANCE   I feel no such carriage.

MERRYGREEK
Do ye feel no pangs of dotage? Answer me right.

DAME CUSTANCE
I dote so, that I make but one sleep all the night.
But what need all these words?

MERRYGREEK   O Jesus, will ye see
What dissembling creatures these same women be?   40
The gentleman ye wot of, whom ye do so love
That ye would fain marry him, if ye durst it move,
Among other rich widows, which are of him glad,
Lest ye for losing of him perchance might run mad,
Is now contented that upon your suit making,   45
Ye be as one in election of taking.

34 *after . . . rate* as usual
36 *lade* burden, afflict
37 *dotage* infatuation
46 *Ye . . . taking* you are as good as accepted

DAME CUSTANCE
  What a tale is this! That I wot of? Whom I love?

MERRYGREEK
  Yea, and he is as loving a worm again as a dove.
  E'en of very pity he is willing you to take,
  Because ye shall not destroy yourself for his sake.   50

DAME CUSTANCE
  Marry, God yield his ma'ship, whatever he be!
  It is gent'manly spoken.

MERRYGREEK   Is it not, trow ye?
  If ye have the grace now to offer yourself, ye speed.

DAME CUSTANCE
  As much as though I did, this time it shall not need.
  But what gent'man is it, I pray you tell me plain,   55
  That wooeth so finely?

MERRYGREEK   Lo where ye be again!
  As though ye knew him not!

DAME CUSTANCE   Tush, ye speak in jest!

MERRYGREEK
  Nay, sure, the party is in good knacking earnest.
  And have you he will, he saith, and have you he must.

DAME CUSTANCE
  I am promised during my life. That is just.   60

MERRYGREEK
  Marry, so thinketh he—unto him alone.

DAME CUSTANCE
  No creature hath my faith and troth but one:
  That is Gawin Goodluck. And if it be not he,
  He hath no title this way, whatever he be.
  Nor I know none to whom I have such word spoken.   65

MERRYGREEK
  Yea, know him not you by his letter and token?

---

48 *worm* tender creature
50 *Because* so that
51 *yield* reward
54 *As . . . did* however true that may be
58 *knacking* downright
60 *just* true
64 *this way* toward me
66 *Yea, . . . token* Baskervill, *et al.* (Ye . . . token Q)

DAME CUSTANCE
　Indeed, true it is that a letter I have,
　But I never read it yet, as God me save.

MERRYGREEK
　Ye a woman, and your letter so long unread?

DAME CUSTANCE
　Ye may thereby know what haste I have to wed!　　70
　But now who it is for my hand, I know by guess.

MERRYGREEK
　Ah, well, I say—

DAME CUSTANCE　　It is Roister Doister, doubtless.

MERRYGREEK
　Will ye never leave this dissimulation?
　Ye know him not—

DAME CUSTANCE　　　　But by imagination.
　For no man there is but a very dolt and lout　　75
　That to woo a widow would so go about.
　He shall never have me his wife while he do live!

MERRYGREEK
　Then will he have you if he may, so mote I thrive!
　And he biddeth you send him word by me
　That ye humbly beseech him ye may his wife be,　　80
　And that there shall be no let in you nor mistrust,
　But to be wedded on Sunday next if he lust,
　And biddeth you to look for him.

DAME CUSTANCE　　　　　　　Doth he bid so?

MERRYGREEK
　When he cometh, ask him whether he did or no.

DAME CUSTANCE
　Go, say that I bid him keep him warm at home,　　85
　For if he come abroad he shall cough me a mome.
　My mind was vexed—I shrew his head, sottish dolt!

71 *for my hand* who seeks my hand in marriage
78 *mote* may
81 *let* hindrance, resistance
82 *lust* wishes

86 *Cough . . . mome* Make a fool of himself. The origin of the expression is obscure; it
　was in use before and after Udall, e.g., by Skelton and Lyly.

MERRYGREEK
　He hath in his head—

DAME CUSTANCE　　　　As much brain as a burbolt!

MERRYGREEK
　Well, Dame Custance, if he hear you thus play choploge—

DAME CUSTANCE
　What will he?

MERRYGREEK　　Play the devil in the horologe.　　　　　　　　90

DAME CUSTANCE
　I defy him! Lout!

MERRYGREEK　　　　Shall I tell him what ye say?

DAME CUSTANCE
　Yea, and add whatsoever thou canst, I thee pray,
　And I will avouch it, whatsoever it be!

MERRYGREEK
　Then let me alone. We will laugh well, ye shall see.
　It will not be long ere he will hither resort.　　　　　　95

DAME CUSTANCE
　Let him come when him lust; I wish no better sport.
　Fare ye well; I will in and read my great letter.
　I shall to my wooer make answer the better.　　　　*Exit*

Act III, Scene iii

MERRYGREEK
　Now that the whole answer in my devise doth rest,
　I shall paint out our wooer in colours of the best.
　And all that I say shall be on Custance's mouth;
　She is author of all that I shall speak, forsooth.

[*Enter* ROISTER DOISTER]

　But yond cometh Roister Doister now, in a trance.　　　5

88　*burbolt* bird-bolt (a blunt-headed arrow for shooting birds)
89　*choploge* choplogic (a contentious, sophisticated arguer)
90　*horologe* clock (Fr., *horloge*)
93　*avouch* confirm
　1　*the . . . rest* the matter is left entirely up to me

90　*Play . . . horologe* Proverbial (Tilley D302). Sow confusion, create chaos, as would
　　the devil (or anyone else) tampering with the works of a clock.

ROISTER DOISTER
    Juno send me this day good luck and good chance!
    I cannot but come see how Merrygreek doth speed.

MERRYGREEK [*Aside*]
    I will not see him, but give him a jut indeed.

                 [*Bumps* ROISTER DOISTER]

    I cry your mastership mercy!

ROISTER DOISTER   And whither now?

MERRYGREEK
    As fast as I could run, sir, in post against you.   10
    But why speak ye so faintly? Or why are ye so sad?

ROISTER DOISTER
    Thou knowest the proverb: because I cannot be had.
    Hast thou spoken with this woman?

MERRYGREEK   Yea, that I have.

ROISTER DOISTER
    And what, will this gear be?

MERRYGREEK   No, so God me save!

ROISTER DOISTER
    Hast thou a flat answer?

MERRYGREEK   Nay, a sharp answer.

ROISTER DOISTER   What?   15

MERRYGREEK
    Ye shall not, she saith, by her will, marry her cat.
    Ye are such a calf, such an ass, such a block,
    Such a lilburne, such a hoball, such a lobcock,

  8 *jut* push, shove
10 *post* haste
    against towards
14 *what, will* eds. (what will Q)
15 s.p. ROISTER DOISTER eds. (M. Mery. Q)
18 *lilburne* lubber, lout
    hoball fool, idiot
    lobcock bumpkin, clown

  6 *Juno* Roister Doister appeals to the Greek goddess of marriage.
12 *Thou ... had* Proverbial (Tilley S14): 'I am sad because I cannot be glad'. Tilley
    conjectures that the proverb went 'because I cannot be glad', but gives no other
    examples (compare 'Then let us say you are sad/Because you are not merry', *The
    Merchant of Venice*, I.i, 47–8). If so, Roister Doister alters it to fit his case, not being
    'had', accepted, by Dame Custance; or it is a misprint.

And because ye should come to her at no season,
She despised your ma'ship out of all reason,   20
'Beware what ye say', ko I, 'of such a gent'man!'
'Nay, I fear him not', ko she, 'do the best he can.
He vaunteth himself for a man of prowess great,
Whereas a good gander, I daresay, may him beat.
And where he is louted and laughed to scorn   25
For the veriest dolt that ever was born,
And veriest lubber, sloven and beast
Living in this world from the west to the east,
Yet of himself hath he such opinion
That in all the world is not the like minion.   30
He thinketh each woman to be brought in dotage
With the only sight of his goodly personage,
Yet none that will have him. We do him lout and flock,
And make him among us our common sporting stock.
And so would I now', ko she, 'save only because—'   35
'Better nay', ko I—'I lust not meddle with daws.'
'Ye are happy', ko I, 'that ye are a woman!
This would cost you your life in case ye were a man.'

ROISTER DOISTER
　Yea, an hundred thousand pound should not save her
　　life!

MERRYGREEK
　No, but that ye woo her to have her to your wife;   40
　But I could not stop her mouth.

ROISTER DOISTER   Heigh ho, alas!

MERRYGREEK
　Be of good cheer, man, and let the world pass.

ROISTER DOISTER
　What shall I do or say, now that it will not be?

MERRYGREEK
　Ye shall have choice of a thousand as good as she.
　And ye must pardon her; it is for lack of wit.   45

21　*Beware* ed. (Bawawe Q)
　　ko quoth, said
25　*louted* mocked
30　*minion* gallant
33　*flock* treat with contempt

42　*Let . . . pass* Proverbial (Tilley W879): 'Let the world wag (slide)'.

ROISTER DOISTER
Yea, for were not I an husband for her fit?
Well, what should I now do?

MERRYGREEK   In faith, I cannot tell.

ROISTER DOISTER
I will go home and die.

MERRYGREEK   Then shall I bid toll the bell?

ROISTER DOISTER
No.

MERRYGREEK   God have mercy on your soul! Ah, good
        gentleman,
That e'er ye should thus die for an unkind woman!   50
Will ye drink once ere ye go?

ROISTER DOISTER   No, no, I will none.

MERRYGREEK
How feel your soul to God?

ROISTER DOISTER   I am nigh gone.

MERRYGREEK
And shall we hence straight?

ROISTER DOISTER   Yea.

MERRYGREEK   *Placebo dilexi.*
Master Roister Doister will straight go home and die.

53–99 *Placebo dilexi... Nequando... Dirige... A porta inferi... Requiem aeternam
... Audivi vocem... Qui Lazarum... In Paradisum* The Latin phrases scattered
through this passage are garbled fragments from various parts of the Office of the
Dead of the Roman Catholic Church. The Vespers service for the dead begins with
the words of Psalm 116:9 (Ps. 114 in the Vulgate), '*Placebo domine...*'; then the
preceding verses of the psalm, beginning '*Dilexi Quoniam...*', are said. Compare
Skelton's *Philip Sparrow* (c. 1505), a mock-requiem for a pet bird, where the same
Latin phrases are used. Also, 'to sing *placebo*' (to play the sycophant) is proverbial
(Tilley P378). '*Neque lux, neque crux, neque* mourners, *neque* clink' (without
candle, nor cross, nor mourners, nor bell) is not in the ritual; Merrygreek may be
echoing the English Reformers' distaste for such Popish 'fooleries' (further
evidence that the play is pre-Marian, perhaps). *A porta inferi* means 'from the gate
of hell'. *Qui Lazarum* alludes to Lazarus whom Jesus resurrected from the tomb
(John 11). *In Paradisum* ('into Paradise') is the beginning of a prayer said as the
corpse was carried to the grave. There are differences in this passage as it appears in
the body of the play (sigs. D4^v–E1) and in the 'Psalmody' appended, with two
songs and the peal of bells, at the end of the text (sigs. J2^{r-v}). A direction in Q, '*ut
infra*', at the end of l. 54, refers to that appendix. Several additional lines are
included there; these have been interpolated in the passage as printed here. For
variants within lines, see p. 211. See Flügel's note (Gayley, pp. 191–3).

[Our Lord Jesus Christ his soul have mercy upon.   55
Thus you see today a man, tomorrow John.]

ROISTER DOISTER
Heigh ho, alas, the pangs of death my heart do break!

MERRYGREEK
Hold your peace, for shame, sir! A dead may may not
    speak!
Nequando. What mourners and what torches shall we
    have?

ROISTER DOISTER
None.

MERRYGREEK   *Dirige.* He will go darkling to his grave,   60
Neque lux, neque crux, neque mourners, *neque* clink;
He will steal to heaven unknowing to God, I think,
A porta inferi. Who shall your goods possess?

ROISTER DOISTER
Thou shalt be my sector and have all, more and less.

MERRYGREEK
Requiem æternam. Now God reward your mastership,   65
And I will cry halfpenny dole for your worship.

            He calls forth the soldier's servants

Come forth, sirs. Hear the doleful news I shall you tell.

[*Enter* DOBINET DOUGHTY, HARPAX *and two other servants*]

Our good master here will no longer with us dwell;
[Yet saving for a woman's extreme cruelty,
He might have lived yet a month or two or three.]   70
But in spite of Custance, which hath him wearied,

55–6 *Our... John* ed. (not in Q; added from text of 'The Psalmody' at end of play)
62 *unknowing* unknown
64 *sector* executor
66 *cry... worship* announce that halfpennies will be distributed to the poor in your
    memory
    s.d. *He... servants* (Evocat servos militis Q)
69–70 *Yet... three* ed. (not in Q; added from appended text)

---

56 *Thus... John* Proverbial (Tilley M404): 'Today a man, tomorrow none'. Merry-
    greek's 'John' for 'none' is inexplicable, but Scheurweghs tries (p. 109).
67 s.d. *two other servants* Four persons, besides the parish clerk, are needed to ring the
    peal of bells (l. 90 s.d.)

Let us see his ma'ship solemnly buried.
And while some piece of his soul is yet him within,
Some part of his funerals let us here begin,
[Yet, sirs, as ye will the bliss of heaven win,   75
When he cometh to the grave, lay him softly in.]
Audivi vocem. All men take heed by this one gentleman,
How you set your love upon an unkind woman.
For these women be all such mad, peevish elves,
They will not be won except it please themselves.   80
But, in faith, Custance, if ever ye come in hell,
Master Roister Doister shall serve you as well.
And will ye needs go from us thus in very deed?

ROISTER DOISTER
    Yea, in good sadness.

MERRYGREEK   Now Jesus Christ be your speed!
    Good night, Roger old knave; farewell Roger old knave,   85
    Good night, Roger, old knave, knave, knap!
    Pray for the late Master Roister Doister's soul.
    And come forth, parish clerk; let the passing bell toll.

                        [*Enter* PARISH CLERK]

[*To the servants*] Pray for your master, sirs, and for him
        ring a peal.
He was your right good master while he was in heal.   90

        [*The peal of bells rung by the* PARISH CLERK *and* ROISTER
                    DOISTER'*s four men.*

                    The first bell, a triple
            When died he? When died he?

                        The second

75–6 *Yet . . . in* ed. (not in Q; added from appended text)
84 *good sadness* all seriousness
86 *knap* knock, rap
88 *passing bell* funeral bell
89 s.d. *To the servants* ed. (Ad servos militis Q)
90 *heal* health
90 s.d.–95 *The peal . . . our own* ed. (not in Q; added from appended text)

85–6 These are presumably words from a popular song. The last word, 'knap'
    suggests that Merrygreek raps or thumps Roister Doister, a liberty he takes at
    every opportunity.
88 s.d. *Enter* PARISH CLERK Although no such character is listed at the beginning of the
    scene, he is called forth here and his presence, with that of Roister Doister's four
    men, is indicated in the heading at l.90 s.d.
91 *triple* The smallest, highest tuned of a set, or peal, of bells; also called the 'treble'.

We have him, we have him.

The third
Roister Doister, Roister Doister.

The fourth bell
He cometh, he cometh.

The great bell
Our own, our own.]   95

MERRYGREEK
Qui Lazarum.

ROISTER DOISTER   Heigh ho!

MERRYGREEK   Dead men go not so fast
In Paradisum.

ROISTER DOISTER   Heigh ho!

MERRYGREEK   Soft, hear what I have cast.

ROISTER DOISTER
I will hear nothing. I am past.

MERRYGREEK   Whough, wellaway!
Ye may tarry one hour and hear what I shall say.
Ye were best, sir, for a while to revive again,   100
And quite them ere ye go.

ROISTER DOISTER   Trowest thou so?

MERRYGREEK   Yea, plain.

ROISTER DOISTER
How may I revive, being now so far past?

MERRYGREEK
I will rub your temples and fet you again at last.

ROISTER DOISTER
It will not be possible.

MERRYGREEK   Yes, for twenty pound.

---

97 *cast* planned
98 *Whough, wellaway* (expressions of dismay)
101 *quite them* pay the servants
    plain indeed
103 *fet* fetch, bring back
104 *for ... pound* I'll wager twenty pounds

ROISTER DOISTER
   Arms! What dost thou?

MERRYGREEK   Fet you again out of your sound.   105
   By this cross, ye were nigh gone indeed! I might feel
   Your soul departing within an inch of your heel.
   Now follow my counsel.

ROISTER DOISTER   What is it?

MERRYGREEK   If I were you,
   Custance should eft seek to me ere I would bow.

ROISTER DOISTER
   Well, as thou wilt have me, even so will I do.   110

MERRYGREEK
   Then shall ye revive again for an hour or two.

ROISTER DOISTER
   As thou wilt I am content, for a little space.

MERRYGREEK
   Good hap is not hasty; yet in space cometh grace.
   To speak with Custance yourself should be very well;
   What good thereof may come, nor I nor you can tell.   115
   But now the matter standeth upon your marriage,
   Ye must now take unto you a lusty courage.
   Ye may not speak with a faint heart to Custance,
   But with a lusty breast and countenance,
   That she may know she hath to answer to a man.   120

ROISTER DOISTER
   Yes, I can do that as well as any can.

MERRYGREEK
   Then because ye must Custance face to face woo,

---

105 *Arms* by his (Christ's) arms
    sound swoon, faint
106 *By . . . cross* (see IV.iii, 9, note)
109 *eft* first
112 *space* time
116 *now . . . upon* now that it is a matter of

---

105 *What doest thou?* Merrygreek has presumably begun rubbing Roister Doister's
    temples with more than the required vigour.
113 *Good . . . hasty* Probably proverbial. Compare Tilley H370 ('Good heed has good
    hap') and H197 ('More haste than good speed').
    in . . . grace Proverbial (Tilley S697-8).

Let us see how to behave yourself ye can do.
Ye must have a portly brag after your estate.

ROISTER DOISTER

Tush, I can handle that after the best rate. 125

MERRYGREEK

Well done! So lo, up, man, with your head and chin!
Up with that snout, man! So lo, now ye begin.
So, that is somewhat like! But, pranky-coat! Nay, when?
That is a lusty brute! Hands under your side, man!
So lo, now is it even as it should be! 130
That is somewhat like for a man of your degree.
Then must ye stately go, jetting up and down—
Tut, can ye no better shake the tail of your gown?
There, lo, such a lusty brag it is ye must make.

ROISTER DOISTER

To come behind and make curtsy, thou must some
    pains take. 135

MERRYGREEK

Else were I much to blame, I thank your mastership.
The Lord one day all to-begrime you with worship!—
Back, Sir Sauce, let gentlefolks have elbow room!
Void, sirs! See ye not Master Roister Doister come?
Make place, my masters.

ROISTER DOISTER   Thou jostlest now too nigh. 140

---

124 *portly brag* noble bearing
    after . . . estate in keeping with your dignity
125 *handle . . . rate* do that perfectly
128 *somewhat like* something like it
    pranky-coat eds. (prankie cote Q)
129 *Hands . . . side* hands on hips, arms a-kimbo
132 *jetting* strutting

---

128 *pranky-coat* The exact meaning is uncertain, and *OED* is unhelpful; it quotes this
    line under *pranky*, meaning 'to play pranks'. But this (which may be a coinage)
    would seem to derive from the verb *prank* which can mean both 'to dress . . . in a
    gay, bright or showy manner' and 'to caper or dance (prance)'. It seems to be used
    here as an adverb: Merrygreek is saying 'Do it like this' and is doubtless
    demonstrating.
138–41 *Back . . . mercy* Merrygreek is acting out, for Roister Doister's benefit, what he
    will say to bystanders when Roister Doister walks out in his finery, with all his
    attendants, to make an impression. He is also playing the imaginary onlookers'
    parts, jostling and shoving Roister Doister (ll. 140, 141), returning to his own
    sardonic person and the present moment at l. 142. He may also be speaking to the
    audience (compare Diccon's 'make here a little roomth!', *GGN*, II.iv, 2).

MERRYGREEK
  Back all rude louts!

ROISTER DOISTER   Tush!

MERRYGREEK   I cry your ma'ship mercy!
  Hoyday! If fair, fine Mistress Custance saw you now,
  Ralph Roister Doister were her own, I warrant you.

ROISTER DOISTER
  Ne'er an *M* by your girdle?

MERRYGREEK   Your good mastership's
  Mastership were her own mistresship's mistresship's.   145
  Ye were take up for hawks, ye were gone, ye were gone!
  But now one other thing more yet I think upon.

ROISTER DOISTER
  Show what it is.

MERRYGREEK   A wooer, be he never so poor,
  Must play and sing before his best-beloved's door.
  How much more, then, you?

ROISTER DOISTER   Thou speakest well, out of
  doubt.   150

MERRYGREEK
  And perchance that would make her the sooner come
  out.

ROISTER DOISTER
  Go call my musicians. Bid them hie apace.

MERRYGREEK
  I will be here with them ere ye can say, 'Trey, ace'!
                                                       Exit

142 *Hoyday* ed. (hoighdagh Q; exclamation of gaiety, wonder)
144 *Ne'er ... girdle* haven't you got an *M* (for 'Master') for me
149 *best-beloved's* eds. (bestbeloves Q)

146 *Ye ... hawks* This would appear at first to make sense only if 'take up' is made a
  noun meaning 'food' or 'bait'; in the context, 'hawks' would be rapacious, husband-
  hunting women. Compare Thomas Preston's *Cambyses* (c. 1561), l. 959: 'That
  husband for hawk's meat of them is up-snatched' (in Baskervill, *et al.*, p. 165). But
  Scheurweghs (p. 102) may be right to cite *take up* in the special sense of
  slaughtering old horses as bait for hawks. 'Take up (i.e., 'taken up') for hawks'
  would then mean 'done for'. No relevant proverb is recorded.
153 *ere ... ace* 'Trey' and 'ace' are, respectively, 'three' and 'one' in dice games. The
  expression was current from the fourteenth century. See B.J. Whiting, *Proverbs,
  Sentences and Proverbial Phrases from English Writings mainly before 1500*
  (Cambridge, Mass., 1968), T478.

ROISTER DOISTER
    This was well said of Merrygreek; I 'low his wit.
    Before my sweetheart's door we will have a fit,   155
    That if my love come forth, that I may with her talk,
    I doubt not but this gear shall on my side walk.
    But lo, how well Merrygreek is returned since!

           [*Enter* MERRYGREEK *and the musicians*]

MERRYGREEK
    There hath grown no grass on my heel since I went
        hence!
    Lo, here have I brought that shall make you pastance.   160

ROISTER DOISTER
    Come, sirs, let us sing to win my dear love Custance.

               They sing
    [I mun be married a Sunday,
    I mun be married a Sunday;
    Whosoever shall come that way,
    I mun be married a Sunday.   165

    Roister Doister is my name,
    Roister Doister is my name;
    A lusty brute, I am the same,
    I mun be married a Sunday.

    Christian Custance have I found,   170
    Christian Custance have I found,
    A widow worth a thousand pound;
    I mun be married a Sunday.

    Custance is as sweet as honey,
    Custance is as sweet as honey,   175
    I her lamb and she my cony;
    I mun be married a Sunday.

---

155 *fit* piece of music
157 *this . . . walk* this affair will go my way
162–82 (Song) eds. (not in Q: added from appended text)
162 *mun* must

---

159 *There . . . heel* Proverbial (Tilley G421). I haven't been standing still. See IV.v, 10.
162–82 The song was obviously composed for the play. There is no indication of the
    tune to which it was set. It is headed 'The Fourth Song' and is placed between 'The
    Second Song' ('Whoso to marry') and 'The Psalmody' on sigs. J2ᵛ–J3 in Q.

When we shall make our wedding feast,
When we shall make our wedding feast,
There shall be cheer for man and beast;   180
I mun be married a Sunday.

I mun be married a Sunday, etc.]

MERRYGREEK
Lo, where she cometh! Some countenance to her make.
And ye shall hear me be plain with her for your sake.

Act III, Scene iv

[*Enter* DAME CUSTANCE]

DAME CUSTANCE
What gauding and fooling is this afore my door?

MERRYGREEK
May not folks be honest, pray you, though they be
poor?

DAME CUSTANCE
As that thing may be true, so rich folks may be fools.

ROISTER DOISTER
Her talk is as fine as she had learned in schools!

MERRYGREEK
Look partly toward her, and draw a little near.   5

DAME CUSTANCE
Get ye home, idle folks!

MERRYGREEK   Why may not we be here?
Nay, and ye will ha' us, ha' us; otherwise, I tell you
plain,
And ye will not ha' us then give us our gear again.

DAME CUSTANCE
Indeed, I have of yours much gay things. God save all.

183 *countenance* sign
  1 *gauding* merry-making
  7 *ha' us, ha' us* ed. (haze, haze Q) have us ...

---

  2 *May ... poor* Proverbial (*ODEP*, p. 638): 'Poor but honest'.
  3 *rich ... fools* Sounds proverbial or aphoristic. Compare 'Fools live poor to die rich'
     (Tilley F539) and 'Riches serve a wise man but command a fool' (R113).

ROISTER DOISTER
　Speak gently unto her, and let her take all.   10

MERRYGREEK
　Ye are too tenderhearted! Shall she make us daws?—
　Nay, dame, I will be plain with you in my friend's
　　cause.

ROISTER DOISTER
　Let all this pass, sweetheart, and accept my service.

DAME CUSTANCE
　I will not be served with a fool in no wise;
　When I choose an husband, I hope to take a man.   15

MERRYGREEK
　And where will ye find one which can do that he can?
　Now this man toward you being so kind,
　You not to make him an answer somewhat to his
　　mind—

DAME CUSTANCE
　I sent him a full answer by you, did I not?

MERRYGREEK
　And I reported it.

DAME CUSTANCE   Nay, I must speak it again.   20

ROISTER DOISTER
　No, no, he told it all!

MERRYGREEK   Was I not meetly plain?

ROISTER DOISTER
　Yes.

MERRYGREEK   But I would not tell all, for, faith, if I had,
　With you, Dame Custance, ere this hour it had been
　　bad,
　And not without cause; for this goodly personage
　Meant no less than to join with you in marriage.   25

DAME CUSTANCE
　Let him waste no more labour nor suit about me.

MERRYGREEK
　Ye know not where your preferment lieth, I see,
　He sending you such a token, ring and letter.

11 *daws* jackdaws, fools
16 *that* that which
21 *meetly* sufficiently

DAME CUSTANCE
  Marry, here it is; ye never saw a better.

MERRYGREEK
  Let us see your letter.

DAME CUSTANCE   Hold, read it if ye can;   30
  And see what letter it is to win a woman!

MERRYGREEK [*Reads*]
  'To mine own dear cony-bird, sweetheart and pigsnye,
  Good Mistress Custance, present these by and by'—
  Of this superscription do ye blame the style?

DAME CUSTANCE
  With the rest as good stuff as ye read a great while.   35

MERRYGREEK [*Reads*]
  'Sweet mistress, whereas I love you nothing at all,
  Regarding your substance and richesse chief of all,
  For your personage, beauty, demeanour and wit,
  I commend me unto you never a whit.
  Sorry to hear report of your good welfare,   40
  For (as I hear say) such your conditions are,
  That ye be worthy favour of no living man,
  To be abhorred of every honest man;
  To be taken for a woman inclined to vice,
  Nothing at all to virtue giving her due price.   45
  Wherefore concerning marriage, ye are thought
  Such a fine paragon, as ne'er honest man bought.
  And now by these presents I do you advertise
  That I am minded to marry you in no wise.
  For your goods and substance, I could be content   50
  To take you as ye are. If ye mind to be my wife,
  Ye shall be assured for the time of my life,
  I will keep ye right well from good raiment and fare;
  Ye shall not be kept but in sorrow and care.
  Ye shall in no wise live at your own liberty;   55

30 *Hold* here, take it
37 *richesse* wealth
48 *advertise* notify

36–70 The essence of the letter episode is Merrygreek's deliberate misreading of it by
  misplacing the punctuation. Thomas Wilson, in his *Rule of Reason* (third edn.,
  1553), cites it as an example of ambiguity (see Introduction, p. xxxiii). Q's
  punctuation has been altered slightly, to make the false 'sense' clear.

Do and say what ye lust, ye shall never please me,
But when ye are merry, I will be all sad,
When ye are sorry, I will be very glad,
When ye seek your heart's ease, I will be unkind;
At no time in me shall ye much gentleness find,   60
But all things contrary to your will and mind
Shall be done; otherwise I will not be behind
To speak. And as for all them that would do you wrong,
I will so help and maintain, ye shall not live long.
Nor any foolish dolt shall cumber you but I;   65
I, whoe'er say nay, will stick by you till I die.
Thus, good Mistress Custance, the Lord you save and
     keep
From me, Roister Doister, whether I wake or sleep.
Who favoureth you no less (ye may be bold)
Than this letter purporteth, which ye have unfold.'   70

DAME CUSTANCE
How by this letter of love? Is it not fine?

ROISTER DOISTER
By the arms of Calais, it is none of mine!

MERRYGREEK
Fie, you are foul to blame! This is your own hand!

DAME CUSTANCE
Might not a woman be proud of such an husband?

MERRYGREEK
Ah, that ye would in a letter show such despite!   75

ROISTER DOISTER
Oh, I would I had him here, the which did it endite!

MERRYGREEK
Why, ye made it yourself, ye told me, by this light!

ROISTER DOISTER
Yea, I meant I wrote it mine own self yesternight.

62 *behind* slow, hesitant
71 *How by* what do you think of
76 *endite* compose
78 *wrote it* copied it out

72 *By... Calais* Perhaps a reference to the very large arsenal at Calais, the English
   toehold upon the Continent until the town was finally retaken by the French in
   1558, after 220 years in English hands. The oath occurs again at IV.vii, 48.

DAME CUSTANCE
    Iwis, sir, I would not have sent you such a mock!

ROISTER DOISTER
    Ye may so take it, but I meant it not so, by Cock!   80

MERRYGREEK
    Who can blame this woman to fume and fret and rage?
    Tut, tut, yourself now have marred your own marriage.
    Well, yet, Mistress Custance, if ye can this remit,
    This gentleman otherwise may your live requit.

DAME CUSTANCE
    No! God be with you both, and seek no more to me!   85
                                                        Exit

ROISTER DOISTER
    Whough! She is gone forever! I shall her no more see!

MERRYGREEK
    What, weep? Fie, for shame! And blubber? For
            manhood's sake,
    Never let your foe so much pleasure of you take!
    Rather play the man's part, and do love refrain.
    If she despise you, e'en despise ye her again!   90

ROISTER DOISTER
    By Gosse and for thy sake, I defy her indeed!

MERRYGREEK
    Yea, and perchance that way ye shall much sooner
            speed.
    For one mad property these women have, in fay:
    When ye will, they will not; will not ye, then will they.
    Ah, foolish woman, ah, most unlucky Custance,   95
    Ah, unfortunate woman, ah, peevish Custance,
    Art thou to thine harms so obstinately bent,
    That you canst not see where lieth thine high
            preferment?

83 *remit* pardon
84 *requit* requite, repay
91 *Gosse* God
93 *in fay* in faith

92–100 This speech is typical of Merrygreek's style when he is with Roister Doister.
    He uses formal rhetorical figures and constructions (e.g., l. 94, and the apostrophe
    to Custance, ll. 95—6), then slips into baby-talk, mocking Roister Doister's foolish
    passion.

Canst thou not lub dis man, which could lub dee so
    well?
Art thou so much thine own foe?

ROISTER DOISTER   Thou dost the truth
    tell.   100

MERRYGREEK
    Well, I lament.

ROISTER DOISTER So do I.

MERRYGREEK   Wherefore?

ROISTER DOISTER   For this thing:
    Because she is gone.

MERRYGREEK   I mourn for another thing.

ROISTER DOISTER
    What is it, Merrygreek, wherefore thou dost grief take?

MERRYGREEK
    That I am not a woman myself for your sake;
    I would have you myself—and a straw for yon Gill!—   105
    And mock much of you, though it were against my
        will.
    I would not, I warrant you, fall in such a rage
    As so to refuse such a goodly personage.

ROISTER DOISTER
    In faith, I heartily thank thee, Merrygreek.

MERRYGREEK
    And I were a woman—

ROISTER DOISTER   Thou wouldest to me seek.   110

MERRYGREEK
    For though I say it, a goodly person ye be.

ROISTER DOISTER
    No, no.

MERRYGREEK   Yes, a goodly man as e'er I did see.

ROISTER DOISTER
    No, I am a poor, homely man, as God made me.

---

99 *lub dis . . . lub dee* (baby talk) love this . . . love thee
105 *Gill* lass, wench
106 *mock* eds. (mocke Q) make (Merrygreek's pun)
107 *rage* fit of madness

MERRYGREEK
   By the faith that I owe to God, sir, but ye be!
   Would I might for your sake spend a thousand pound
      land.   115

ROISTER DOISTER
   I daresay thou wouldest have me to thy husband.

MERRYGREEK
   Yea, and I were the fairest lady in the shire,
   And knew you as I know you and see you now here—
   Well, I say no more.

ROISTER DOISTER   Gramercies, with all my heart.

MERRYGREEK
   But since that cannot be, will ye play a wise part?   120

ROISTER DOISTER
   How should I?

MERRYGREEK   Refrain from Custance a while now,
   And I warrant her soon right glad to seek to you.
   Ye shall see her anon come on her knees creeping,
   And pray you to be good to her, salt tears weeping.

ROISTER DOISTER
   But what and she come not?

MERRYGREEK   In faith, then, farewell she!   125
   Or else, if ye be wroth, ye may avenged be.

ROISTER DOISTER
   By Cock's precious potstick, and e'en so I shall!
   I will utterly destroy her and house and all.
   But I would be avenged, in the mean space,
   On that vile scribbler that did my wooing disgrace.   130

MERRYGREEK
   'Scribbler', ko you? Indeed, he is worthy no less!
   I will call him to you and ye bid me, doubtless.

ROISTER DOISTER
   Yes, for although he had as many lives

---

115 *might ... land* had an income of a thousand pounds from my lands (as a dowry)
126 *wroth* angry
129 *mean space* meantime

---

127 *By ... potstick* The same unusual oath occurs in the interlude *Jack Juggler* (c. 1555), which has been attributed to Udall. A potstick is simply an utensil for stirring anything cooking in a pot.

As a thousand widows and a thousand wives,
As a thousand lions and a thousand rats,   135
A thousand wolves and a thousand cats,
A thousand bulls and a thousand calves,
And a thousand legions divided in halves,
He shall never 'scape death on my sword's point,
Though I should be torn therefore joint by joint!   140

MERRYGREEK
Nay, if ye will kill him, I will not fet him;
I will not in so much extremity set him.
He may yet amend, sir, and be an honest man;
Therefore pardon him, good soul, as much as ye can.

ROISTER DOISTER
Well, for thy sake, this once with his life he shall pass.   145
But I will hew him all to pieces, by the mass!

MERRYGREEK
Nay, faith, ye shall promise that he shall no harm have,
Else I will not fet him.

ROISTER DOISTER   I shall, so God me save!
But I may chide him a-good?

MERRYGREEK   Yea, that do, hardily.

ROISTER DOISTER
Go then.

MERRYGREEK   I return, and bring him to you by and by.   150
                                                    Exit

Act III, Scene v

ROISTER DOISTER
What is a gentleman but his word and his promise?
I must now save this villain's life in any wise;
And yet at him already my hands do tickle,
I shall uneth hold them, they will be so fickle.
But lo and Merrygreek have not brought him since.   5

     [*Enter* MERRYGREEK *and the* SCRIVENER, *conversing*]

141 *fet* fetch
149 *hardily* ed. (hardely Q) by all means
  2 *in . . . wise* whatever happens
  4 *uneth* hardly
    fickle uncontrollable
  5 *lo and* see if
    since already

MERRYGREEK
  Nay, I would I had of my purse paid forty pence.

SCRIVENER
  So would I too; but it needed not that stound.

MERRYGREEK
  But the gent'man had rather spent five thousand
        pound,
  For it disgraced him at least five times so much.

SCRIVENER
  He disgraced himself, his loutishness is such!   10

ROISTER DOISTER [*Aside*]
  How long they stand prating!—Why comst thou not
        away?

MERRYGREEK [*To* SCRIVENER]
  Come now to himself, and hark what he will say.

SCRIVENER
  I am not afraid in his presence to appear.

ROISTER DOISTER
  Art thou come, fellow?

SCRIVENER   How think you? Am I not here?

ROISTER DOISTER
  What hindrance hast thou done me, and what villainy?   15

SCRIVENER
  It hath come of thyself, if thou hast had any.

ROISTER DOISTER
  All the stock thou comest of, later or rather,
  From thy first father's grandfather's father's father,
  Nor all that shall come of thee to the world's end,
  Though to threescore generations they descend,   20
  Can be able to make me a just recompense
  For this trespass of thine and this one offence!

SCRIVENER
  Wherein?

ROISTER DOISTER   Did not you make me a letter, brother?

SCRIVENER
  Pay the like hire, I will make you such another!

  7 *that stound* at that time
  17 *rather* earlier

ROISTER DOISTER
Nay, see and these whoreson Pharisees and scribes   25
Do not get their living by polling and bribes!
If it were not for shame—[*Threatens to strike* SCRIVENER]

SCRIVENER   Nay, hold thy hands still!

[*Strikes* ROISTER DOISTER]

MERRYGREEK [*To* ROISTER DOISTER]
Why, did ye not promise that ye would not him spill?

SCRIVENER
Let him not spare me.

ROISTER DOISTER   Why, wilt thou strike me again?

SCRIVENER
Ye shall have as good as ye bring of me, that is plain.   30

MERRYGREEK
I cannot blame him, sir, though your blows would him
        grieve,
For he knoweth present death to ensue of all ye give.

ROISTER DOISTER [*To* SCRIVENER]
Well, this man for once hath purchased thy pardon.

SCRIVENER
And what say ye to me? Or else I will be gone.

ROISTER DOISTER
I say the letter thou madest me was not good.   35

SCRIVENER
Then did ye wrong copy it, of likelihood.

ROISTER DOISTER
Yes, out of thy copy word for word I it wrote.

26 *polling* extortion
28 *spill* kill
30 *have . . . me* get from me as good as you give
32 *present* instant

25 *Pharisees . . . scribes* In the New Testament, particularly the Gospels, the Pharisees,
an ancient Hebrew sect, who practised strict observance of Jewish law and claimed
spiritual superiority thereby, and the scribes, the professional interpreters of the
law, are frequently referred to in pejorative terms. Specifically, they represent the
Jewish establishment, hostile to Jesus and intent on trapping him in doctrinal error;
for example, Matthew 7:28–9, Luke 6:7. Generally the terms connote hypocrisy
and intolerance.

SCRIVENER
Then was it as ye prayed to have it, I wot,
But in reading and pointing there was made some fault.

ROISTER DOISTER
I wot not, but it made all my matter to halt.   40

SCRIVENER
How say you, is this mine original or no?

ROISTER DOISTER
The selfsame that I wrote out of, so mote I go!

SCRIVENER
Look you on your own fist, and I will look on this,
And let this man be judge whether I read amiss:
    [*Reads*] 'To mine own dear cony-bird, sweetheart, and
        pigsnye,   45
Good Mistress Custance, present these by and by'—
How now? Doth not this superscription agree?

ROISTER DOISTER
Read that is within and there ye shall the fault see.

SCRIVENER [*Reads*]
    'Sweet mistress, whereas I love you, nothing at all
Regarding your richesse and substance, chief of all   50
For your personage, beauty, demeanour and wit,
I commend me unto you; never a whit
Sorry to hear report of your good welfare,
For (as I hear say) such your conditions are
That ye be worthy favour. Of no living man   55
To be abhorred, of every honest man
To be taken for a woman inclined to vice
Nothing at all; to virtue giving her due price.
Wherefore, concerning marriage, ye are thought
Such a fine paragon as ne'er honest man bought.   60
And now by these presents, I do you advertise
That I am minded to marry you; in no wise
For your goods and substance—I can be content
To take you as you are. If ye will be my wife,
Ye shall be assured for the time of my life,   65
I will keep you right well; from good raiment and fare

38 *prayed* asked
39 *But* unless
   pointing punctuating
42 *so ... go* (oath) so may I thrive
43 *fist* hand (writing)
45 *cony-bird* ed. (coney birde, Q; cony, bird eds.)

Ye shall not be kept, but in sorrow and care
Ye shall in no wise live. At your own liberty,
Do and say what ye lust: ye shall never please me
But when ye are merry. I will be all sad 70
When ye are sorry; I will be very glad
When ye seek your heart's ease. I will be unkind
At no time; in me shall ye much gentleness find.
But all things contrary to your will and mind
Shall be done otherwise; I will not be behind 75
To speak. And as for all them that would do you wrong
(I will so help and maintain ye), shall not live long.
Nor any foolish dolt shall cumber you; but I,
I, whoe'er say nay, will stick by you till I die.
Thus, good Mistress Custance, the Lord you save and
    keep. 80
From me, Roister Doister, whether I wake or sleep,
Who favoureth you no less (ye may be bold)
Than this letter purporteth, which ye have unfold.'
Now, sir, what default can ye find in this letter?

ROISTER DOISTER
Of truth, in my mind, there cannot be a better. 85

SCRIVENER
Then was the fault in reading and not in writing;
No, nor, I daresay, in the form of enditing.
But who read this letter, that it sounded so nought?

MERRYGREEK
I read it, indeed.

SCRIVENER   Ye read it not as ye ought.

ROISTER DOISTER [*To* MERRYGREEK]
Why, thou wretched villain, was all this same fault in
    thee? 90

[*Threatens to strike* MERRYGREEK]

MERRYGREEK
I knock your costard if ye offer to strike me!

[*Hits* ROISTER DOISTER]

ROISTER DOISTER
Strikest thou indeed? And I offer but in jest?

76 *them* ed. (they Q)
77 *shall* they shall
88 *nought* worthless
91 *costard* head

MERRYGREEK
   Yea, and rap you again except ye can sit in rest!
   And I will no longer tarry here, me believe!

ROISTER DOISTER
   What, wilt thou be angry, and I do thee forgive?—   95
   Fare thou well, scribbler. I cry thee mercy indeed!

SCRIVENER
   Fare ye well, bibbler, and worthily may ye speed. [*Exit*]

ROISTER DOISTER
   If it were another but thou, it were a knave.

MERRYGREEK
   Ye are another yourself, sir, the Lord us both save,
   Albeit in this matter I must your pardon crave.   100
   Alas, would ye wish in me the wit that ye have?
   But as for my fault, I can quickly amend:
   I will show Custance it was I that did offend.

ROISTER DOISTER
   By so doing, her anger may be reformed.

MERRYGREEK
   But if by no entreaty she will be turned,   105
   Then set light by her and be as testy as she,
   And do your force upon her with extremity.

ROISTER DOISTER
   Come on, therefore, let us go home, in sadness.

MERRYGREEK
   That, if force shall need, all may be in a readiness.
   And as for this letter, hardily let all go;   110
   We will know whe'er she refuse you for that or no.
                      Exeunt

---

97 *bibbler* drinker, drunkard
106 *set ... her* treat her contemptuously
108 *in sadness* in earnest, indeed
109 *if ... need* if it becomes necessary to resort to force
111 *whe'er* ed. (where Q) whether

Act IV, Scene i

[*Enter* SIM SURESBY]

SURESBY

Is there any man but I, Sim Suresby, alone,
That would have taken such an enterprise him upon,
In such an outrageous tempest as this was,
Such a dangerous gulf of the sea to pass?
I think, verily, Neptune's mighty godship   5
Was angry with some that was in our ship,
And but for the honesty which in me he found,
I think for the others' sake we had been drowned.
But fie on that servant which for his master's wealth
Will stick for to hazard both his life and his health!   10
My master, Gawin Goodluck, after me a day,
Because of the weather, thought best his ship to stay;
And now that I have the rough surges so well past,
God grant I may find all things safe here at last.
Then will I think all my travail well spent.   15
Now the first point wherefore my master hath me sent
Is to salute Dame Christian Custance, his wife
Espoused, whom he tendereth no less than his life.
I must see how it is with her, well or wrong,
And whether for him she doth not now think long.   20
Then to other friends I have a message or tway,
And then so to return and meet him on the way.
Now will I go knock that I may dispatch with speed—
But lo, forth cometh herself, happily indeed.

10 *stick* hesitate
15 *travail* labour (but also here, 'travel')
18 *tendereth* values
20 *now . . . long* grow impatient

5–8 Perhaps an allusion to the Old Testament story of Jonah, in which the prophet, attempting to flee from God because he does not want to prophesy to the Ninevites, boards a ship. When a tempest threatens the lives of those aboard, they believe that one among them has offended his god, bringing down this punishment upon all in the ship. They cast lots, Jonah is the loser, and he is thrown overboard, whereupon the storm abates (Jonah 1:1–15).

Act IV, Scene ii

[*Enter* CHRISTIAN CUSTANCE]

DAME CUSTANCE
I come to see if any more stirring be here.
But what stranger is this which doth to me appear?

SURESBY
I will speak to her.—Dame, the Lord you save and see!

DAME CUSTANCE
What, friend Sim Suresby? Forsooth, right welcome ye be!
How doth mine own Gawin Goodluck? I pray thee, tell.   5

SURESBY
When he knoweth of your health, he will be perfect well.

DAME CUSTANCE
If he have perfect health, I am as I would be.

SURESBY
Such news will please him well; this is as it should be.

DAME CUSTANCE
I think now long for him.

SURESBY   And he as long for you.

DAME CUSTANCE
When will he be at home?

                                His heart is here e'en now;   10

SURESBY
His body cometh after.

DAME CUSTANCE   I would see that fain.

SURESBY
As fast as wind and sail can carry it amain.

[*Enter* ROISTER DOISTER *and* MERRYGREEK]

---

14 *fain* willingly
15 *amain* at full speed

---

15 s.d. *Enter* . . . MERRYGREEK Roister Doister and Merrygreek presumably appear just
before Suresby remarks on their approach. As usual, Q simply lists their names with
the other characters' at the beginning of scene iii.

But what two men are yond coming hitherward?

DAME CUSTANCE
Now I shrew their best Christmas cheeks both
    togetherward!

Act IV, Scene iii

DAME CUSTANCE [*Aside*]
What mean these lewd fellows thus to trouble me still?
Sim Suresby here perchance shall thereof deem some ill,
And shall suspect in me some point of naughtiness,
And they come hitherward.

SURESBY   What is their business?

DAME CUSTANCE
I have nought to them nor they to me, in sadness.   5

SURESBY
Let us harken them.—[*Aside*] Somewhat there is,
    I fear it.

ROISTER DOISTER [*To* MERRYGREEK]
I will speak out aloud, best that she may hear it.

MERRYGREEK
Nay, alas, ye may so fear her out of her wit.

ROISTER DOISTER
By the cross of my sword, I will hurt her no whit.

---

1 *lewd* good-for-nothing, naughty
3 *naughtiness* wickedness (i.e., loose morals)
4 *And* if
7 *aloud, best* ed. (aloud best, Q)

---

14 *Now . . . togetherward* This line and the reference to Christmas Day at I.iv, 73 have
  been cited as evidence that the play was performed at court at Christmas, 1553 (but
  see Introduction, p. xxxiii). Cursing someone's cheeks or beard and teeth was a
  common expression of defiance. Dame Custance uses it again at V.iv, 28, without
  'Christmas'. Compare 'maugre (Fr. *malgré*, 'in spite of') thy cheeks' as in *Piers
  Plowman*, B.vi. 158, and 'maugre thy head', frequent in Malory's *Le Morte Darthur*.
9 *By . . . sword* Roister Doister swears upon his sword, the guard of which forms a
  cross with the hilt and blade. Malory's Sir Percival actually had a crucifix in the hilt
  of his sword (*The Works of Sir Thomas Malory*, ed. Eugène Vinaver, 2nd edn.
  (1967), II, 918). Compare III.iii, 106 and IV.vii, 11.

MERRYGREEK
  Will ye do no harm indeed? Shall I trust your word?   10

ROISTER DOISTER
  By Roister Doister's faith, I will speak but in bourd.—
  Sirs, see that my harness, my target and my shield
  Be made as bright now as when I was last in field,
  As white as I should to war again tomorrow;
  For sick shall I be but I work some folk sorrow!   15
  Therefore see that all shine as bright as Saint George,
  Or as doth a key newly come from the smith's forge.
  I would have my sword and harness to shine so bright
  That I might therewith dim mine enemies' sight;
  I would have it cast beams as fast, I tell you plain,   20
  As doth the glittering grass after a shower of rain.
  And see that, in case I should need to come to arming,
  All things may be ready at a minute's warning!
  For such chance may chance in an hour; do ye hear?

MERRYGREEK
  As perchance shall not chance again in seven year!   25

ROISTER DOISTER
  Now draw we near to her, and hear what shall be said.

MERRYGREEK
  But I would not have you make her too much afraid.

ROISTER DOISTER
  Well found, sweet wife, I trust, for all this your sour
      look!

---

11 *bourd* jest
11–12 *bourd . . . Sirs* (two lines omitted) ed.
12 *harness* armour
   target a small, light shield
14 *as I should* as if I should go

11–12 Between these two lines in Q, occur two others which appear to be alternatives
   to ll. 6–7. Probably they should have been cancelled: SURESBY: Let us harken
   them; somewhat there is, I fear it./ROISTER DOISTER: I will speak out aloud, I care
   not who hear it.
12 *Sirs* Roister Doister must here be calling, or pretending to call, to his retainers who
   are offstage, presumably in his house. That only he and Merrygreek enter at the
   beginning of the scene is clear from IV.ii, 13.
16 *Saint George* A third or fourth century soldier, martyred for his Christian faith
   under the emperor Diocletian. He was patron saint of soldiers long before he was
   adopted as England's national saint subsequent to Edward III's founding of the
   Order of the Garter under his patronage.

DAME CUSTANCE
Wife! Why call ye me wife?

SURESBY [*Aside*]   Wife! This gear goeth
acrook!

MERRYGREEK
Nay, Mistress Custance, I warrant you, our letter   30
Is not as we read e'en now, but much better,
And where ye half stomached this gentleman afore,
For this same letter, ye will love him now therefore;
Nor it is not this letter, though ye were a queen,
That should break marriage between you twain, I ween.   35

DAME CUSTANCE
I did not refuse him for the letter's sake!

ROISTER DOISTER
Then ye are content me for your husband to take?

DAME CUSTANCE
You for my husband to take? Nothing less, truly!

ROISTER DOISTER
Yea, say so, sweet spouse, afore strangers hardily.

MERRYGREEK
And though I have here his letter of love with me,   40
Yet his ring and tokens he sent keep safe with ye.

DAME CUSTANCE
A mischief take his tokens, and him and thee too!
But what prate I with fools? Have I nought else to do?
Come in with me, Sim Suresby, to take some repast.

SURESBY
I must, ere I drink, by your leave, go in all haste   45
To a place or two with earnest letters of his.

DAME CUSTANCE
Then come drink here with me.

SURESBY   I thank you.

DAME CUSTANCE   Do not miss.

29 *gear* business, matter
    acrook awry
32 *half stomached* were partly offended with
43 *what* why

You shall have a token to your master with you.

SURESBY
No tokens this time, gramercies! God be with you. *Exit*

DAME CUSTANCE [*Aside*]
Surely this fellow misdeemeth some ill in me,   50
Which thing, but God help, will go near to spill me.

ROISTER DOISTER
Yea, farewell, fellow, and tell thy master Goodluck
That he cometh too late of this blossom to pluck!
Let him keep him there still, or at leastwise make no
    haste,
As for his labour hither he shall spend in waste.   55
His betters be in place now!

MERRYGREEK [*Aside*]   As long as it will hold.

DAME CUSTANCE
I will be even with thee, thou beast, thou mayst be
    bold!

ROISTER DOISTER
Will ye have us then?

DAME CUSTANCE   I will never have thee!

ROISTER DOISTER
Then will I have you?

DAME CUSTANCE   No, the devil shall have thee!
I have gotten this hour more shame and harm by thee   60
Than all thy life days thou canst do me honesty!

MERRYGREEK
Why, now may ye see what it cometh to in the end,
To make a deadly foe of your most loving friend!
And iwis, this letter, if ye would hear it now—

DAME CUSTANCE
I will hear none of it!

MERRYGREEK   In faith, would ravish you!   65

DAME CUSTANCE
He hath stained my name forever, this is clear.

---

50 *misdeemeth* suspects
51 *spill* undo, ruin
55 *As for* since
57 *thou ... bold* you may be sure

ROISTER DOISTER
  I can make all as well in an hour—

MERRYGREEK   As ten year.
  How say ye, will ye have him?

DAME CUSTANCE   No.

MERRYGREEK   Will ye take him?

DAME CUSTANCE
  I defy him!

MERRYGREEK At my word?

DAME CUSTANCE   A shame take him!
  Waste no more wind, for it will never be.   70

MERRYGREEK
  This one fault with twain shall be mended, ye shall see.
  Gentle Mistress Custance now, good Mistress Custance,
  Honey Mistress Custance now, sweet Mistress Custance,
  Golden Mistress Custance now, white Mistress
    Custance,
  Silken Mistress Custance now, fair Mistress Custance—   75

DAME CUSTANCE
  Faith, rather than to marry with such a doltish lout,
  I would match myself with a beggar, out of doubt!

MERRYGREEK
  Then I can say no more. [*To* ROISTER DOISTER] To speed
    we are not like,
  Except ye rap out a rag of your rhetoric.

DAME CUSTANCE
  Speak not of winning me, for it shall never be so!   80

ROISTER DOISTER
  Yes, dame, I will have you whether ye will or no!
  I command you to love me! Wherefore should ye not?
  Is not my love to you chafing and burning hot?

MERRYGREEK
  To her! That is well said!

ROISTER DOISTER   Shall I so break my brain
  To dote upon you, and ye not love us again?   85

MERRYGREEK
  Well said yet!

74 *white* fair; pure; dear
77 *out of doubt* without question
79 *Except . . . rhetoric* Unless you can produce some eloquent, persuasive speech

DAME CUSTANCE   Go to, you goose!

ROISTER DOISTER   I say, Kit Custance,
In case ye will not ha' us—well, better yes, perchance!

DAME CUSTANCE
Avaunt, lozel, pick thee hence!

MERRYGREEK   Well, sir, ye perceive
For all your kind offer, she will not you receive.

ROISTER DOISTER
Then a straw for her! And a straw for her again!   90
She shall not be my wife, would she never so fain!
No, and though she would be at ten thousand pound
    cost!

MERRYGREEK
Lo, dame, ye may see what an husband ye have lost!

DAME CUSTANCE
Yea, no force; a jewel much better lost than found!

MERRYGREEK
Ah, ye will not believe how this doth my heart wound!   95
How should a marriage between you be toward,
If both parties draw back and become so froward?

ROISTER DOISTER
Nay, dame, I will fire thee out of thy house,
And destroy thee and all thine, and that by and by!

MERRYGREEK
Nay, for the passion of God, sir, do not so!   100

ROISTER DOISTER
Yes, except she will say 'yea' to that she said 'no'!

87 *ha' us* ed. (haze Q)
88 *Avaunt* Be gone! Away!
   lozel scoundrel
   pick take
92 *and . . . cost* even though she would be willing to pay ten thousand pounds to marry
   me
94 *no force* no matter
96 *toward* about to take place
97 *froward* uncooperative

98–9 These lines do not rhyme, one of only a handful of such instances in the play. As
   neither line is obviously corrupt, it is idle to conjecture.

DAME CUSTANCE

And what, be there no officers, trow we, in town,
To check idle loiterers bragging up and down?
Where be they by whom vagabonds shall be repressed,
That poor silly widows might live in peace and rest?   105
Shall I never rid thee out of my company?
I will call for help. What ho! Come forth, Truepenny!

[*Enter* TRUEPENNY]

TRUEPENNY

Anon! What is your will, mistress? Did ye call me?

DAME CUSTANCE

Yea. Go run apace, and as fast as may be,
Pray Tristram Trusty, my most assured friend,   110
To be here by and by, that he may me defend.

TRUEPENNY

That message so quickly shall be done, by God's grace,
That at my return ye shall say I went apace!   *Exit*

DAME CUSTANCE

Then shall we see, I trow, whether ye shall do me harm!

ROISTER DOISTER

Yes, in faith, Kit, I shall thee and thine so charm,   115
That all women incarnate by thee may beware!

DAME CUSTANCE

Nay, as for charming me, come hither if thou dare!
I shall clout thee till thou stink, both thee and thy
          train,

105 *silly* helpless
108 *Anon!* Coming!
109 *apace* swiftly
111 *by and by* at once

103–4 *idle loiterers ... vagabonds* Dame Custance's words echo the language of a
    succession of Tudor statutes intended to suppress vagrancy, such as that of 1547:
    'Whosoever ... shall be lurking in any house or houses, or loitering, or idle
    wandering by the highway's side, or in streets, cities, towns or villages ... shall be
    taken for a vagabond ... and it shall be lawful ... to bring or cause to be brought
    the said person to two of the next justices of the peace ... '. A vagabond or vagrant,
    was any person who had no means of support and remained unemployed for three
    days or more. A first conviction carried the sentence of branding with a 'V' and two
    years' enslavement. This Act was repealed in 1549 (it was clearly not being
    enforced) and a succession of Elizabethan Poor Laws were somewhat less barbaric.
    Vagrancy continued to be a major concern of Tudor governments. See John Pound,
    Poverty and Vagrancy in Tudor England (1971).

And coil thee mine own hands and send thee home
    again!

ROISTER DOISTER
    Yea, sayst thou me that, dame? Dost thou me threaten?   120
    [*To* MERRYGREEK] Go we, I will see whether I shall be
    beaten!

MERRYGREEK
    Nay, for the pash of God! Let me now treat peace,
    For bloodshed will there be in case this strife increase.
    Ah, good Dame Custance, take better way with you!

DAME CUSTANCE
    Let him do his worst!

MERRYGREEK   Yield in time!

ROISTER DOISTER [*To* MERRYGREEK]   Come hence, thou!   125

            Exeunt ROISTER DOISTER *and* MERRYGREEK

Act IV, Scene iv

DAME CUSTANCE
    So, sirrah!—If I did not with him take this way,
    I should not be rid of him, I think, till doomsday.
    I will call forth my folks, that without any mocks,
    If he come again, we may give him raps and knocks.
    Madge Mumblecrust, come forth, and Tibet Talkapace!   5
    Yea, and come forth too, Mistress Annot Alyface!

    [*Enter* ANNOT ALYFACE, TIBET TALKAPACE *and* MADGE
                 MUMBLECRUST]

ANNOT
    I come.

TIBET   And I am here.

MADGE   And I am here too, at length.

DAME CUSTANCE
    Like warriors, if need be, ye must show your strength.
    The man that this day hath thus beguiled you

119 *coil thee* beat thee with
122 *pash* passion
    treat negotiate
124 *take . . . you* behave more reasonably

Is Ralph Roister Doister, whom ye know well enow,   10
The most lout and dastard that ever on ground trod.

TIBET
I see all folk mock him when he goeth abroad—

DAME CUSTANCE
What, pretty maid, will ye talk when I speak?

TIBET
No, forsooth, good mistress.

DAME CUSTANCE   Will ye my tale break?
He threateneth to come hither with all his force to
    fight.   15
I charge you, if he come, on him with all your might!

MADGE
I with my distaff will reach him one rap!

TIBET
And I with my new broom will sweep him one swap,
And then with our great club I will reach him one rap!

ANNOT
And I with our skimmer will fling him one flap!   20

TIBET
Then Truepenny's firefork will him shrewdly fray,
And you with the spit may drive him quite away!

DAME CUSTANCE
Go make all ready, that it may be e'en so.

TIBET
For my part, I shrew them that last about it go!

                    Exeunt [TIBET TALKAPACE, ANNOT
                ALYFACE *and* MADGE MUMBLECRUST]

---

11 *dastard* base coward
21 *shrewdly* sharply
    fray attack

---

20 *skimmer* A shallow, perforated spoon-like utensil, used for skimming liquids.
21 *firefork* A fork-shaped instrument used, like a poker, to stir up the fire.

Act IV, Scene v

DAME CUSTANCE
   Truepenny did promise me to run a great pace,
   My friend Tristram Trusty to fet into this place.
   Indeed, he dwelleth hence a good start, I confess;
   But yet a quick messenger might twice since, as I guess,
   Have gone and come again. Ah, yond I spy him now.   5

    [*Enter* TRUEPENNY *and* TRISTRAM TRUSTY]

TRUEPENNY
   Ye are a slow goer, sir, I make God avow!
   My Mistress Custance will in me put all the blame.
   Your legs be longer than mine—come apace, for shame!

DAME CUSTANCE
   I can thee thank, Truepenny; thou hast done right well.

TRUEPENNY
   Mistress, since I went no grass hath grown on my heel,   10
   But Master Tristram Trusty here maketh no speed.

DAME CUSTANCE
   That he came at all, I thank him in very deed,
   For now have I need of the help of some wise man.

TRUSTY
   Then may I be gone again, for none such I am.

TRUEPENNY
   Ye may be by your going; for no alderman   15
   Can go, I daresay, a sadder pace than ye can.

DAME CUSTANCE
   Truepenny, get thee in. Thou shalt among them know
   How to use thyself like a proper man, I trow.

TRUEPENNY
   I go.   *Exit*

---

  3 *a good start* some distance
15 *by your going* to judge by the way you walk
16 *sadder* soberer, more deliberate
17 *them* (i.e., the maids)

---

10 *No . . . heel* Proverbial (Tilley G421). See III, iii, 159.
15–16 *for . . . ye can* Proverbial (Tilley A98): 'Paced like an alderman'. This occurrence
   is not noted by Tilley, and is the earliest recorded in *ODEP*.

DAME CUSTANCE   Now, Tristram Trusty, I thank you
     right much,
For at my first sending to come ye never grutch.   20

TRUSTY
   Dame Custance, God ye save, and while my life shall
     last,
For my friend Goodluck's sake, ye shall not send in
     waste.

DAME CUSTANCE
   He shall give you thanks.

TRUSTY   I will do much for his sake.

DAME CUSTANCE
   But, alack, I fear great displeasure shall he take!

TRUSTY
   Wherefore?

DAME CUSTANCE   For a foolish matter.

TRUSTY   What is your cause?   25

DAME CUSTANCE
   I am ill accumbered with a couple of daws.

TRUSTY
   Nay, weep not, woman, but tell me what your cause is.
   As concerning my friend, is anything amiss?

DAME CUSTANCE
   No, not on my part; but here was Sim Suresby—

TRUSTY
   He was with me and told me so.

DAME CUSTANCE   And he stood by   30
While Ralph Roister Doister, with help of Merrygreek,
For promise of marriage did unto me seek.

TRUSTY
   And had ye made any promise before them twain?

DAME CUSTANCE
   No! I had rather be torn in pieces and slain!
   No man hath my faith and troth but Gawin Goodluck;   35
   And that before Suresby did I say, and there stuck.

20 *grutch* complain
24 *he* ed. (be Q)
26 *accumbered* encumbered, oppressed
36 *there stuck* stuck by what I said

But of certain letters there were such words spoken—

TRUSTY
He told me that too.

DAME CUSTANCE   And of a ring and token,
That Suresby, I spied, did more than half suspect
That I my faith to Gawin Goodluck did reject.   40

TRUSTY
But there was no such matter, Dame Custance, indeed?

DAME CUSTANCE
If ever my head thought it, God send me ill speed!
Wherefore I beseech you with me to be a witness,
That in all my life I never intended thing less;
And what a brainsick fool Ralph Roister Doister is,   45
Yourself know well enough.

TRUSTY   Ye say full true, iwis.

DAME CUSTANCE
Because to be his wife I ne grant nor apply,
Hither will he come, he sweareth, by and by,
To kill both me and mine and beat down my house flat.
Therefore I pray your aid.

TRUSTY   I warrant you that.   50

DAME CUSTANCE
Have I so many years lived a sober life,
And showed myself honest, maid, widow and wife,
And now to be abused in such a vile sort?
Ye see how poor widows live all void of comfort!

TRUSTY
I warrant him do you no harm nor wrong at all.   55

DAME CUSTANCE
No, but Matthew Merrygreek doth me most appal,
That he would join himself with such a wretched lout.

TRUSTY
He doth it for a jest; I know him, out of doubt.
And here cometh Merrygreek.

DAME CUSTANCE   Then shall we hear his
          mind.

47 *ne* neither
50 *warrant* promise

Act IV, Scene vi

[Enter MERRYGREEK*]*

MERRYGREEK
Custance and Trusty both. I do you here well find.

DAME CUSTANCE
Ah, Matthew Merrygreek, ye have used me well!

MERRYGREEK
Now for altogether, ye must your answer tell:
Will ye have this man, woman, or else will ye not?
Else will he come, never boar so brim nor toast so hot.   5

TRUSTY *and* DAME CUSTANCE
But why join ye with him?

TRUSTY   For mirth?

DAME CUSTANCE   Or else in
sadness?

MERRYGREEK
The more fond of you both! Hardily, the matter guess!

TRUSTY
Lo, how say ye, dame?

MERRYGREEK   Why, do ye think, Dame
Custance,
That in this wooing I have meant ought but pastance?

DAME CUSTANCE
Much things ye spake, I wot, to maintain his dotage.   10

MERRYGREEK
But well might ye judge I spake it all in mockage.
For why, is Roister Doister a fit husband for you?

---

3 *for altogether* once and for all
5 *brim* fierce
6 *in sadness* in earnest
7 *fond* foolish, mistaken
  Hardily . . . guess really, now, what do you think
9 *pastance* amusement
10 *dotage* foolish affection
12 *For why* because

---

5 *toast . . . hot* Proverbial (Tilley T363): 'As hot(warm) as a toast'. Common from the fifteenth century to modern times.

TRUSTY
  I daresay ye never thought it.

MERRYGREEK   No, to God I vow!
  And did not I know afore of the insurance
  Between Gawin Goodluck and Christian Custance?   15
  And did not I, for the nonce, by my conveyance,
  Read his letter in a wrong sense for dalliance?
  That if you could have take it up at the first bound,
  We should thereat such a sport and pastime have
        found,
  That all the whole town should have been the merrier!   20

DAME CUSTANCE
  Ill ache your heads both! I was never wearier,
  Nor never more vexed since the first day I was born!

TRUSTY
  But very well I wist he here did all in scorn.

DAME CUSTANCE
  But I feared thereof to take dishonesty.

MERRYGREEK
  This should both have made sport and showed your
        honesty,   25
  And Goodluck, I dare swear, your wit therein would
        'low.

TRUSTY
  Yea, being no worse than we know it to be now.

MERRYGREEK
  And nothing yet too late; for when I come to him,
  Hither will he repair with a sheep's look full grim,
  By plain force and violence to drive you to yield.   30

DAME CUSTANCE
  If ye two bid me, we will with him pitch a field,
  I and my maids together.

MERRYGREEK   Let us see! Be bold!

14 *insurance* betrothal
16 *for the nonce* on purpose
   conveyance cunning execution, contrivance
17 *dalliance* sport
23 *scorn* mockery (of Roister Doister)
24 *take* be thought guilty of
26 *'low* (allow) approve
31 *pitch a field* do battle

DAME CUSTANCE
Ye shall see women's war!

TRUSTY   That fight will I behold!

MERRYGREEK
If occasion serve, taking his part full brim,
I will strike at you, but the rap shall light on him.   35
When we first appear—

DAME CUSTANCE   Then will I run away
As though I were afeared.

TRUSTY   Do you that part well play,
And I will sue for peace.

MERRYGREEK   And I will set him on.
Then will he look as fierce as a Cotswold lion!

TRUSTY
But when go'st thou for him?

MERRYGREEK   That do I very now.   40

DAME CUSTANCE
Ye shall find us here.

MERRYGREEK   Well, God have mercy on you!
                                                        Exit

TRUSTY
There is no cause of fear. The least boy in the street—

DAME CUSTANCE
Nay, the least girl I have will make him take his feet.
But hark, methink they make preparation.

TRUSTY
No force, it will be a good recreation.   45

DAME CUSTANCE
I will stand within, and step forth speedily,
And so make as though I ran away dreadfully.

37 *afeared* afraid
38 *set him on* incite him
40 *very* right
43 *take his feet* run away
49 *so* then
   dreadfully in fright

---

39 *Cotswold lion* Proverbial (Tilley L323). Humorous name for a sheep (compare
   1.29). Occurs in *Thersites* (1537) and as late as 1600 in the anonymous *Sir John
   Oldcastle*, Part I.
44 *But ... preparation* Presumably there are 'noises off' coming from the direction of
   Roister Doister's house.

Act IV, Scene vii

[*Enter* ROISTER DOISTER, MERRYGREEK, DOUGHTY, HARPAX,
and other servants, armed, with drum, ensign, etc.]

ROISTER DOISTER
Now, sirs, keep your 'ray, and see your hearts be stout!
But where be these caitiffs? Methink they dare not rout!
How sayst thou, Merrygreek? What doth Kit Custance
 say?

MERRYGREEK
I am loath to tell you.

ROISTER DOISTER   Tush! Speak, man—yea or nay?

MERRYGREEK
Forsooth, sir, I have spoken for you all that I can.   5
But if ye win her, ye must e'en play the man;
E'en to fight it out, ye must a man's heart take.

ROISTER DOISTER
Yes, they shall know, and thou knowest I have a
 stomach.

MERRYGREEK
'A stomach', quod you? Yea, as good as e'er man had!

ROISTER DOISTER
I trow they shall find and feel that I am a lad.   10

MERRYGREEK
By this cross, I have seen you eat your meat as well

 1 *'ray* array, formation
 2 *caitiffs* wretches, villains
  rout assemble
 8 *have a stomach* am brave
10 *lad* man of spirit (also someone of low birth or condition, a varlet)

s.d. *Enter . . . etc.* Editors vary in their translations into full stage directions of the lists of
 characters here and at scene viii in Q. The latter includes 'two drums with their
 ensigns', which Boas transfers to sc. vii. But this ed. takes it, as does Adams, that
 one drum (i.e., drummer) and one ensign (standard-bearer) belong to Roister
 Doister's 'army' and one of each to Dame Custance's; hers does not enter until sc.
 viii.
 11–20 *eat your meat . . . your stomach cloyed* Merrygreek insists on taking 'stomach' very
 literally.

As any that e'er I have seen of or heard tell!
'A stomach', quod you? He that will that deny
I know was never at dinner in your company!

ROISTER DOISTER
Nay, the stomach of a man it is that I mean!   15

MERRYGREEK
Nay, the stomach of an horse or a dog, I ween!

ROISTER DOISTER
Nay, a man's stomach with a weapon, mean I!

MERRYGREEK
Ten men can scarce match you with a spoon in a pie!

ROISTER DOISTER
Nay, the stomach of a man to try in strife!

MERRYGREEK
I never saw your stomach cloyed yet in my life.   20

ROISTER DOISTER
Tush, I mean in strife or fighting to try.

MERRYGREEK
We shall see how ye will strike now being angry.

ROISTER DOISTER
Have at thy pate then, and save thy head if thou may!
                    [*Strikes at him*]

MERRYGREEK
Nay, then have at your pate again, by this day!
                    [*Strikes back*]

ROISTER DOISTER
Nay, thou may not strike at me again in no wise.   25

MERRYGREEK
I cannot in fight make to you such warrantise;
But as for your foes here, let them the bargain 'by.

ROISTER DOISTER
Nay, as for they, shall every mother's child die!
And in this my fume, a little thing might make me
To beat down house and all, and else the devil take me!   30

12 *seen . . . tell* seen or heard tell of
20 *cloyed* satiated
23 *pate* head
26 *warrantise* guarantee
27 *'by* abide (i.e., suffer the consequences)
29 *fume* fit of anger

MERRYGREEK
  If I were as ye be, by Gog's dear mother,
  I would not leave one stone upon another
  Though she would redeem it with twenty thousand
     pounds.

ROISTER DOISTER
  It shall be even so, by his lily wounds!

MERRYGREEK
  Be not at one with her upon any amends!　　　　35

ROISTER DOISTER
  No, though she make to me never so many friends!
  Not if all the world for her would undertake;
  No, not God himself neither shall not her peace make!
  On, therefore! March forward! Soft! Stay awhile yet!

MERRYGREEK
  On!

ROISTER DOISTER　　Tarry!

MERRYGREEK　　　　　　Forth!

ROISTER DOISTER　　　　　　Back!

MERRYGREEK　　　　　　　　On!

ROISTER DOISTER　　　　　　　　Soft! Now
  forward set!　　　　　　　　　　　　　　40

[Enter DAME CUSTANCE]

DAME CUSTANCE
  What business have we here? Out, alas! Alas!　　*[Exit]*

ROISTER DOISTER
  Ha, ha, ha, ha, ha!
  Didst thou see that, Merrygreek? How afraid she was?
  Didst thou see how she fled apace out of my sight?
  Ah, good sweet Custance! I pity her, by this light!

MERRYGREEK
  That tender heart of yours will mar altogether;　　45
  Thus will ye be turned with wagging of a feather!

33 *she* (i.e., Dame Custance)
34 *by...wounds* by Christ's lovely wounds
35 *Be...amends* do not make peace with her whatever compensation she may offer
37 *undertake* pledge, stand surety

ROISTER DOISTER
  On, sirs! Keep your 'ray!

MERRYGREEK   On! Forth, while this gear is
  hot!

ROISTER DOISTER
  Soft! The arms of Calais! I have one thing forgot!

MERRYGREEK
  What lack we now?

ROISTER DOISTER   Retire, or else we be all slain!

MERRYGREEK
  Back, for the pash of God! Back, sirs! Back again!   50
  What is the great matter?

ROISTER DOISTER   This hasty forth going
  Had almost brought us all to utter undoing!
  It made me forget a thing most necessary.

MERRYGREEK
  Well remembered of a captain, by Saint Mary!

ROISTER DOISTER
  It is a thing must be had.

MERRYGREEK   Let us have it then.   55

ROISTER DOISTER
  But I wot not where nor how.

MERRYGREEK   Then wot not I when.
  But what is it?

ROISTER DOISTER   Of a chief thing I am to seek.

MERRYGREEK
  Tut, so will ye be when ye have studied a week.
  But tell me what it is.

ROISTER DOISTER   I lack yet an headpiece.

48 *The . . . Calais* (see III. iv, 72n.)
50 *pash* passion
54 *of* by

MERRYGREEK
    The kitchen collocavit—the best hence to Greece!   60
    Run fet it, Dobinet and come at once withal,
    And bring with thee my potgun hanging by the wall.
                           [Exit DOUGHTY]
    I have seen your head with it full many a time,
    Covered as safe as it had been with a scrine.
    And I warrant it save your head from any stroke,   65
    Except perchance to be amazed with the smoke.
    I warrant your head therewith, except for the mist,
    As safe as if it were fast locked up in a chest.
    And lo, here our Dobinet cometh with it now!

    [*Enter* DOUGHTY *with a pail and a pistol*]

DOUGHTY
    It will cover me to the shoulders well enow.   70

MERRYGREEK
    Let me see it on.

ROISTER DOISTER   In faith, it doth meetly well.

MERRYGREEK
    There can be no fitter thing. Now ye must us tell
    What to do.

ROISTER DOISTER   Now, forth in 'ray, sirs, and stop no more!

---

60 *collocavit* (from *collock*) kitchen pail or tub (only recorded example of this mock-Latin form)
    the best . . . Greece the best from here to Greece
62 *potgun* popgun, pistol
64 *scrine* ed. (skrine Q) strongbox
66 *amazed* stunned
71 *meetly* tolerably

---

60 *collocavit* The would-be knight, armed with kitchen pail for a helmet and broom or other household implement for a weapon, was a popular comic figure. Roister Doister's martial exploits in the kitchen have already been mentioned (I.iv, 63–4, 73–4). A stage direction for the entry of the Vice, Ambidexter, in *Cambyses*, reads: 'Enter the Vice with an old capcase on his head, an old pail about his hips for harness, a scummer and a potlid by his side, and a rake on his shoulder'. Compare the weapons to be used by Dame Custance's maids (IV.iv, 17–22). Wickham considers it probable that the servants A and B fight each other with similar implements in Medwall's *Fulgens and Lucrece*, part i, ll. 1165ff. (*English Moral Interludes*, p. 71n.).

MERRYGREEK
  Now Saint George to borrow! Drum, 'dub-a-dub' afore!
                    [*Enter* TRUSTY]

TRUSTY
  What mean you to do, sir? Commit manslaughter?   75

ROISTER DOISTER
  To kill forty such is a matter of laughter!

TRUSTY
  And who is it, sir, whom ye intend thus to spill?

ROISTER DOISTER
  Foolish Custance here forceth me against my will.

TRUSTY
  And is there no mean your extreme wrath to slake?
  She shall some amends unto your good ma'ship make.   80

ROISTER DOISTER
  I will none amends.

TRUSTY   Is her offence so sore?

MERRYGREEK
  And he were a lout, she could have done no more.
  She hath called him fool, and dressed him like a fool,
  Mocked him like a fool, used him like a fool.

TRUSTY
  Well, yet the sheriff, the justice or constable   85
  Her misdemeanour to punish might be able.

ROISTER DOISTER
  No, sir! I mine own self will in this present cause
  Be sheriff and justice and whole judge of the laws;
  This matter to amend, all officers be I shall,
  Constable, bailiff, sergeant—

MERRYGREEK   And hangman and all.   90

TRUSTY
  Yet a noble courage and the heart of a man
  Should more honour win by bearing with a woman.
  Therefore take the law, and let her answer thereto.

---

74 *Drum . . . afore* (order to the drummer to begin playing at the front of the troops)
79 *slake* appease
83 *dressed* treated
93 *take . . . law* seek redress through legal means

---

74 *Saint . . . borrow* Semi-proverbial (*ODEP*, p. 693). Literally, St. George being
  security for one's good faith. Here simply an asseveration.

ROISTER DOISTER
Merrygreek, the best way were even so to do.
What honour should it be with a woman to
    fight?   95

MERRYGREEK
And what then? Will ye thus forego and lose your
    right?

ROISTER DOISTER
Nay, I will take the law on her withouten grace!

TRUSTY
Of if your ma'ship could pardon this one trespass—
I pray you, forgive her.

ROISTER DOISTER   Ho!

MERRYGREEK   Tush, tush, sir, do not!

[TRUSTY]
Be good master to her.

ROISTER DOISTER   Ho!

MERRYGREEK   Tush, I say, do not!   100
And what, shall your people here return straight home?

ROISTER DOISTER
Yea, levy the camp, sirs, and hence again, each one.
But be still in readiness if I hap to call;
I cannot tell what sudden chance may befall.

MERRYGREEK
Do not off your harness, sirs, I you advise,   105
At the least for this fortnight, in no manner wise.
Perchance in an hour when all ye think least,
Our master's appetite to fight will be best.

---

97 *withouten grace* without mercy
99 *Ho* halt, stop (addressed to his men)
100 s.p. TRUSTY eds. (omitted in Q)
102 *levy* raise, break
103–4 (assigned to ROISTER DOISTER) eds. (TRUSTY Q)

---

100 The half-line is obviously Trusty's, not Merrygreek's; it contradicts the latter's
    urging that the assault be carried out. 'Be good master' (not 'be good, master' as
    in some eds.) means 'show yourself a noble, generous superior' to her; Trusty is
    flattering Roister Doister. The concept of 'good lordship' derives from the feudal
    relationship of lord and vassal.
103–4 These lines clearly belong to Roister Doister; the Q s.p. may have been displaced
    from l. 100 where it should have been.

But, soft! Ere ye go, have once at Custance's house!

ROISTER DOISTER
Soft! What wilt thou do?

MERRYGREEK   Once discharge my
    harquebouse,   110
And for my heart's ease, have once more with my
    potgun.

ROISTER DOISTER
Hold thy hands! Else is all our purpose clean fordone!

MERRYGREEK
And it cost me my life—

ROISTER DOISTER   I say thou shalt not!

MERRYGREEK
By the matte, but I will! Have once more with hail shot!
I will have some pennyworth, I will not lose all!   115

Act IV, Scene viii

[*Enter* DAME CUSTANCE]

DAME CUSTANCE
What caitiffs are those that so shake my house wall?

MERRYGREEK
Ah, sirrah! Now, Custance, if ye had so much wit,
I would see you ask pardon and yourselves submit.

DAME CUSTANCE
Have I still this ado with a couple of fools?

MERRYGREEK
Hear ye what she saith?

109 *have once* fire one round
112 *clean fordone* utterly lost
114 *matte* mass
     hail shot small shot which scatters when fired
115 *I will have . . . all* I will not waste all this preparation

---

109–15 Merrygreek discharges his firearms several times during this exchange. Stage
    directions to that effect might be placed after ll. 112 and 115.
110 *harquebouse* The harquebus, an early type of portable gun or musket, was usually
    supported upon a forked rest when being fired.

DAME CUSTANCE   Maidens, come forth with your
    tools!   5

      [*Enter* TIBET TALKAPACE, ANNOT ALYFACE, MADGE
    MUMBLECRUST *and* TOM TRUEPENNY, *armed, with drum,*
                ensign, etc.]

ROISTER DOISTER [*To his men*]
  In array!

MERRYGREEK   'Dub-a-dub', sirrah!

ROISTER DOISTER   In array!
  They come suddenly on us!

MERRYGREEK   'Dub-a-dub'!

ROISTER DOISTER   In array!
  That ever I was born! We are taken tardy!

MERRYGREEK
  Now, sirs, quit ourselves like tall men and hardy!

DAME CUSTANCE
  On afore, Truepenny! Hold thine own, Annot!   10
  On toward them, Tibet, for 'scape us they cannot!
  Come forth, Madge Mumblecrust! So stand fast together.

MERRYGREEK
  God send us a fair day!

ROISTER DOISTER   See, they march on hither!

TIBET
  But, mistress—

DAME CUSTANCE What sayst thou?

TIBET   Shall I go fet our goose?

DAME CUSTANCE
  What to do?

TIBET   To yonder captain I will turn her loose.   15
  And she gape and hiss at him as she doth at me,
  I durst jeopard my hand she will make him flee!

---

    5 s.d. *Enter . . . etc.* (see sc. vii, headnote)
    8 *taken tardy* caught unprepared
    9 *quit* acquit
      tall brave
  16 *And* if
  17 *jeopard* hazard

DAME CUSTANCE
  On! Forward!

ROISTER DOISTER   They come!

MERRYGREEK   Stand!

ROISTER DOISTER   Hold!

MERRYGREEK   Keep!

ROISTER DOISTER   There!

MERRYGREEK   Strike!

ROISTER DOISTER   Take heed!

DAME CUSTANCE
  Well said, Truepenny!

TRUEPENNY   Ah, whoresons!

DAME CUSTANCE   Well done, indeed!

MERRYGREEK
  Hold thine own, Harpax! Down with them, Dobinet!   20

DAME CUSTANCE
  Now, Madge! There, Annot! Now stick them, Tibet!

TIBET
  All my chief quarrel is to this same little knave
  That beguiled me last day—nothing shall him save!

DOUGHTY
  Down with this little quean that hath at me such spite!
  Save you from her, master! It is a very sprite!   25

DAME CUSTANCE
  I myself will Monsieur Grand Capitaine undertake!

ROISTER DOISTER
  They win ground!

MERRYGREEK   Save yourself, sir, for God's sake!

19 *Well said* well done
22–3 *this . . . day* (i.e., Doughty)
24 *quean* whore
25 *you* yourself
   sprite spirit, devil
26 *Monsieur Grand Capitaine* ed. (mounsire graunde captaine Q)

18ff. Battle is joined, with Dame Custance's side on the attack.
27–32 As the dialogue indicates, Merrygreek is carrying out the trick that he spoke of
   to Dame Custance and Trusty at IV.vi, 34–5. He evidently does so again at l. 51.

ROISTER DOISTER
  Out, alas! I am slain! Help!

MERRYGREEK   Save yourself!

ROISTER DOISTER   Alas!

MERRYGREEK
  Nay then, have at you, mistress!

ROISTER DOISTER   Thou hittest me, alas!

MERRYGREEK
  I will strike at Custance here!

ROISTER DOISTER   Thou hittest me!

MERRYGREEK   So I will!   30
  Nay, Mistress Custance!

ROISTER DOISTER   Alas, thou hittest me still!
  Hold!

MERRYGREEK   Save yourself, sir!

ROISTER DOISTER   Help! Out, alas! I am slain!

MERRYGREEK
  Truce! Hold your hands! Truce, for a pissing while or
    twain!
  Now, how say you, Custance? For saving of your life,
  Will ye yield and grant to be this gent'man's wife?   35

DAME CUSTANCE
  Ye told me he loved me! Call ye this love?

MERRYGREEK
  He loved a while, even like a turtledove.

DAME CUSTANCE
  Gay love, God save it! So soon hot, so soon cold!

MERRYGREEK
  I am sorry for you. He could love you yet, so he could.

ROISTER DOISTER
  Nay, by Cock's precious, she shall be none of mine!   40

MERRYGREEK
  Why so?

---

28 *Out, alas* (exclamation of dismay)

---

38 *love . . . cold* Proverbial (Tilley L483): 'Hot love is soon cold'. Compare H732:
'Soon hot, soon cold'.

ROISTER DOISTER   Come away! By the matte, she is
   mankine!
  I durst adventure the loss of my right hand
  If she did not slay her other husband!
  And see if she prepare not again to fight!

MERRYGREEK
  What then? Saint George to borrow, our Lady's knight!   45

ROISTER DOISTER
  Slay else whom she will, by Gog, she shall not slay me!

MERRYGREEK
  How then?

ROISTER DOISTER   Rather than to be slain, I will flee!

DAME CUSTANCE
  To it again, my knightesses! Down with them all!

ROISTER DOISTER
  Away, away, away! She will else kill us all!

MERRYGREEK
  Nay, stick to it, like an hardy man and a tall!   50

ROISTER DOISTER
  Oh, bones! Thou hittest me! Away, or else die we shall!

MERRYGREEK
  Away, for the pash of our sweet Lord Jesus Christ!

DAME CUSTANCE
  Away, lout and lubber, or I shall be thy priest!

    Exeunt [ROISTER DOISTER, MERRYGREEK *and their men*]

  So, this field is ours; we have driven them all away.

TIBET
  Thanks to God, mistress, ye have had a fair day.   55

DAME CUSTANCE [*To her servants*]
  Well, now go ye in and make yourself some good cheer.

ALL
  We go.

      [*Exeunt* TIBET, ANNOT, MADGE *and* TRUEPENNY,
                    their drum, ensign, etc.]

41 *mankine* furious, mad
45 *our Lady's* the Virgin Mary's
53 *I . . . priest* (ironically) give you the last rites
   s.d. *Exeunt . . . men* ed. (Exeant om [nes] Q)
57 s.p. ALL (all the servants) eds. (O [mn] es pariter Q)
   s.d. *Exeunt . . . etc.* eds.

TRUSTY   Ah sir, what a field we have had here!

DAME CUSTANCE
    Friend Tristram, I pray you be a witness with me.

TRUSTY
    Dame Custance, I shall depose for your honesty.
    And now fare ye well, except something else ye would.   60

DAME CUSTANCE
    Not now, but when I need to send, I will be bold.
    I thank you for these pains.   *Exit* [TRUSTY]
                                    And now I will get me in.
    Now Roister Doister will no more wooing begin!   *Exit*

Act V, Scene i

[*Enter* GAWIN GOODLUCK *and* SIM SURESBY]

GOODLUCK
    Sim Suresby, my trusty man, now advise thee well,
    And see that no false surmises thou me tell:
    Was there such ado about Custance, of a truth?

SURESBY
    To report that I heard and saw to me is ruth,
    But both my duty and name and property   5
    Warneth me to you to show fidelity.
    It may be well enough, and I wish it so to be;
    She may herself discharge and try her honesty.
    Yet their claim to her methought was very large,
    For with lettrs, rings and tokens they did her charge;   10
    Which when I heard and saw, I would none to you
            bring.

GOODLUCK
    No, by Saint Mary, I allow thee in that thing.
    Ah, sirrah, now I see truth in the proverb old:

59 *depose* make a statement under oath
62 s.d. *Exit* TRUSTY eds. (Exeat (at l. 61) Q)
 4 *ruth* a matter of regret
 5 *property* character
 8 *try* prove
12 *allow . . . thing* approve your action in that respect

57 'Ah sir' may sound like Dame Custance addressing Trusty (and some eds. reassign
    the line to her) but it is he who is saluting her as the victorious 'general'; and 'she'
    would of course have been played by a boy.

'All things that shineth is not by and by pure gold'.
If any do live a woman of honesty,   15
I would have sworn Christian Custance had been she.

SURESBY

Sir, though I to you be a servant true and just,
Yet do not ye therefore your faithful spouse mistrust;
But examine the matter and if ye shall it find
To be all well, be not ye, for my words, unkind.   20

GOODLUCK

I shall do that is right, and as I see cause why.
But here cometh Custance forth. We shall know by
    and by.

Act V, Scene ii

[*Enter* DAME CUSTANCE]

DAME CUSTANCE [*Aside*]

I come forth to see and harken for news good,
For about this hour is the time, of likelihood,
That Gawin Goodluck, by the sayings of Suresby,
Would be at home. And lo, yond I see him, I!—
What! Gawin Goodluck, the only hope of my life!   5
Welcome home, and kiss me, your true espoused wife!

GOODLUCK

Nay, soft, Dame Custance! I must first, by your licence,
See whether all things be clear in your conscience.
I hear of your doings, to me very strange.

DAME CUSTANCE

What fear ye? That my faith towards you should
    change?   10

GOODLUCK

I must needs mistrust ye be elsewhere entangled,
For I hear that certain men with you have wrangled
About the promise of marriage by you to them made.

20 *for . . . words* because of what I have reported
 7 *by your licence* with your permission
12 *wrangled* disputed

14 *'all . . . gold'* Proverbial (Tilley A146). An ancient and familiar proverb, which
appears in its best-known form in *The Merchant of Venice:* 'All that glisters is not
gold' (II.vii, 65).

DAME CUSTANCE
  Could any man's report your mind therein persuade?

GOODLUCK
  Well, ye must therein declare yourself to stand clear,   15
  Else I and you, Dame Custance, may not join this year.

DAME CUSTANCE
  Then would I were dead and fair laid in my grave!
  Ah, Suresby, is this the honesty that ye have,
  To hurt me with your report, not knowing the thing?

SURESBY
  If ye be honest, my words can hurt you nothing.   20
  But what I heard and saw, I might not but report.

DAME CUSTANCE
  Ah Lord, help poor widows destitute of comfort!
  Truly, most dear spouse, nought was done but for
        pastance.

GOODLUCK
  But such kind of sporting is homely dalliance.

DAME CUSTANCE
  If ye knew the truth, ye would take all in good part.   25

GOODLUCK
  By your leave, I am not half well skilled in that art.

DAME CUSTANCE
  It was none but Roister Doister, that foolish mome—

GOODLUCK
  Yea, Custance, better (they say) a bad 'scuse than
        none.

DAME CUSTANCE
  Why, Tristram Trusty, sir, your true and faithful
        friend,
  Was privy both to the beginning and the end: 30
  Let him be the judge and for me testify.

17 *fair* quite
19 *thing* facts
24 *homely dalliance* undignified, frivolous activity
26 *that art* the art of divining the truth
27 *mome* blockhead

---

28 *better . . . none* Proverbial (Tilley E214).

GOODLUCK

> I will the more credit that he shall verify,
> And because I will the truth know e'en as it is,
> I will to him myself, and know all without miss.
> Come on, Sim Suresby, that before my friend thou may   35
> Avouch the same words which thou didst to me say.
>
> *Exeunt* [GOODLUCK *and* SURESBY]

Act V, Scene iii

DAME CUSTANCE

> Oh Lord, how necessary it is now of days,
> That each body live uprightly all manner ways;
> For let never so little a gap be open,
> And be sure of this, the worst shall be spoken!
> How innocent stand I in this, for deed or thought,   5
> And yet see what mistrust towards me it hath wrought!
> But thou, Lord, knowest all folks' thoughts and eke
>   intents,
> And thou art the deliverer of all innocents.
> Thou didst help the advoutress that she might be
>   amended;
> Much more then, help, Lord, that never ill intended.   10
> Thou didst help Susanna, wrongfully accused,

36 *Avouch* declare, affirm
   s.d. *Exeunt . . .* SURESBY eds. (Exeant Q)
 1 *now of days* nowadays
 7 *eke* also
 9 *advoutress* adultress
10 *that* one who

---

 9 *Thou . . . amended* Dame Custance alludes to the story of the woman taken in
   adultery and brought before Jesus by the Pharisees, who ask him if he does not
   agree that she should be stoned according to Mosaic law. He replies 'He that is
   without sin among you, let him first cast a stone at her'. The accusers depart
   ashamed, and Jesus dismisses the woman: 'Go and sin no more' (John 8:1–11). The
   biblical allusions in this speech serve to enforce Udall's moralizing of his Roman
   model and as a reminder of the heroine's full name, Christian Custance
   (Constancy).
11 *Susanna . . . accused* In the Apocryphal story of Susanna, the young woman refuses
   to yield herself to two lustful elders who have hidden in her garden to watch her
   bathing. In revenge, they accuse her of adultery with another man and she is
   condemned to death. But God sends a wise young judge, Daniel, who uncovers the
   two men's falsehood. They are executed in Susanna's place and she is restored to
   her husband and family. At verses 42–3, she prays, as Dame Custance does, that her
   innocence be revealed.

And no less dost thou see, Lord, how I am now abused.
Thou didst help Hester when she should have died;
Help also, good Lord, that my truth may be tried.
Yet if Gawin Goodluck with Tristram Trusty speak,　　15
I trust of ill report the force shall be but weak.
And lo, yond they come sadly talking together.
I will abide, and not shrink for their coming hither.

Act V, Scene iv

[*Enter* GOODLUCK, TRUSTY *and* SURESBY]

GOODLUCK [*To* TRUSTY]
And was it none other than ye to me report?

TRUSTY
No; and here were ye wished to have seen the sport.

GOODLUCK
Would I had, rather than half of that in my purse!

SURESBY
And I do much rejoice the matter was no worse.
And like as to open it I was to you faithful,　　5
So of Dame Custance' honest truth I am joyful;
For God forfend that I should hurt her by false report.

GOODLUCK
Well, I will no longer hold her in discomfort.

DAME CUSTANCE [*Aside*]
Now come they hitherward—I trust all shall be well.

GOODLUCK
Sweet Custance, neither heart can think nor tongue tell　　10

---

13 *Hester* Esther
14 *tried* proved
17 *sadly* earnestly
 7 *forfend* forbid

---

13 *Thou . . . died* In the Old Testament book of Esther, the heroine, though she is
queen to King Ahaseurus, risks death by coming into his presence unbidden. She
takes the risk in order to plead for her people, the Jews, who are being persecuted
by the King's wicked counsellor, Haman. But the king is pleased to see Esther, she
is spared, and her wish is granted (Esther 4–5). Both Esther and Susanna were the
subjects of English plays in the sixteenth century, the anonymous *Godly Queen
Hester* (c. 1527) and Thomas Garter's *The Most Virtuous and Godly Susanna* (c.
1569).

How much I joy in your constant fidelity.
Come now, kiss me, the pearl of perfect honesty!

DAME CUSTANCE
God let me no longer to continue in life
Than I shall towards you continue a true wife!

GOODLUCK
Well now, to make you for this some part of amends, 15
I shall desire first you, and then such of our friends
As shall to you seem best, to sup at home with me,
Where at your fought field we shall laugh and merry
    be.

SURESBY
And mistress, I beseech you, take with me no grief;
I did a true man's part, not wishing your reprief. 20

DAME CUSTANCE
Though hasty reports, through surmises growing,
May of poor innocents be utter overthrowing,
Yet because to thy master thou hast a true heart,
And I know mine own truth, I forgive thee, for my
    part.

GOODLUCK
Go we all to my house, and of this gear no more. 25
Go prepare all things, Sim Suresby; hence, run afore.

SURESBY
I go.   *Exit*

GOODLUCK   But who cometh yond? Matthew Merrygreek?

DAME CUSTANCE
Roister Doister's champion, I shrew his best cheek!

TRUSTY
Roister Doister self, your wooer, is with him too.
Surely some thing there is with us they have to do. 30

18 *fought field* battle
19 *take ... grief* do not be angry with me
20 *man's* servant's
   reprief reproof, disgrace
28 *shrew ... cheek* (see IV.ii, 14, note)
29 *self* himself

Act V, Scene v

[*Enter* ROISTER DOISTER *and* MERRYGREEK]

MERRYGREEK
  Yond I see Gawin Goodluck, to whom lieth my
      message.
  I will first salute him after his long voyage,
  And then make all thing well concerning your behalf.

ROISTER DOISTER
  Yea, for the pash of God!

MERRYGREEK   Hence, out of sight, ye calf,
  Till I have spoke with them, and then I will you fet.   5

ROISTER DOISTER
  In God's name!   [*Exit*]
  What, Master Gawin Goodluck, well met!

MERRYGREEK
  And from your long voyage I bid you right welcome
      home.

GOODLUCK
  I thank you.

MERRYGREEK I come to you from an honest mome.

GOODLUCK
  Who is that?

MERRYGREEK Roister Doister, that doughty kite.

DAME CUSTANCE
  Fie! I can scarce abide ye should his name recite!   10

MERRYGREEK
  Ye must take him to favour, and pardon all past;
  He heareth of your return and is full ill aghast.

GOODLUCK
  I am right well content he have with us some cheer.

---

6 s.d. *Exit* eds. (not in Q)
9 *doughty* valiant
12 *full ill aghast* terribly frightened

---

9 *kite* A bird of the falcon family, primarily a scavenger, hence the pejorative sense
  implied in its figurative application to persons. Scavengers are not valiant, so
  'doughty kite' is oxymoronic. Merrygreek is perhaps also punning on 'knight', as
  the 'k' would still have been sounded in Udall's time.

DAME CUSTANCE
  Fie upon him, beast! then will not I be there!

GOODLUCK
  Why Custance, do ye hate him more than ye love me?   15

DAME CUSTANCE
  But for your mind, sir, where he were would I not be!

TRUSTY
  He would make us all laugh.

MERRYGREEK   Ye ne'er had better sport.

GOODLUCK
  I pray you, sweet Custance, let him to us resort.

DAME CUSTANCE
  To your will I assent.

MERRYGREEK   Why, such a fool it is,
  As no man for good pastime would forego or miss.   20

GOODLUCK
  Fet him to go with us.

MERRYGREEK   He will be a glad man!   *Exit*

TRUSTY
  We must, to make us mirth, maintain him all we can.
  And lo, yond he cometh, and Merrygreek with him.

DAME CUSTANCE
  At his first entrance, ye shall see I will him trim!
  But first let us harken the gentleman's wise talk.   25

TRUSTY
  I pray you, mark, if ever ye saw crane so stalk!

---

16 *But . . . mind* did you not desire it

---

23 *yond he cometh* One might be justified in having Roister Doister and Merrygreek
  enter here, though Dame Custance says 'At his first entrance' (l. 24). But
  presumably the characters 'see' those who are about to enter approaching before
  they become visible to the audience. In performance, the precise moment at which
  the new 'scene' begins need not be and is not so arbitrarily marked as it is on the
  printed page. Here, Merrygreek and Roister Doister remain apart from the others
  until l. 18 or so of sc. vi.
26 *crane* A large wading bird with very long legs, neck and bill, related to the stork and
  the heron. Trusty continues Merrygreek's disparaging ornithological imagery with
  reference to Roister Doister.

Act V, Scene vi

[*Enter* ROISTER DOISTER *and* MERRYGREEK]

ROISTER DOISTER
May I then be bold?

MERRYGREEK   I warrant you on my word.
They say they shall be sick but ye be at their board.

ROISTER DOISTER
They were not angry then?

MERRYGREEK   Yes, at first, and made
        strange;
But when I said your anger to favour should change,
And therewith had commended you accordingly,   5
They were all in love with your ma'ship by and by,
And cried you mercy that they had done you wrong.

ROISTER DOISTER
For why no man, woman nor child can hate me long.

MERRYGREEK
'We fear', quod they, 'he will be avenged one day;
Then for a penny give all our lives we may!'   10

ROISTER DOISTER
Said they so indeed? Did they? Yea, even with one
        voice?

MERRYGREEK
'He will forgive all', quod I. O, how they did rejoice!

ROISTER DOISTER
Ha, ha, ha!

MERRYGREEK
'Go fet him', say they, 'while he is in good mood,
For have his anger who lust, we will not, by the rood!'   15

ROISTER DOISTER
I pray God that it be all true that thou hast me told,
And that she fight no more.

    2 *but* unless
    3 *made strange* resisted, demurred
    8 *For why* because
    15 *have . . . lust* let whoever wishes to do so feel his anger
        rood cross

MERRYGREEK   I warrant you, be bold.
  To them and salute them.

ROISTER DOISTER   Sirs, I greet you all well.

ALL
  Your mastership is welcome.

DAME CUSTANCE   Saving my quarrel,
  For sure, I will put you up into the Exchequer!   20

MERRYGREEK
  Why so? Better nay! Wherefore?

DAME CUSTANCE   For an usurer!

ROISTER DOISTER
  I am no usurer, good mistress, by his arms!

MERRYGREEK
  When took he gain of money to any man's harms?

DAME CUSTANCE
  Yes, a foul usurer he is, ye shall see else.

ROISTER DOISTER [*To* MERRYGREEK]
  Didst not thou promise she would pick no mo'
    quarrels?   25

DAME CUSTANCE
  He will lend no blows, but he have in recompense
  Fifteen for one, which is too much, of conscience!

ROISTER DOISTER
  Ah dame, by the ancient law of arms, a man
  Hath no honour to foil his hands on a woman.

---

20 *put ... Exchequer* take you to court
23 *took ... money* made a profit from lending money
29 *foil* defile

---

20 *Exchequer* The court of Exchequer, now no longer a separate court, which dealt
  primarily with matters of revenue.
21–31 Usury, the lending of money at interest, was forbidden by the medieval
  Church. Successive councils had laid down injunctions against it in all forms; the
  Council of Vienne (1312) threatened with excommunication any ruler or
  magistrate who knowingly sanctioned it. The issue continued to exercise
  theologians and moralists after the Reformation; Udall's friend, Thomas Wilson,
  published *A Discourse on Usury* in 1572. See R.H. Tawney, *Religion and the Rise of
  Capitalism* (1926; repr. 1938, etc.). Dame Custance is, of course, accusing Roister
  Doister of 'usury' in a humorous sense, of receiving fifteen blows for every one he
  gave (l. 27).

DAME CUSTANCE
  And where other usurers take their gains yearly,   30
  This man is angry but he have his by and by!

GOODLUCK
  Sir, do not for her sake bear me your displeasure.

MERRYGREEK
  Well, he shall with you talk thereof more at leisure.
  Upon your good usage, he will now shake your hand.

ROISTER DOISTER
  And much heartily welcome from a strange land.   35

MERRYGREEK
  Be not afeared, Gawin, to let him shake your fist.

GOODLUCK
  Oh, the most honest gentleman that e'er I wist!
  I beseech your ma'ship to take pain to sup with us.

MERRYGREEK
  He shall not say you nay, and I too, by Jesus,
  Because ye shall be friends and let all quarrels pass.   40

ROISTER DOISTER
  I will be as good friends with them as e'er I was.

MERRYGREEK
  Then let me fet your choir that we may have a song.

ROISTER DOISTER
  Go.   [*Exit* MERRYGREEK]

GOODLUCK   I have heard no melody all this year long.

[*Enter* MERRYGREEK *with* DOUGHTY, HARPAX *and musicians*]

MERRYGREEK
  Come on, sirs, quickly!

ROISTER DOISTER   Sing on, sirs, for my friends' sake.

---

34 *upon . . . usage* if you promise to behave yourself
43 s.d. *Exit* MERRYGREEK eds. (not in Q)
   s.d. *Enter . . . musicians* eds. (not in Q)

---

43 s.d. In view of the speed with which he returns. Merrygreek might do little more
   than cross to Roister Doister's house or to the stage entrance and call to the
   musicians.

DOUGHTY
   Call ye these your friends?

ROISTER DOISTER   Sing on, and no mo' words
   make!   45

Here they sing

GOODLUCK
   The Lord preserve our most noble Queen of renown,
   And her virtues reward with the heavenly crown.

DAME CUSTANCE
   The Lord strengthen her most excellent Majesty,
   Long to reign over us in all prosperity.

TRUSTY
   That her godly proceedings the faith to defend   50
   He may 'stablish and maintain through to the end.

MERRYGREEK
   God grant her, as she doth, the Gospel to protect,
   Learning and virtue to advance and vice to correct.

ROISTER DOISTER
   God grant her loving subjects both the mind and grace
   Her most godly proceedings worthily to embrace.   55

HARPAX
   Her highness' most worthy counsellors God prosper,
   With honour and love of all men to minister.

ALL
   God grant the nobility her to serve and love,
   With all the whole commonty as doth them behove.

AMEN

---

59 *commonty* commons

---

45 s.d. *Here they sing* There seems no good reason not to suppose that the prayer which
   follows is not the song, though some editors have questioned it.
46 *Queen* If, as seems likely, the play was written and performed in 1552 when Edward
   VI was still alive, this reference and the personal pronouns were altered later,
   assuming the prayer was included in the original performance. The queen in
   question is probably Elizabeth, who was reigning when the play was published in
   1566 (see Introduction, p. xxxiii). The text could, in any case, have easily been
   emended, for performance or printing.

The Psalmody

Placebo dilexi
Master Roister Doister will straight go home and die;
Our Lord Jesus Christ his soul have mercy upon.
Thus you see today a man, tomorrow John.

Yet saving for a woman's extreme cruelty,   5
He might have lived yet a month or two or three.
But in spite of Custance, which hath him wearied,
His ma'ship shall be worshipfully buried.
And while some piece of his soul is yet him within,
Some part of his funerals let us here begin.   10

> *Dirige.* He will go darkling to his grave,
> *Neque lux, neque crux, nisi solum* clink.
> Never gent'man so went toward heaven, I think.

Yet, sirs, as ye will the bliss of heaven win,
When he cometh to the grave, lay him softly in.   15
And all men take heed by this one gentleman,
How you set your love upon an unkind woman;
For these women be all such mad, peevish elves,
They will not be won except it please themselves.
But, in faith, Custance, if ever ye come in hell,   20
Master Roister Doister shall serve you as well.

> Good night, Roger, old knave; farewell, Roger,
>   old knave;
> Good night, Roger, old knave, knave, knap.
> *Nequando. Audivi vocem. Requiem aeternam.*

 8 (compare III.iii, 72)
12–13 (compare III.iii, 61–2)
16 (compare III.iii, 77)
24 (compare III.iii, 59, 77, 65 respectively)

The Psalmody. In Q, immediately below AMEN, the following heading is printed:
'Certain songs to be sung by those which shall use this comedy or interlude'. There
follow texts of 'The Second Song' ('Whoso to marry a minion wife'), 'The Fourth
Song' ('I mun be married a Sunday'), 'The Psalmody' and 'The peal of bells rung
by the parish clerk and Roister Doister's four men'. In this edition, all of these have
been inserted in their appropriate places in the text of the play. The appended text
of 'The Psalmody' is given here, however, as it varies somewhat from that printed
in Act III, scene iii in Q.

THE
Old Wiues Tale.

A pleasant conceited Comedie, played by the Queenes Ma-
iesties players.

Written by *G. Peele*

Printed at London by *Iohn Danter* , and are to
be sold by *Raph Hancocke* , and *Iohn*
Hardie. 1 5 9 5 .

[Dramatis Personae

ANTIC
FROLIC } *pages*
FANTASTIC
CLUNCH, *a smith*
MADGE, *an old woman, the smith's wife*   5

FIRST BROTHER (Calypha) } *brothers to Delia*
SECOND BROTHER (Thelea)
OLD MAN *at the cross* (Erestus)
VENELIA, *his betrothed*
LAMPRISCUS   10
HUANEBANGO, *a braggart knight*
BOOBY, *the Clown, his companion and rival*
SACRAPANT, *the Conjurer*
DELIA, *daughter to the King of Thessaly, abducted by Sacrapant*
EUMENIDES, *the Wandering Knight, in love with Delia*   15

1–3 *pages* Based on the reference by Fantastic in ll. 11–12 to 'our young master'.

4 CLUNCH Named at 32, and called 'Smith' in Q speech prefixes. The word means 'a lumpish fellow, clodhopper or boor', but Peele's use of it as a name suggests no more than a rustic or a country fellow. It must have been current by the time the play was written, though the earliest recorded occurrence of the noun in *OED* is 1602 (see C. W. Whitworth, 'Some Words in Two Thomas Lodge Romances (1591–2)', *N&Q*, N.S.24 (1977), 516).

5 MADGE Named by the Smith at 53. Called 'Old Woman' in Q speech prefixes.

6 FIRST BROTHER Named 'Calypha' at 388. This edition retains Q's titles for the two brothers in speech prefixes; their names occur late and almost incidentally, and it is their status as Delia's brothers which identifies them in the play.

7 SECOND BROTHER Not named as 'Thelea' until 853.

8 OLD MAN Called 'Erestus' only at the end of the play (852). His function as a kind of benevolent presiding figure, a counterpart to the evil Sacrapant, is suggested by his namelessness, and this edition retains Q's speech prefixes.

11 HUANEBANGO M.C. Bradbrook thinks 'Juan y Bango' is meant, suggesting a Spanish braggart (*ES*, 43, p. 325). The braggart soldier, or captain, was a familiar character in all European comedy, and was a principal figure in *commedia dell'arte* where he often bore a Spanish name, e.g. 'Sangre y Fuego'.

12 BOOBY So called in Q throughout his first scene (248–325); thereafter called 'Corebus'. This change of name is the source of a major confusion in the play, as one of Jack's friends who try to get the Churchwarden to bury him is also called Corebus. This edition retains the name 'Booby' for Huanebango's companion throughout. He is designated as 'the Clown' at his entrances both as 'Booby' at 248 and as 'Corebus' at 537.

13 SACRAPANT Peele may have taken the name from Ariosto's epic *Orlando Furioso* (Sacrapante) or from Robert Greene's play of the same name, where it is spelled 'Sacripant'.

15 EUMENIDES Possibly from the romantic hero of John Lyly's play *Endymion* (1588).

WIGGEN ⎫ *friends of Jack*
COREBUS ⎭

CHURCHWARDEN (Steven Loach)

SEXTON

ZANTIPPA, *the Curst Daughter* ⎫ *daughters to Lampriscus*   20
CELANTA, *the Foul Wench*   ⎭

A VOICE *in the well*

A HEAD *in the well*

JACK, *a ghost*

HOSTESS   25

Friar, Echo, Two Furies, Harvest-men and women, Fiddlers]

20 *Curst* shrewish

---

18 CHURCHWARDEN So called in stage directions and speech prefixes, except at 447,
   where the s.p. is 'Simon'; this may refer to the name of an actor, John Symons (see
   Chambers, II, 111). He refers to himself as 'Stephen Loach' at 483.

20 ZANTIPPA From 'Xanthippe', name of the shrewish wife of the Greek philosopher
   Socrates.

22-3 A VOICE . . . A HEAD This edition distinguishes between the VOICE, which speaks
   from the well, and the HEAD, which is mute, rising and descending from the well
   with gifts. Q conflates them, using the speech prefix 'Head' at 621, and 'Voice' at
   756.

The Old Wife's Tale

Enter ANTIC, FROLIC *and* FANTASTIC

ANTIC

How now, fellow Frolic! What, all amort? Doth this
sadness become thy madness? What though we have lost
our way in the woods? Yet never hang the head as though
thou hadst no hope to live till tomorrow. For Fantastic
and I will warrant thy life tonight for twenty in   5
the hundred.

FROLIC

Antic and Fantastic, as I am frolic franion, never in all my
life was I so dead slain. What, to lose our way in the wood,
without either fire or candle, so uncomfortable? *O coelum!*
O terra! O maria! O Neptune!   10

FANTASTIC

Why makes thou it so strange, seeing Cupid hath led our
young master to the fair lady, and she is the only saint he
hath sworn to serve?

FROLIC

What resteth then, but we commit him to his wench, and
each of us take his stand up in a tree and sing out our ill   15
fortune to the tune of 'O man in desperation'?

ANTIC

Desperately spoken, fellow Frolic, in the dark; but seeing
it falls out thus, let us rehearse the old proverb:

1 *Frolic* eds. (Franticke Q)
  all amort (Fr., *à la mort;* literally 'mortally sick') dejected, dispirited
5 *warrant ... hundred* lay five-to-one odds against your being killed
7 *franion* gay, reckless fellow
8 *dead slain* exhausted *or* frightened to death
11 *makes ... strange* do you carry on so

9–10 *O coelum ... Neptune* O heaven! O earth! O sea (and/or 'Mary')! O Neptune!
The classical source is Terence's *Adelphoe (The Brothers)*, 1. 790: *'o caelum, o terra, o
maria Neptuni'.* Hook (p. 422n.) notes that it is similarly misquoted in Kyd's
Soliman and Perseda, IV.ii, 67.
12–13 *she ... serve* A parallel is suggested between the action of the play-within where
Eumenides has sworn his love to Delia with whom he is united at last, and that of
the frame, or 'outer' world. This has led some critics to consider *OWT* as an
afterpiece, others to conclude that it was written and played for a marriage feast
(see Introduction, p. xlii).
16 *'O ... desperation'* A popular tune, to which many songs were set.

Three merry men, and three merry men,
And three merry men be we;   20
I in the wood, and thou on the ground,
And Jack sleeps in the tree.

[A dog barks]

FANTASTIC
Hush! A dog in the wood, or a wooden dog! O
comfortable hearing! I had even as lief the chamberlain of
the White Horse had called me up to bed.   25

FROLIC
Either hath this trotting cur gone out of his circuit, or else
are we near some village,

Enter a smith with a lantern and candle

which should not be far off, for I perceive the glimmering
of a glow-worm, a candle, or a cat's eye, my life for a
halfpenny.—In the name of my own father, be thou ox or   30
ass that appearest, tell us what thou art!

CLUNCH
What am I? Why, I am Clunch the smith. What are you?
What make you in my territories at this time of the night?

23 *wooden* (wood) mad
24 *even as lief* just as soon
29–30 *my... halfpenny* (oath)
32 *(and passim)* s.p. CLUNCH eds. (Smith Q)
33 *make you* are you doing

19–22 *Three merry men... in the tree* Another popular song, recorded elsewhere with
the same words sung here. It had its own tune, so was not 'to the tune of "O man in
desperation" '; the pages sing something 'merry' rather than 'desperate', although
in some versions the 'tree' in question is a gallows, as in *Rollo, Duke of Normandy*,
by John Fletcher *et al.* (ed. J.D. Jump, 1948), III.ii. The story is quoted in several
plays of the period and Sir Toby Belch sings the first line in *Twelfth Night* (II.iii,
74); the new Arden and New Penguin editions of that play print the tunes. See also
W. Chappell, *Popular Music of the Olden Time* (1859; repr. 1965), I, 216–18, and
P.J. Seng, *The Vocal Songs in the Plays of Shakespeare* (1967), pp. 101–3.

25 *White Horse* Many London taverns have this name. The reference is probably to
the one in Friday Street, near St. Paul's, frequented by Peele himself, according to
an anecdote in *The Merry Conceited Jests of George Peele* (1607) (ed. Bullen, *The
Works of George Peele* (1888), II, 386).

26 *trotting... circuit* Perhaps an allusion to the use of dogs to work treadmills, or
tread-wheels, to pump water, turn spits, etc. Dromio of Syracuse, in *The Comedy of
Errors*, fears being 'transformed ... to a curtal dog, and made [to] turn i' the wheel'
(III.ii, 144).

ANTIC

What do we make, dost thou ask? Why, we make faces for
fear; such as if thy mortal eye could behold, would make   35
thee water the long seams of thy side slops, smith.

FROLIC

And, in faith, sir, unless your hospitality do relieve us, we
are like to wander with a sorrowful 'heigh-ho' among the
owlets and hobgoblins of the forest. Good Vulcan, for
Cupid's sake that hath cozened us all, befriend us as thou   40
mayest, and command us howsoever, wheresoever, when-
soever, in whatsoever, for ever and ever.

CLUNCH

Well, masters, it seems to me you have lost your way in
the wood. In consideration whereof, if you will go with
Clunch to his cottage, you shall have house-room and a   45
good fire to sit by, although we have no bedding to put
you in.

ALL

O blessed smith, O bountiful Clunch!

CLUNCH

For your further entertainment, it shall be as it may be, so
and so.   50

Hear a dog bark

Hark! This is Ball, my dog, that bids you welcome in his
own language. Come, take heed for stumbling on the
threshold. Open door, Madge; take in guests.

Enter old woman

---

36 *side slops* wide, baggy breeches
40 *cozened* tricked

---

39 *Vulcan* Vulcanus, the Roman name for the Greek god of fire, Hephaestus. He built
palaces for the other Olympian gods and fashioned armour and jewellery from
metal, hence his traditional role as patron of smiths.
49 *it . . . be* Proverbial (Tilley T202): 'Things must be as they may'.
50 s.d. *Hear . . . bark* An example of the authorial stage direction, telling us that the
characters hear something, rather than providing an instruction for the sound to be
made at this point. Some editors emend to 'Here a dog barks'.
52–3 *stumbling . . . threshold* A bad omen.

MADGE
> Welcome, Clunch, and good fellows all, that come with
> my good man. For my good man's sake, come on, sit   55
> down. Here is a piece of cheese and a pudding of my own
> making.

ANTIC
> Thanks, gammer. A good example for the wives of our
> town.

FROLIC
> Gammer, thou and thy good man sit lovingly together.   60
> We come to chat and not to eat.

CLUNCH
> Well, masters, if you will eat nothing, take away. Come,
> what do we to pass away the time? Lay a crab in the fire to
> roast for lamb's-wool. What, shall we have a game at
> trump or ruff to drive away the time? How say you?   65

FANTASTIC
> This smith leads a life as merry as a king with Madge his
> wife. Sirrah Frolic, I am sure thou art not without some
> round or other; no doubt but Clunch can bear his part.

FROLIC
> Else think you me ill brought up! So set to it when you
> will.   70

They sing

Song

> Whenas the rye reach to the chin,
> And chopcherry, chopcherry ripe within,
> Strawberries swimming in the cream,
> And schoolboys playing in the stream.
> Then 'O', then 'O', then 'O' my true love said,   75

54 *(and passim)* s.p. MADGE eds. *(variously,* Ol., Old woman, Old wom., etc. Q)
55 *good man. For* ed. (good man for Q)
63 *crab* crabapple

---

64 *lamb's-wool* A drink consisting of hot ale mixed with the pulp of roasted apples or
crabapples and sugared and spiced.
65 *trump or ruff* Card games similar to but less complicated than whist and bridge, and
popular in the sixteenth century.
71 *Song* No early tune seems to have survived. Benjamin Britten set it to music in his
Spring Symphony (1949).
72 *chopcherry* 'A game in which one tries to catch a suspended cherry with the teeth;
bob-cherry' *(OED)*.

Till that time come again,
She could not live a maid.

ANTIC
This sport does well. But methinks, gammer, a merry
winter's tale would drive away the time trimly. Come, I
am sure you are not without a score.   80

FANTASTIC
I' faith, gammer, a tale of an hour long were as good as an
hour's sleep.

FROLIC
Look you, gammer, of the giant and the king's daughter,
and I know not what. I have seen the day, when I was a
little one, you might have drawn me a mile after you with   85
such a discourse.

MADGE
Well, since you be so importunate, my good man shall fill
the pot and get him to bed. They that ply their work must
keep good hours. One of you go lie with him; he is a
clean-skinned man, I tell you, without either spavin or   90
windgall. So I am content to drive away the time with an
old wife's winter's tale.

FANTASTIC
No better hay in Devonshire. A' my word, gammer, I'll be
one of your audience.

FROLIC
And I another, that's flat.   95

ANTIC
Then must I to bed with the good man. *Bona nox*,
gammer. Good night, Frolic.

92 *wife's* ed. (wives Q)
93 *A'* at, upon
95 *flat* definite
96 *Bona nox* good night
97 *Good* eds. (God Q)

90 *spavin* A hard, bony tumour resulting from inflammation of cartilage joining bones
     in a horse's leg.
91 *windgall* A soft tumour on either side of a horse's leg just above the fetlock.
93 *No . . . Devonshire* Proverbial? (unrecorded). There's no better way to spend our
     time.

CLUNCH

Come on, my lad. Thou shalt take thy unnatural rest with me.

Exeunt ANTIC *and the smith*

FROLIC

Yet this vantage shall we have of them in the morning, to   100
be ready at the sight thereof extempore.

MADGE

Now this bargain, my masters, must I make with you, that
you will say 'hum' and 'ha' to my tale; so shall I know you
are awake.

BOTH

Content, gammer; that will we do.   105

MADGE

Once upon a time, there was a king or a lord or a duke
that had a fair daughter, the fairest that ever was, as white
as snow, and as red as blood; and once upon a time, his
daughter was stolen away, and he sent all his men to seek
out his daughter, and he sent so long that he sent all his   110
men out of his land.

FROLIC

Who dressed his dinner then?

MADGE

Nay, either hear my tale or kiss my tail!

FANTASTIC

Well said! On with your tale, gammer.

MADGE

O Lord, I quite forgot! There was a conjurer, and this   115
conjurer could do anything, and he turned himself into a
great dragon and carried the king's daughter away in his
mouth to a castle that he made of stone, and there he kept
her I know not how long, till at last all the king's men
went out so long that her two brothers went to seek her.   120

112 *dressed* served

---

98 *unnatural* Because a man and a boy are sharing a bed.
99 s.d. *Exeunt... smith* The actors playing these two parts are presumably needed to
 play other roles in the inner play; Madge, Frolic and Fantastic remain onstage as
 audience for the inner play.
100–1 *Yet... extempore* But we shall see the dawn as soon as it appears, unlike those
 who will be asleep.

O, I forget: she—he, I would say—turned a proper young
man in to a bear in the night and a man in the day, and
keeps by a cross that parts three several ways, and he
made his lady run mad. God's me bones! Who comes
here?   125

Enter the two brothers

FROLIC
Soft, gammer, here some come to tell your tale for you.

FANTASTIC
Let them alone; let us hear what they will say.

FIRST BROTHER
Upon these chalky cliffs of Albion
We are arrived now with tedious toil,
And compassing the wide world round about   130
To seek our sister, to seek fair Delia forth,
Yet cannot we so much as hear of her.

SECOND BROTHER
O fortune cruel, cruel and unkind,
Unkind in that we cannot find our sister,
Our hapless sister in her cruel chance—   135
Soft! Who have we here?

Enter the OLD MAN *at the cross, stooping to gather*

124 *God's* ed. (gods Q)
136 s.d *the* OLD MAN ed. (Senex Q)

---

123 *keeps . . . cross* This formulation may lend weight to the suggestion that the Old
Man (Erestus) remains onstage (though perhaps not always visible) at his station,
the cross, throughout the inner play (see below, 234 s.d. and note), and indicates a
feature of the setting ('three several ways'). Madge is not to be relied upon for
consistency or preciseness, however. This passage (115–25) and her previous one
(106–11) set the fairy-tale, 'Once upon a time' atmosphere of her tale, and her
forgetfulness as regards certain details (115, 121) and the imprecise use of
pronouns—'she', 'he' (121, 123), omission of 'he' (123)—enhance the effect. We
do not see Sacrapant's stone castle (118), only a cell or study (326 s.d.), and Madge
neglects to say that Erestus is turned into an *old* man (122).
136 s.d. *Enter . . . gather* The Old Man cannot both 'enter' and be 'at the cross'
simultaneously, of course (see above, 123n.), and 'at the cross' here may be
intended as identification rather than as indicating location. He must, however, get
onstage for the first time, as the inner play begins. A director might want to have
him in place as the brothers enter, especially if he is to be seen as a sort of presiding
figure; 'who comes here' (124–5) and 'here some come' (126) might include him as
well as the brothers. They then become aware of him at 136; compare 294 and see
234n., below.

FIRST BROTHER

Now father, God be your speed. What do you gather there?

OLD MAN

Hips and haws, and sticks and straws, and things that I gather on the ground, my son.   140

FIRST BROTHER

Hips and haws, and sticks and straws! Why, is that all your food, father?

OLD MAN

Yea, son.

SECOND BROTHER

Father, here is an alms-penny for me, and if I speed in that I go for, I will give thee as good a gown of grey as   145 ever thou didst wear.

FIRST BROTHER

And father, here is another alms-penny for me, and if I speed in my journey, I will give thee a palmer's staff of ivory and a scallop shell of beaten gold.

OLD MAN

Was she fair?   150

SECOND BROTHER

Ay, the fairest for white and the purest for red, as the blood of the deer or the driven snow.

---

139 *Hips* fruit of the wild rose
   haws fruit of the hawthorn
144 *alms-penny* penny given for charity
   speed am successful
148 *palmer's* pilgrim's

---

145 *gown of grey* Traditional garb of a pilgrim.
148 *palmer's . . . gold* A pilgrim to the Holy Land brought a palm branch back with him; hence the name 'palmer'. The staff would be simply a walking stick. The scallop shell was a badge or sign, like the palm: pilgrims to the shrine of St. James of Compostella in Spain wore or carried one back with them (whence the French name for scallops, *coquilles Saint Jacques*). Hook (p. 425) quotes Sir Walter Raleigh's poem 'The Passionate Man's Pilgrimage', which mentions staff and shell.
150 *Was she fair?* It is not necessary to assume, as some editors have, that something is omitted in the text just before the Old Man asks this question. He has perhaps overheard the two brothers talking about their sister, or reads their minds, or simply divines the object of their quest.

OLD MAN

Then hark well and mark well my old spell:
  Be not afraid of every stranger,
  Start not aside at every danger;   155
  Things that seem are not the same.
  Blow a blast at every flame;
  For when one flame of fire goes out,
  Then comes your wishes well about.
  If any ask who told you this good,   160
  Say the White Bear of England's wood.

FIRST BROTHER

Brother, heard you not what the old man said?
  'Be not afraid of every stranger,
  Start not aside for every danger;
  Things that seem are not the same.   165
  Blow a blast at every flame;
  [For when one flame of fire goes out,
  Then comes your wishes well about.]
  If any ask who told you this good,
  Say the White Bear of England's wood.'   170

SECOND BROTHER

Well, if this do us any good,
Well fare the White Bear of England's wood!

Exeunt [*the two brothers*]

OLD MAN

Now sit thee here and tell a heavy tale.
Sad in thy mood and sober in thy cheer,
Here sit thee now and to thyself relate   175

---

161 (also 170, 172) *White Bear* eds. (white Beare Q)
167–8 *For... about* eds. (not in Q)
172 s.d. *Exeunt... brothers* eds. (ex. Q)

---

159 *comes* The third person singular verb with a plural noun is common in Elizabethan
    English; some other examples in this play occur at 412, 505 and 660.
161 *White... wood* No heraldic significance has been discovered which would make
    this a reference to a particular person or family. Gummere (p. 345) observes that
    Merlin appears in the form of a bear in the old ballad 'Childe Rowland'.
167–8 Most editors have followed Dyce in supplying these two lines from the Old
    Man's preceding speech (158–9). There is no good reason for the brother to omit
    them when repeating the instructions, and the exact repetition of such charms,
    incantations and the like heightens their portent and serves to fix them in the
    memory, both the characters' and the audience's.

The hard mishap of thy most wretched state.
In Thessaly I lived in sweet content,
Until that Fortune wrought my overthrow;
For there I wedded was unto a dame
That lived in honour, virtue, love and fame.   180
But Sacrapant, that cursed sorcerer,
Being besotted with my beauteous love,
My dearest love, my true betrothed wife,
Did seek the means to rid me of my life.
But worse than this, he with his chanting spells   185
Did turn me straight into an ugly bear;
And when the sun doth settle in the west,
Then I begin to don my ugly hide.
And all the day I sit as now you see,
And speak in riddles, all inspired with rage,   190
Seeming an old and miserable man;
And yet I am in April of my age.

Enter VENELIA *his lady, mad; and goes in again*

See where Venelia, my betrothed love,
Runs madding all enraged about the woods,
All by his cursed and enchanting spells.   195

Enter LAMPRISCUS *with a pot of honey*

But here comes Lampriscus, my discontented neighbour.—
How now, neighbour? You look toward the ground as well as I.
You muse on something.

---

190 *rage* prophetic inspiration

---

177 *Thessaly* A division of ancient Greece, on the eastern (Aegean) side, now part of
Macedonia. Hook cites Apuleius, *The Golden Ass* (second century A.D.), whose
narrator says: 'I was very desirous to know and see some marvellous and strange
things, remembering with myself that I was in the midst parts of all Thessaly,
where, by the common report of all the world, is the birthplace of sorceries and
enchantments' (Loeb edition, p. 49).
179 *wedded* There is no need to worry unduly about the apparent impreciseness in the
Old Man's account of his relationship with Venelia: *wedded . . . betrothed wife*
(183) . . . *betrothed love* (193). Her status is similar to that of Juliet and, later,
Mariana in *Measure for Measure*, where the latter is referred to by the Duke as
'neither maid, widow nor wife' (V.i, 178). Venelia is 'neither wife, widow nor maid'
(417), and is thus the one who will break Sacrapant's glass, destroying his power.
192 *April . . . age* The cliché is repeated at 654 and 675. Youth and old age, actual and
apparent, are a major motif in the play, one of several aspects of the central truth-
and-illusion theme.

LAMPRISCUS

Neighbour, on nothing but on the matter I so often
moved to you. If you do anything for charity, help me; if   200
for neighbourhood or brotherhood, help me. Never was
one so cumbered as is poor Lampriscus. And to begin, I
pray, receive this pot of honey to mend your fare.

OLD MAN

Thanks, neighbour, set it down. [*Aside*] Honey is always
welcome to the bear.—And now, neighbour, let me hear   205
the cause of your coming.

LAMPRISCUS

I am, as you know, neighbour, a man unmarried, and
lived so unquietly with my two wives that I keep every
year holy the day wherein I buried them both. The first
was on Saint Andrew's Day, the other on Saint Luke's.   210

OLD MAN

And now, neighbour, you of this country say, your
custom is out. But on with your tale, neighbour.

LAMPRISCUS

By my first wife, whose tongue wearied me alive, and
sounded in my ears like the clapper of a great bell, whose
talk was a continual torment to all that dwelt by her or   215

200 *moved* spoke about
202 *cumbered* encumbered, burdened
203 *mend your fare* improve your diet
204 s.d. *Aside* Binnie
211 *this country* (i.e., England)
212 *custom* obligatory service, as to a feudal master
    out over, done
213 *alive* when she was alive

204–5 *Honey... bear* This looks as if it may be a line of verse in Q; Binnie prints it as
     one in view of its 'gnomic flavour'. But Q's arrangement may be meant to indicate
     only that the line is spoken aside. Bears' taste for honey is recognized in proverbs,
     e.g. Tilley B130 and H551.
210 *Saint Andrew's... Saint Luke's* November 30th and October 18th, respectively.
     Both days were traditionally believed to be propitious for choosing a husband
     and/or discovering the identity of a future spouse. In *Measure for Measure*, the
     'dejected Mariana', who is to be reunited with her betrothed who had abandoned
     her, resides at Saint Luke's. Hook notes (p. 426) that St. Luke was patron of
     horned creatures (from his symbol, a winged ox), including cuckolds, an ironic
     association in view of his feast day's supposed propitiousness where lovers and their
     desires were concerned. Lampriscus's good luck was to have buried his two
     insupportable wives on these favourable days.

lived nigh her, you have heard me say I had a handsome daughter.

OLD MAN
True, neighbour.

LAMPRISCUS
She it is that afflicts me with her continual clamours and hangs on me like a bur. Poor she is, and proud she is; as 220 poor as a sheep new-shorn, and as proud of her hopes as a peacock of her tail well-grown.

OLD MAN
Well said, Lampriscus! You speak it like an Englishman.

LAMPRISCUS
As curst as a wasp, and as froward as a child new-taken from the mother's teat. She is to my age as smoke to the 225 eyes, or as vinegar to the teeth.

OLD MAN
Holily praised, neighbour. As much for the next.

LAMPRISCUS
By my other wife I had a daughter, so hard-favoured, so foul and ill-faced, that I think a grove full of golden trees, and the leaves of rubies and diamonds, would not be a 230 dowry answerable to her deformity.

OLD MAN
Well, neighbour, now you have spoke, hear me speak.

---

224 *curst* shrewish, ill-tempered
   froward refractory

---

220 *hangs... bur* Proverbial (Tilley B723).
   Poor... proud Proverbial (Tilley, P474, P475): 'Poor and proud...'. Poverty and pride are linked in many other proverbs, e.g. Tilley P572, P577, P579, P580; and *ODEP:* 'A proud beggar that makes his own alms'.
220–1 *as poor... new-shorn* Proverbial (Tilley S295): 'As rich as a new-shorn sheep' (used ironically); *ODEP* cites this line from *OWT*, but Tilley does not.
221–2 *as proud... tail* Proverbial (Tilley P157). 'Her' is the wrong pronoun for the pea*cock*, the male, but the pea*hen* does not have a fine tail.
224 *As... wasp* Proverbial (Tilley W76): 'As angry as a wasp'.
225–6 *as smoke... teeth* Scriptural: 'As vinegar to the teeth, and as smoke to the eyes, so is the sluggard to them that send him' (Proverbs 10:26). This explains the Old Man's comment 'Holily praised' in the next line.

Send them to the well for the water of life; there shall they
find their fortunes unlooked for. Neighbour, farewell.

[*Withdraws*]

LAMPRISCUS
Farewell and a thousand! And now goeth poor Lampris- 235
cus to put in execution this excellent counsel.

Exit

FROLIC
Why, this goes round without a fiddling stick. But do you
hear, gammer, was this the man that was a bear in the
night and a man in the day?

MADGE
Ay, this is he; and this man that came to him was a beggar 240
and dwelt upon a green. But soft, who comes here? O,
these are the harvest-men. Ten to one, they sing a song of
mowing.

Enter the Harvest-men a-singing, with this song double repeated

All ye that lovely lovers be, pray you for me.
Lo, here we come a-sowing, a-sowing,   245

---

234 s.d. *Withdraws* Binnie (Exit Q)
235 *Farewell ... thousand* a thousand times farewell
236 s.d. *Exit* eds. (Exeunt Q)
243 s.d. *double repeated* (a pleonasm) repeated

---

233 *well ... water of life* Possibly an echo of the story of Jesus and the Samaritan woman
at Jacob's Well (John 4:5–26), in which he speaks to her of 'living water' (v. 10)
and 'a well of water springing up into everlasting life' (v. 14).
234 s.d. I follow Binnie's suggestion that the Old Man does not actually leave the stage.
At 294–5, Booby says 'Soft, here is an old man at the cross', and no entrance is
marked, implying that he has been there at the cross and is only then noticed by
Booby, or perhaps emerges from his hut by the cross. See 123 n. and 136 n., above.
237 *this ... stick* This tale is moving along rapidly, even without the help of a musical
accompaniment. The expression may be proverbial; Hook cites 'The devil rides on
a fiddlestick' (Tilley D263).
242–3 *Ten ... mowing* Madge would lose her bet, logical though it is: the Harvest-men's
song is of sowing. Although a misprint is possible, the juxtaposition of spring and
autumn activities in rural festivals was common (Hook, pp. 427–8). The sudden,
unrelated appearance of the Harvest-men with their song is simply part of the
dream-like fantasy quality of the play; Madge has no control over who or what may
intrude into her 'tale'.

And sow sweet fruits of love:
In your sweethearts well may it prove.

Exeunt [Harvest-men]

Enter HUANEBANGO *with his two-hand sword, and* BOOBY *the Clown*

FANTASTIC
Gammer, what is he?

MADGE
O, this is one that is going to the conjurer. Let him alone;
hear what he says.   250

HUANEBANGO
Now by Mars and Mercury, Jupiter and Janus, Sol and
Saturnus, Venus and Vesta, Pallas and Proserpina, and by
the honour of my house Polimackeroeplacidus, it is a
wonder to see what this love will make silly fellows
adventure, even in the wane of their wits and and infancy   255
of their discretion. Alas, my friend, what fortune calls
thee forth to seek thy fortune among brazen gates,
enchanted towers, fire and brimstone, thunder and
lightning? Beauty, I tell thee, is peerless, and she precious
whom thou affectest. Do off these desires, good country-   260
man; good friend, run away from thyself, and so soon as
thou canst, forget her whom none must inherit but he
that can monsters tame, labours achieve, riddles absolve,
loose enchantments, murder magic, and kill conjuring
—and that is the great and mighty Huanebango!   265

BOOBY
Hark you, sir, hark you. First, know I have here the

256 *my friend* i.e., Booby (?)
260 *affectest* love; seek to obtain
263 *absolve* solve
266 *here* i.e., in his hat

---

247 s.d. *two-hand sword* A two-hand sword, long, heavy and obsolete in the sixteenth
century, was the standard weapon for braggarts and bullies and for giants and other
performers in mummings and pageants. References in the accounts for Midsummer
and Lord Mayor's shows to this essential property are frequent (see MSC, III
(1954), e.g. pp. 17, 23, 24, 29, 65). Because of its obsoleteness, it was also the
weapon ascribed, humorously or insultingly, to old men, as in *2 Henry VI*, II.i, 46
and *Romeo and Juliet*, I.i, 73–4.
253 *Polimackeroeplacidus* The name is borrowed from Plautus's *Pseudolus;* the person so
named (Polymachaeroplagides) does not appear, but is mentioned. He is the
master of Harpax, whose name Udall borrowed in *RD*.

flirting feather, and have given the parish the start for the long stock. Now, sir, if it be no more but running through a little lightning and thunder, and 'Riddle me, riddle me, what's this?', I'll have the wench from the conjurer if he 270 were ten conjurers.

HUANEBANGO

I have abandoned the court and honourable company, to do my devoir against this sore sorcerer and mighty magician. If this lady be so fair as she is said to be, she is mine, she is mine! *Meus, mea, meum, in contemptum* 275 *omnium grammaticorum.*

BOOBY

O falsum Latinum! The fair maid is *minum, cum apurti-nantibus gibletes* and all.

HUANEBANGO

If she be mine, as I assure myself the heavens will do somewhat to reward my worthiness, she shall be allied to 280 none of the meanest gods, but be invested in the most famous stock of Huanebango Polimackeroeplacidus, my grandfather; my father, Pergopolineo; my mother, Dio-nora de Sardinia, famously descended—

---

267 *flirting* ed. (flurting Q) tossing, waving jauntily
273 *devoir* duty (Fr.)

267-8 *have...stock* Have startled the whole parish (or, perhaps, got ahead of them where fashion is concerned) with my long stockings. Booby is showing off his clothes, which may be not quite of the latest fashion, despite his boast. As the clown, he is identified by his outlandish dress, as Huanebango is identified by his outlandish speech and manners. For a resumé of various interpretations of *stock*, see Hook, p. 428. *OED* gives no example of 'give a (the) start to' as 'startle' before the nineteenth century. Compare 'got the start of you' at 615-16.

275-6 *Meus...grammaticorum* 'Mine, mine, mine, in disregard of all grammars'. Huanebango uses all three Latin genders (masculine, feminine, neuter) to refer to his lady, to whom, of course, only the feminine is appropriate.

277 *O...minum* Booby's Latin is also false; *minum* is nonsense. Dyce arranged these lines as verse and was followed by other editors. But internal rhymes occur in other prose passages in Q (e.g. 139, 153).

277-8 *cum...gibletes* More nonsense. *Cum appertinentibus* (or *pertinentiis*) was a legal phrase, meaning 'with its appurtenances'; *gibletes* (presumably 'giblets') was 'corrected' by Dyce to *gibletis*, and some other editors have followed him.

283 *Pergopolineo* Another Plautine name. Pyrgopolynices is the braggart soldier of *Miles Gloriosus.*

283-4 *Dionora de Sardinia* Untraced. Perhaps just another exotic-sounding name, invented by Peele.

BOOBY

Do you hear, sir? Had not you a cousin that was called 285
Gusteceridis?

HUANEBANGO

Indeed I had a cousin that sometime followed the court
infortunately, and his name, Bustegusteceridis.

BOOBY

O Lord, I know him well! He is the Knight of the Neat's
Feet. 290

HUANEBANGO

O, he loved no capon better. He hath oftentimes deceived
his boy of his dinner. That was his fault, good Bustegusteceridis.

BOOBY

Come, shall we go along? Soft, here is an old man at the
cross. Let us ask him the way thither.—Ho you, gaffer! I 295
pray you tell where the wise man, the conjurer, dwells.

HUANEBANGO

Where that earthly goddess keepeth her abode, the
commander of my thoughts, and fair mistress of my heart.

OLD MAN

Fair enough, and far enough from thy fingering, son.

HUANEBANGO

I will follow my fortune after mine own fancy, and do 300
according to mine own discretion.

OLD MAN

Yet give something to an old man before you go.

---

288 *infortunately* without success
292 *boy* page, servant
295 *you, gaffer* ed. (you gaffer Q, eds.)

---

286 *Gusteceridis* This and the longer name at 288 are Peele's versions of such Plautine
monstrosities as 'Bumbomachides Clutomistaridysarchides', mentioned by Pyrgopolynices near the beginning of *Miles Gloriosus* (I,14).

289–90 *Knight... Feet* Neat's, or ox's, feet were scraps, used to make brawn. Binnie
suggests something like 'Knight of the Leftovers' as conveying the meaning of the
epithet. In the light of Huanebango's next speech, Hook's comment that the cousin
was 'a noble trencherman' is obviously accurate.

294–5 *Soft... cross* See note on 234, above. Editors who retain Q's exit for the Old Man
at 234 are obliged to provide an entrance here.

HUANEBANGO

Father, methinks a piece of this cake might serve your turn.

OLD MAN

Yea, son.   305

HUANEBANGO

Huanebango giveth no cakes for alms; ask of them that give gifts for poor beggars.—Fair lady, if thou wert once shrined in this bosom, I would buckler thee! Haratantara!

Exit

BOOBY

Father, do you see this man? You little think he'll run a mile or two for such a cake, or pass for a pudding. I tell   310 you, father, he has kept such a begging of me for a piece of this cake! Whoo! He comes upon me with a 'superfantial substance and the foison of the earth', that I know not what he means. If he came to me thus, and said 'My friend Booby' or so, why I could spare him a piece, with   315 all my heart. But when he tells me how God hath enriched me above other fellows with a cake, why, he makes me blind and deaf at once! Yet, father, here is a piece of cake for you, as hard as the world goes.

308 *buckler* shield, protect
     thee! Haratantara! Binnie (thee haratantara Q)
310 *pass for* care for
312–13 a *'superfantial... earth'* McIlwraith (*quotation marks*)
313 *foison* plentiful harvest
319 *as... goes* even though times are hard

312–13 *superfantial... earth* Booby is imitating Huanebango's bombast. As McIlwraith notes, *OED*, like Booby, is ignorant of 'superfantial'. As it stands it is sheer nonsense, and that is sufficient in the context, whether Booby is correctly quoting or misquoting Huanebango. It is just possible, however, that Peele wrote 'superstantial'; a compositor might have misread a manuscript 'st' as 'f' (especially with so many other 's's', 'st's' and 'f's' in the immediate vicinity). Two medieval Latin philosophical terms, *superstantia* and *supersubstantia*, meant, respectively, 'formally (but not physically) existent' and 'transcending substance'. Thus 'superstantial substance' would be *clever* nonsense: it would be literally self-contradictory. It would thus also continue the Latin wordplay of 275–8, and it *sounds* as if it means 'super-abundance', i.e. 'foison'.

318 *blind... once* Booby, speaking figuratively of the effect upon him of Huanebango's verbal barrage, anticipates the fate pronounced by the Old Man a few lines later.

OLD MAN

Thanks, son, but list to me: 320
He shall be deaf when thou shalt not see.
Farewell, my son; things may so hit,
Thou mayst have wealth to mend thy wit.

BOOBY

Farewell, father, farewell, for I must make haste after my
two-hand sword that is gone before.   325

[*Exit* BOOBY. OLD MAN *withdraws*]

Enter SACRAPANT *in his study*

SACRAPANT

The day is clear, the welkin bright and gray,
The lark is merry and records her notes;
Each thing rejoiceth underneath the sky,
But only I whom heaven hath in hate,
Wretched and miserable Sacrapant.   330
In Thessaly was I born and brought up;
My mother Meroe hight, a famous witch,
And by her cunning I of her did learn
To change and alter shapes of mortal men.
There did I turn myself into a dragon,   335

325 s.d. *Exit . . . withdraws* ed. (Exeunt omnes Q)
326 *welkin* sky
329 *But only* except
332 *hight* is called

---

325 s.d. *withdraws* Again, the decision whether to leave the Old Man onstage or not is
one that a director must make. His 'exit' might, in any case, be into a hut or hovel,
his 'station' near the cross, and thus not really 'off'. This edition repeats 'withdraws'
here for consistency's sake. See notes on 136, 234 and 294–5 above, and 419 below.
s.d. *Enter . . . study* This probably means that a curtain is drawn, revealing
Sacrapant already 'in his study'. Compare, for example, Marlowe's *Doctor Faustus*,
I.i ('Enter Faustus in his study' (A-text, 1604, only)) and *The Jew of Malta*, I.i
('Enter Barabas in his counting-house'). The study is also referred to as a 'cell'
(614 s.d.). This may be the so-called 'discovery-space', of the Elizabethan public
theatre, a recessed area at the rear of the stage which could be curtained off, or a
portable curtained booth, set up for productions in which it was needed. A curtain
is drawn later to reveal the sleeping Delia (822 s.d.), and the two brothers propose
to 'enter' (402). See the discussion of staging in the Introduction, p. 1vi.
326 *gray* Q's spelling; some eds. emend to *grey*, though *OED* states that both forms have
equal weight. It seems to mean here 'blue', or 'bluish', and not 'overcast' or 'dull'.
332 *Meroe* According to *The Golden Ass* (Loeb edn., pp. 13–35), a Thessalonian witch
who specialized in changing men into beasts. Hook (p. 337) notes that only
Apuleius and Peele ascribe the name to a woman; elsewhere, Meroe is an island in
the Nile in Ethiopia.

And stole away the daughter to the king,
Fair Delia, the mistress of my heart,
And brought her hither to revive the man
That seemeth young and pleasant to behold,
And yet is aged, crooked, weak and numb.   340
Thus by enchanting spells I do deceive
Those that behold and look upon my face;
But well may I bid youthful years adieu.

Enter DELIA *with a pot in her hand*

See where she comes from whence my sorrows grow.—
How now, fair Delia, where have you been?   345

DELIA
At the foot of the rock for running water, and gathering
roots for your dinner, sir.

SACRAPANT
Ah, Delia, fairer art thou than the running water, yet
harder far than steel or adamant.

DELIA
Will it please you to sit down, sir?   350

SACRAPANT
Ay, Delia, sit and ask me what thou wilt. Thou shalt have
it brought into thy lap.

DELIA
Then I pray you, sir, let me have the best meat from the
king of England's table, and the best wine in all France,
brought in by the veriest knave in all Spain.   355

SACRAPANT
Delia, I am glad to see you so pleasant. Well, sit thee
down.
Spread, table, spread; meat, drink and bread.
Ever may I have what I ever crave,
When I am spread, for meat for my black cock,   360
And meat for my red.

Enter a Friar with a chine of beef and a pot of wine

355 *veriest* most extreme, worst
361 s.d. *chine of beef* part of the backbone

338–43 *the man ... adieu* Sacrapant is thus in the opposite case to that to which he has
    condemned Erestus, who is young but appears old (189–92). Jack explains at the
    end (846–50).
344 *sorrows* Because his love for her is unrequited.

SACRAPANT
Here, Delia; will ye fall to?

DELIA
Is this the best meat in England?

SACRAPANT
Yea.

DELIA
What is it?   365

SACRAPANT
A chine of English beef, meat for a king and a king's
followers.

DELIA
Is this the best wine in France?

SACRAPANT
Yea.

DELIA
What wine is it?   370

SACRAPANT
A cup of neat wine of Orleans, that never came near the
brewers in England.

DELIA
Is this the veriest knave in all Spain?

SACRAPANT
Yea.

DELIA
What is he? A friar?   375

SACRAPANT
Yea, a friar indefinite and a knave infinite.

362 *fall to* begin eating
371 *neat* undiluted

---

371 *Orleans* On the Loire River, whose valley is one of the major wine-producing
    regions in France.
372 *brewers* Dealers who bought wine and diluted or mixed it before selling it.
376 *friar indefinite* Perhaps a friar of no particular order (Dominican, Franciscan,
    Carmelite, etc.), or, as Hook suggests (p. 431), the opposite of a 'limiter' like
    Chaucer's friar in *The Canterbury Tales* (I, 209), who had a license to beg in a
    particular area only. Or merely a play on words.

DELIA
  Then I pray ye, sir friar, tell me before you go: which is
  the most greediest Englishman?

FRIAR
  The miserable and most covetous usurer.

SACRAPANT
  Hold thee there, friar!   380

                                          Exit FRIAR

  But soft, who have we here? Delia, away, begone!

                    Enter the two brothers

  Delia, away, for beset are we!
  But heaven or hell shall rescue her for me!

                    [*Exeunt* SACRAPANT *and* DELIA]

FIRST BROTHER
  Brother, was not that Delia did appear?
  Or was it but her shadow that was here?   385

SECOND BROTHER
  Sister, where art thou? Delia, come again!
  He calls, that of thy absence doth complain.
  Call out, Calypha, that she may hear,
  And cry aloud, for Delia is near.

ECHO
  Near.   390

380 *Hold thee there* stick to that opinion
383 *But . . . me* neither heaven nor hell shall rescue her if I can prevent it
     s.d. *Exeunt . . .* DELIA eds.

---

378 *most greediest* The double superlative is a common Elizabethan form. Compare, e.g.,
     'the most unkindest cut of all' (*Julius Caesar*, III.ii, 183).
383 s.d. Sacrapant and Delia clearly go out here, since the former re-enters at 403 and
     Delia is not seen again until 560. They would doubtless retreat into the study or
     cell, wherever it is located and whatever form it has; see 325 s.d., note.
388 *Calypha* The first time the First Brother is named. See Dramatis Personae, 6n.
390–6 The echo device was popular in Elizabethan drama. Earlier examples than this
     are in Thomas Lodge's *The Wounds of Civil War* (c. 1587) and Robert Wilson's *The
     Cobbler's Prophecy* (c. 1590), a play that may have influenced Peele (see
     Bradbrook, *ES*, 43 (1962), pp. 325–6). In Wilson's play, the echo is 'artificial' and
     leads the person who hears it astray (ed. W. W. Greg, MSR (1914), 11.502–22).
     Likewise, this echo which seems to be helpful, is not; it leads the brothers into
     danger. The lines would be most effective if seen to be spoken by Sacrapant, from
     hiding; the brothers would think it an echo, the audience would know better. It
     indicates 'this' way, i.e., toward Sacrapant's cell.

FIRST BROTHER
Near! Oh, where? Hast thou any tidings?

ECHO
Tidings.

SECOND BROTHER
Which way is Delia then? Or that, or this?

ECHO
This.

FIRST BROTHER
And may we safely come where Delia is?   395

ECHO
Yes.

SECOND BROTHER
Brother, remember you the White Bear of England's
wood:
   'Start not aside for every danger,
   Be not afeared of every stranger;   400
   Things that seem are not the same.'

FIRST BROTHER
Brother, why do we not then courageously enter?

SECOND BROTHER
Then, brother, draw thy sword and follow me.

Enter the Conjurer; it lightens and thunders. The SECOND BROTHER
falls down

FIRST BROTHER
What, brother, dost thou fall?

SACRAPANT
Ay, and thou too, Calypha.   405

Fall FIRST BROTHER. *Enter two Furies*

399–401 *'Start . . . same'* The Second Brother misremembers slightly; see 154–6.
403 s.d. *Enter . . . Conjurer* Peele reverts to Sacrapant's function here; it is as conjurer
    that he will now act.
405 *Calypha* Sacrapant has presumably overheard the brothers' conversation from his
    hiding place; the Second Brother called Calypha by name at 388.

Adeste Daemones! Away with them!
Go carry them straight to Sacrapanto's cell,
There in despair and torture for to dwell.
                    [*Exeunt Furies with the two brothers*]

These are Thenore's sons of Thessaly,
That come to seek Delia their sister forth.   410
But with a potion I to her have given,
My arts hath made her to forget herself.

He removes a turf, and shows a light in a glass

See here the thing which doth prolong my life.
With this enchantment I do anything.
And till this fade, my skill shall still endure;   415
And never none shall break this little glass,
But she that's neither wife, widow nor maid.
Then cheer thyself; this is thy destiny,
Never to die but by a dead man's hand.

                                              Exit

Enter EUMENIDES, *the Wandering Knight, and the*
            OLD MAN *at the cross*

EUMENIDES
Tell me, Time, tell me, just Time,   420
When shall I Delia see?
When shall I see the lodestar of my life?
When shall my wandering course end with her sight,
Or I but view my hope, my heart's delight?—
[*Sees* OLD MAN] Father, God speed! If you tell fortunes, I 425
pray, good father, tell me mine.

406 Adeste eds. (Adestes Q) come forth, attend
    Daemones spirits
408 s.d. *Exeunt . . . brothers* eds. (no s.d. in Q)
412 *arts hath* (see 159 n.)
419 s.d. *Exit* eds. (Exeunt Q)
422 *lodestar* guiding light

---

419 s.d. *Exit* Q's *Exeunt* includes the Furies and the brothers. But editors since Dyce
    have sent them off after 408, as Sacrapant's speech (409–19) seems to be addressed
    to the audience, and the Furies have been sent away at 406–7.
    s.d. *Enter . . . cross* If the Old Man has withdrawn to the cross or into a hut at 325
    (see note), he enters, or comes forward, from there. Eumenides then sees him at
    425 (compare 294–5).

OLD MAN

   Son, I do see in thy face
   Thy blessed fortune work apace.
   I do perceive that thou hast wit;
   Beg of thy fate to govern it,   430
   For wisdom governed by advice
   Makes many fortunate and wise.
   Bestow thy alms, give more than all,
   Till dead men's bones come at thy call.
   Farewell, my son; dream of no rest,   435
   Till thou repent that thou didst best.

                                  [Withdraws]

EUMENIDES

   This man hath left me in a labyrinth:
   He biddeth me give more than all,
   'Till dead men's bones come at thy call'.
   He biddeth me dream of no rest,   440
   Till I repent that I do best.   *[Lies down and sleeps]*

     Enter WIGGEN, COREBUS, CHURCHWARDEN *and* SEXTON

WIGGEN

You may be ashamed, you whoreson scald sexton and
churchwarden, if you had any shame in those shameless
faces of yours, to let a poor man lie so long above ground
unburied! A rot on you all, that have no more compassion 445
of a good fellow when he is gone!

CHURCHWARDEN

What, would you have us to bury him, and to answer it
ourselves to the parish?

---

431 *advice* ed. (advise Q)
436 s.d. *Withdraws* ed. (Exit Old m. Q)
439 *'Till . . . call'* (quotation marks) Bullen
441 s.d. *Lies . . . sleeps* eds.
      s.d. COREBUS eds. (Corobus Q)
442 *scald* scurvy, contemptible
447 s.p. CHURCHWARDEN eds. (Simon Q; see Dramatis Personae, 18n.)
447–8 *answer . . . parish* pay the fee (for burial) to the parish treasury out of our own
      pockets

---

441 s.d. *Lies . . . sleeps* Despite the fact that it contradicts the Old Man's injunction to
     'dream of no rest', repeated by Eumenides, this seems to be required by Q's
     direction at 466: 'Eumenides awakes . . .'.

SEXTON

Parish me no parishes! Pay me my fees and let the rest run
on in the quarter's accounts, and put it down for one of 450
your good deeds, a' God's name, for I am not one that
curiously stands upon merits.

COREBUS

You whoreson sodden-headed sheep's face! Shall a good
fellow do less service and more honesty to the parish, and
will you not when he is dead let him have Christmas 455
burial?

WIGGEN

Peace, Corebus! As sure as Jack was Jack, the frolic'st
franion amongst you, and I, Wiggen, his sweet sworn
brother, Jack shall have his funerals, or some of them
shall lie on God's dear earth for it, that's once! 460

CHURCHWARDEN

Wiggen, I hope thou wilt do no more than thou darest
answer.

WIGGEN [*Beats* CHURCHWARDEN]

Sir, sir, dare or dare not, more or less, answer or not
answer, do this, or have this!

SEXTON

Help, help, help! Wiggen sets upon the parish with a 465
pikestaff!

452 *curiously* fastidiously
453 s.p. COREBUS eds. (Corobus Q)
455 *Christmas* Christian (a malapropism)
460 *once* final, certain

449–52 *Pay . . . merits* The sexton is saying that as long as he receives his own fee for
burying Jack, he doesn't mind if the other costs are borne by the parish ('one of
your good deeds') out of existing funds; he isn't 'particular' about anything—
except his fee.
454 *less . . . honesty* Corebus means *more* service. Such confusions and malapropisms as
well as vivid epithets are characteristics of his speech.
463–4 The rhythm of the speech suggests the action of the beating that Wiggen is
administering. The sexton's next speech confirms that this action has been going on
during Wiggen's speech.
465–6 *Wiggen . . . pikestaff* Some editors (but not Gummere, McIlwraith, Hook,
Binnie) have followed Dyce in making this a stage direction.
465 *parish* From the context, the churchwarden would seem to be meant; he is the
representative of the parish. *OED* records no such usage of the word. The sexton is
unlikely to be referring to himself in the third person. Brooke and Paradise assume
that *both* officers are being referred to, but Wiggen's 'Sir, sir' and Corebus's 'this
shake-rotten parish' (468–9) sound like the singular. Elsewhere, *parish* is given its
common meaning.

EUMENIDES *awakes and comes to them*

EUMENIDES [*To* WIGGEN]
Hold thy hands, good fellow.

COREBUS
Can you blame him, sir, if he take Jack's part against this shake-rotten parish that will not bury Jack?

EUMENIDES
Why, what was that Jack?   470

COREBUS
Who, Jack, sir? Who, our Jack, sir? As good a fellow as ever trod upon neat's leather.

WIGGEN
Look you, sir: he gave fourscore and nineteen mourning gowns to the parish when he died, and because he would not make them up a full hundred they would not bury   475
him. Was this not good dealing?

CHURCHWARDEN
O Lord, sir, how he lies! He was not worth a halfpenny, and drunk out every penny; and now his fellows, his drunken companions, would have us to bury him at the charge of the parish. And we make many such matches,   480
we may pull down the steeple, sell the bells, and thatch the chancel. He shall lie above ground till he dance a galliard about the churchyard, for Steven Loach!

469 *shake-rotten* (term of abuse; *OED*'s only example)
472 *neat* cow, ox
     neat's leather shoes
480 *And* if
483 *galliard* quick, lively dance
     for . . . Loach as far as I'm concerned

473–4 *mourning gowns* In which to dress poor members of the parish who would walk in the funeral procession as official mourners.
481–2 *thatch the chancel* To replace the lead or slate roof sold, with the bell, to raise money.
483 *Steven Loach* The Churchwarden's own name; confirmed by Wiggen's address to him in the next line. See Dramatis Personae, 18n. A loach is a small, barbelled freshwater fish; the Churchwarden's name may connote his appearance. The word is used figuratively (e.g., in *The Merry Conceited Jests of George Peele*) for 'simpleton'.

WIGGEN

Sic argumentaris, domine Loach: 'And we make many such
matches, we may pull down the steeple, sell the bells, and   485
thatch the chancel.' In good time, sir, and hang yourselves
in the bell-ropes when you have done! *Domine, opponens
praepono tibi hanc questionem:* whether will you have the
ground broken or your pates broken first? For one of
them shall be done presently, and to begin mine, I'll seal   490
it upon your coxcomb!

EUMENIDES

Hold thy hands! I pray thee, good fellow, be not too hasty.

COREBUS [*To* CHURCHWARDEN]

You capon's face! We shall have you turned out of the
parish one of these days with never a tatter to your arse.
Then you are in worse taking than Jack.   495

EUMENIDES

Faith, and he is bad enough. [*To* CHURCHWARDEN *and*
SEXTON] This fellow does but the part of a friend, to seek
to bury his friend. How much will bury him?

WIGGEN

Faith, about some fifteen or sixteen shillings will bestow
him honestly.   500

SEXTON

Ay, even thereabouts, sir.

EUMENIDES

Here, hold it then. [*Aside*] And I have left me but one
poor three half-pence. Now do I remember the words the
old man spake at the cross: 'Bestow all thou hast'—and

---

484 *Sic ... Loach* Thus you argue, Master Loach
487–8 *Domine ... questionem* Sir, in opposition, I propose to you this question
489 *broken first? For* eds. (broken: first, for Q)
490 *presently* immediately
     to begin mine to implement my preference
491 *coxcomb* head
495 *taking* condition
499 *bestow* dispose of, provide for
502 *hold it* take it
504–6 *'Bestow ... call'* (*prose* Q) (*verse* Hook, Binnie) (*quotation marks* eds.)

---

484 *Sic ... Loach; Domine ... questionem* Formulae from formal disputation, still an
    obligatory part of university education in Peele's day.
503 *three half-pence* An Elizabethan silver coin worth one-and-a-half pence.

this is all—'till dead men's bones comes at thy 505
call'.—Here, hold it, and so farewell.

[Exit]

WIGGEN

God and all good be with you, sir.—Nay, you cormorants,
I'll bestow one peal of Jack at mine own proper costs and
charges.

COREBUS

You may thank God the long staff and the bilbo-blade 510
crossed not your coxcomb. Well, we'll to the church stile
and have a pot and so, trill-lill.

BOTH

Come, let's go.   *Exeunt*

FANTASTIC

But, hark you, gammer, methinks this Jack bore a great
sway in the parish.   515

MADGE

O, this Jack was a marvellous fellow! He was but a poor
man, but very well beloved. You shall see anon what this
Jack will come to.

Enter the Harvest-men singing, with women in their hands

---

505 *bones comes* (see 159 n.)
506 s.d. *Exit* ed. (no s.d. in Q)
507 *cormorants* large, voracious sea birds; hence, greedy persons
508 *bestow . . . Jack* pay for a peal of bells to be rung in Jack's memory
510 *bilbo-blade* eds. (bilbowe blade Q)
512 *trill-lill* (sound of drink flowing down the throat)
513 s.p. BOTH (i.e., Wiggen and Corebus)
518 s.d. *in . . . hands* hand in hand

---

510 *bilbo-blade* A sword from Bilbao in northern Spain, highly prized for its temper;
      generally any sword.
511–12 *church stile . . . pot* The church and the alehouse, focal points of social life, were
      often in close proximity, as Sir Thomas Overbury observed in his sketch of 'A
      Sexton' in *Characters* (1616): 'He could willingly all his life time be confinde to the
      church-yard; at least within five foot on't: for at every church stile, commonly ther's
      an ale-house' (*Works*, ed. E. F. Rimbault (1856; repr. 1890), p.145).
513 s.d. *Exeunt* Wiggen and Corebus would go out together, and the Churchwarden
      and the Sexton would follow, or go out a different way, perhaps 'counting the
      money that has come in so unexpectedly' (Hook, p. 435).

FROLIC
Soft, who have we here? Our amorous harvesters.

FANTASTIC
Ay, ay; let us sit still and let them alone.   520

Here they begin to sing, the song doubled

Lo, here we come a-reaping, a-reaping,
To reap our harvest fruit;
And thus we pass the year so long,
And never be we mute.

Exeunt the Harvest-men [and women]

Enter HUANEBANGO

FROLIC
Soft, who have we here?   525

MADGE
O, this is a choleric gentleman! All you that love your
lives, keep out of the smell of his two-hand sword. Now
goes he to the conjurer.

FANTASTIC
Methinks the conjurer should put the fool into a juggling
box.   530

HUANEBANGO
Fee, fa, fum!
Here is the Englishman—
Conquer him that can—

---

519 *harvesters* eds. (harvest starres Q)
524 s.d. *Exeunt* eds. (Exit Q)
527 *smell* reach, vicinity
531–2 *Fee . . . fum!/Here . . . Englishman* eds. (one line in Q)
533–4 *Conquer . . . can—/Came . . . bright* eds. (one line in Q)

---

520 s.d. *Here . . . doubled* If they 'begin to sing' here, what were they singing when they
    entered (518 s.d.)? These are more authorial stage directions, indicating that they
    sing, but not concerned with the specifics of stage business. 'Doubled' means
    simply 'repeated' (Compare 243 s.d.) in which case it would presumably be
    repeated several times.
526–8 Madge introduces Huanebango, although we already know who and what he is.
    She (or Peele) is forgetful.
529–30 *juggling box* If any specific apparatus is meant, it is unknown. 'Juggling' meant
    the practice of magic or legerdemain, or deception generally.
531–2 *Fee . . . Englishman* A version of the familiar folk tale giant's roar, as in 'Jack the
    Giant-Killer', 'Jack and the Beanstalk' and 'Childe Rowland'.

Came for his lady bright,
To prove himself a knight,   535
And win her love in fight.

[*Enter* BOOBY *the Clown*]

BOOBY
Hoo-haw, Master Bango, are you here? Hear you, you
had best sit down here and beg an alms with me.

HUANEBANGO
Hence, base cullion! Here is he that commandeth ingress
and egress with his weapon, and will enter at his   540
voluntary, whosoever saith no.

A voice and flame of fire. HUANEBANGO *falleth down*

VOICE
No.

MADGE
So with that they kissed, and spoiled the edge of as good a
two-hand sword as ever God put life in. Now goes Booby
in, spite of the conjurer.   545

536 s.d. *Enter . . . Clown* Dyce, Bullen (part of 524 s.d. in Q)
     BOOBY ed. (Corebus Q)
537 s.p. BOOBY ed. (Cor. Q)
     Hoo-haw ed. (Who hawe Q)
539 *cullion* vile fellow, rascal
539–40 *ingress and egress* entry and exit
541 *voluntary* will
544 *Booby* ed. (Corebus Q)
545 *spite of* in spite of
     s.d. *Enter . . . Furies* eds. (*Enter the Conjurer, and strike Corebus blind* Q)

---

536 s.d. Dyce and Bullen are right, given Booby's 'are you here?' in 537. Also Madge
     refers only to Huanebango in 526–8; Fantastic's 'the fool' would thus refer to him,
     and not to the 'clown'.
540 *enter* Like the brothers at 402–3, Huanebango is about to enter Sacrapant's cell to
     rescue Delia.
542 s.p. VOICE This is not the voice from the well (see Dramatis Personae), but
     Sacrapant's. He intervenes verbally from hiding (compare the Echo at 390–6), then
     casts his spell on the intruder. The stage direction indicates that the voice's saying
     'No', the appearance of the flame and Huanebango's falling down all occur more or
     less simultaneously.
543–4 *they . . . sword* Madge's way of saying that Huanebango and the earth met
     ('kissed'), and his sword stuck into the ground, which is detrimental to its cutting
     efficiency.
545 s.d. The Furies are needed to carry Huanebango away on Sacrapant's command
     (546).

Enter the Conjurer [and two Furies]

SACRAPANT
Away with him into the open fields
To be a ravening prey to crows and kites.

[*Exeunt Furies with* HUANEBANGO]

And for this villain, let him wander up and down,
In nought but darkness and eternal night.

[*Strikes* BOOBY *blind*]

BOOBY
Here hast thou slain Huan, a slashing knight,   550
And robbed poor Booby of his sight!

SACRAPANT
Hence, villain, hence!   *Exit* [BOOBY]

Now I have unto Delia
Given a potion of forgetfulness,
That when she comes she shall not know her brothers.
Lo, where they labour like to country slaves,   555

547 s.d. *Exeunt* ... HUANEBANGO eds. (no s.d. in Q)
549 s.d. *Strikes* ... *blind* eds. (part of 545 s.d. in Q)
        BOOBY ed. (Corebus Q)
550 s.p. BOOBY ed. (Cor Q)
551 *Booby* ed. (Corebus Q)
552 s.d. *Exit* eds. (after 551 Q)
        BOOBY ed.
552-3 *Now* ... *Delia/Given* ... *forgetfulness* eds. (one line in Q)

547 *ravening* ... *kites* An example of the rhetorical and poetical figure *hypallage*. The
     modifier which belongs with *crows and kites* is displaced to give the unexpected and
     hence striking construction, *ravening prey*, which is itself an oxymoron.
     s.d. This seems the appropriate place for the Furies to go out carrying
     Huanebango; no exit is provided in Q. Sacrapant then turns to Booby.
550 *slashing knight* A swashbuckler. A character called 'Bold Slasher' or 'Captain
     Slasher' appears in some mummers' plays.
551 Substitution of 'Booby' for 'Corebus' means the loss of a syllable. As Q stands, 550
     is in trochaic pentameter, lacking the final unstressed syllable (a masculine ending
     on 'knight' is appropriate); and with 'robbéd' spoken as two syllables, 551 is in
     iambic pentameter. With the emendation, the trochaic metre is maintained (with,
     perhaps, a spondaic first foot), and the line has the same number of syllables—
     nine—as 550. See Dramatis Personae, 12n.
555-6 No editor has suggested that the brothers should be visible here; their entry is
     announced in the conventional way by Delia at 572. Sacrapant may gesture 'off' as
     he speaks these lines. But a director could have them visible in the 'distance' and
     bring them forward at 572.

With spade and mattock on this enchanted ground.
Now will I call her by another name,
For never shall she know herself again
Until that Sacrapant hath breathed his last.
See where she comes.   560

Enter DELIA

Come hither, Delia; take this goad. Here hard
At hand two slaves do work and dig for gold.
Gore them with this and thou shalt have enough.

He gives her a goad

DELIA
Good sir, I know not what you mean.

SACRAPANT [*Aside*]
She hath forgotten to be Delia,   565
But not forgot the same she should forget.
But I will change her name.—
Fair Berecynthia (so this country calls you),
Go ply these strangers, wench; they dig for gold.

Exit SACRAPANT

DELIA
O heavens! How am I beholding to this fair young man!   570
But I must ply these strangers to their work.
See where they come.

561–2 *Come . . . hard/At . . . gold* eds. (Come . . . goad,/Here . . . gold Q)
561 *goad* pointed rod or stick, for driving cattle
565 s.d. *Aside* eds.
569 *ply* drive, keep at work
570 *beholding* beholden, indebted

565–6 She has forgotten her name (575–6), but still remembers too much of her former
    life. Sacrapant gives her a new name to replace the old and orders her, in effect, to
    exorcise the remains of that life, and of reality, by beating her brothers whom he
    describes as 'slaves' and 'strangers'. He also appeals to human greed, harping on
    gold (562–3, 569); this marks him as wicked, in contrast to those in the play who
    give freely.
568 *Berecynthia* A surname of Cybele, ancient Greek earth-goddess, from the mountin
    in Phrygia where she was supposed to reside.
570–2 No amount of rearranging these lines will produce four regular verse lines; Dyce
    tried several different ways. They are here left as they are in Q.

Enter the two brothers in their shirts, with spades, digging

FIRST BROTHER
O brother, see where Delia is!

SECOND BROTHER
O Delia, happy are we to see thee here!

DELIA
What tell you me of Delia, prating swains?   575
I know no Delia, nor know I what you mean.
Ply you your work or else you are like to smart!

FIRST BROTHER
Why, Delia, knowst thou not thy brothers here?
We come from Thessaly to seek thee forth;
And thou deceivest thyself, for thou art Delia.   580

DELIA
Yet more of Delia? Then take this and smart!

[Pricks them with the goad]

What, feign you shifts for to defer your labour?
Work, villains, work! It is for gold you dig.

SECOND BROTHER
Peace, brother, peace; this vile enchanter
Hath ravished Delia of her senses clean,   585
And she forgets that she is Delia.

FIRST BROTHER [*To* DELIA]
Leave, cruel thou, to hurt the miserable.—
Dig, brother, dig, for she is hard as steel.

Here they dig and descry the light under a little hill

SECOND BROTHER
Stay, brother, what hast thou descried?

575 *swains* labourers, servants
581 s.d. *Pricks . . . goad* eds.
582 *feign you shifts* are you devising tricks
585 *clean* quite
588 s.d. *descry* perceive, discover

588 s.d. *Here . . . hill* Another authorial direction in which he narrates the action as he
visualizes it rather than simply indicating what occurs on stage. Compare 50 s.d.
and 804 s.d. The repetition of the verb 'descried' in the next line of dialogue is
revealing.

DELIA

Away and touch it not! It is something that my lord hath   590
hidden there.

She covers it again. Enter SACRAPANT

SACRAPANT

Well said! Thou plyest these pioneers well.—Go, get you
in, you labouring slaves!
Come, Berecynthia, let us in likewise,
And hear the nightingale record her notes.   595

Exeunt

Enter ZANTIPPA, *the Curst Daughter, to the well, with a pot in her
hand*

ZANTIPPA

Now for a husband, house and home! God send a good
one or none, I pray God! My father hath sent me to the
well for the water of life, and tells me if I give fair words I
shall have a husband.

Enter [CELANTA], *the Foul Wench, to the well for water, with a pot
in her hand*

But here comes Celanta, my sweet sister. I'll stand by and   600
hear what she says.

[*Withdraws*]

590–1 *Away . . . there* (*prose* Q) (that/My eds.; some thing,/That Hook)
592–3 (*prose* Q (well./Go) eds.)
592 *Well said* well done
     pioneers diggers
601 s.d. *Withdraws* Binnie

590–1 Why Delia should shift to prose here is unclear, but attempts to sort the
seventeen syllables into two lines of verse are not very satisfactory; Hook's is the
best. It would be irregular, like much other verse in the play. But Peele may be
using prose for contrast (see 592–3).
592–3 These lines divide more easily into verse than the preceding ones, though they
would be tetrameters, while 594–5 are pentameters. But Peele may have wanted
prose, to contrast the harshness of Delia's and Sacrapant's words to the brothers
with both their preceding sorrowful exchange in verse (584–8) and Sacrapant's
romantic invitation to Delia (594–5).

CELANTA

My father hath sent me to the well for water, and he tells
me if I speak fair, I shall have a husband and none of the
worst. Well, though I am black I am sure all the world
will not forsake me; and as the old proverb is, 'Though I   605
am black, I am not the devil'.

ZANTIPPA [*Approaching*]

Marry gup, with a murrain! I know wherefore thou
speakest that, but go thy ways home as wise as thou
camest, or I'll set thee home with a wanion!

*Here she strikes her pitcher against her sister's, and breaks them both
and goes her way*

CELANTA

I think this be the curstest quean in the world! You see   610
what she is—a little fair but as proud as the devil, and the
veriest vixen that lives upon God's earth. Well, I'll let her
alone, and go home and get another pitcher, and for all
this, get me to the well for water.

                                                          Exit

Enter two Furies out of the Conjurer's cell and lay HUANEBANGO *by
the well of life, [then exeunt]*

Enter ZANTIPPA *with a pitcher to the well*

ZANTIPPA

Once again for a husband, and in faith, Celanta, I have   615

604 *black* dark-complexioned
607 s.d *Approaching* Binnie
609 *with a wanion* with a vengence
610 *curstest* cursedest
    quean hussy
614 s.d. *lay* eds. (*laies* Q)
615–16 *have... of* have a headstart on

605–6 *Though... devil* Proverbial (Tilley D297).
607 *Marry... murrain* Interjection expressing indignation or irritation. 'Marry',
    originally from 'Mary', thus an oath, had come by the late sixteenth century to
    signify no more than an expression of impatience or surprise. 'Gup' (*go up*) is an
    exclamation of derision or remonstrance, often coupled with 'Marry' as here. 'With
    a murrain', i.e. 'the plague on it', is another common colloquial exclamation of
    anger; compare *GGN*, I.iii, 29.
611 *as... devil* Proverbial (Tilley L572): 'As proud as Lucifer'.

got the start of you! Belike husbands grow by the well-
side. Now my father says I must rule my tongue. Why,
alas, what am I then? A woman without a tongue is as a
soldier without his weapon. But I'll have my water and be
gone.   620

Here she offers to dip her pitcher in, and a [VOICE] *speaks in the well*

VOICE
Gently dip, but not too deep,
For fear you make the golden beard to weep.

[*A* HEAD *comes up with ears of corn*]

Fair maiden, white and red,
Comb me smooth, and stroke my head,
And thou shalt have some cockle-bread.   625

616 *Belike* maybe
620 s.d. VOICE ed. (head Q)
621 s.p. VOICE ed. (Head Q)
622 *beard* eds. (birde Q)
      s.d. *A* HEAD . . . corn ed. (no s.d. in Q)
624 *Comb* . . . *stroke* ed. (Stroke . . . combe Q)

616–17 *Belike . . . well-side* Zantippa has not yet seen Huanebango, so this is wishful
      thinking, which immediately comes true.
618–19 *A woman . . . weapon* Proverbial (Tilley W675): 'A woman's weapon is her
      tongue'.
620 s.d. VOICE See Dramatis Personae, 22–3n.
622 *beard* Although the four extant copies of Q agree on 'birde' here, most editors
      emend to 'beard' because when the voice speaks again at 756–7, the two corrected
      copies read 'beard', which seems right; by metonymy, 'beard' stands for 'head'.
      What does a bird have to do with it? On the other hand, what has logic or
      likelihood to do with this play-world?
      s.d. By analogy with 757 s.d. The Head must appear for Zantippa to break her
      pitcher on it (631 s.d.).
624 Unless we assume that Zantippa misquotes, the line should read 'Comb me smooth
      and stroke my head'. Compare also 759 and 764.
625 *cockle-bread* Cockle is a weed, sometimes called 'corn cockle', which grows in corn-
      and wheatfields. Cockle-bread may have been a kind of cornbread, or perhaps
      inferior bread with cockle mixed, in the harvesting, with the corn; the Head is
      bearing ears of corn. *OED* records no such literal meaning, however. John Aubrey,
      writing in the late seventeenth century, records a 'wanton sport' of 'young wenches'
      called 'moulding of Cocklebread': '*viz.* they get upon a Table-board, and then
      gather-up their knees and their Coates with their hands as high as they can, and
      then they wabble to and fro with their Buttocks as if they were kneading of Dough
      with their Arses', reciting a rhyme meanwhile (*Three Prose Works*, ed. J. Buchanan-
      Brown (1972), p. 254). Another reference associates it with 'playing at
      barleybreak . . . and such like profane exercises' (*OED*). So the Voice may be
      indulging in a bawdy joke. The offer of cockle-bread clearly provokes Zantippa,
      but not her sister (767).

ZANTIPPA
    What is this?
    'Fair maiden, white and red,
    Comb me smooth and stroke my head,
    And thou shalt have some cockle-bread.'
    'Cockle' callest thou it, boy? Faith, I'll give you cockle- 630
    bread!

She breaks her pitcher upon [the] HEAD; *[it descends.] Then it thunders and lightens, and* HUANEBANGO *rises up.* HUANEBANGO *is deaf and cannot hear*

HUANEBANGO
    Phylyda phylerydos, Pamphylyda floryda flortos,
    'Dub-dub-a-dub, bounce!' quoth the guns, with a sulphu-
       rous huff-snuff!
    Waked with a wench, pretty peat, pretty love, and my
       sweet pretty pigsnie.
    Just by thy side shall sit surnamed great Huanebango;   635
    Safe in my arms will I keep thee, threat Mars or thunder
       Olympus!

ZANTIPPA *[Aside]*
    Foh! What greasy groom have we here? He looks as
    though he crept out of the backside of the well, and
    speaks like a drum perished at the west end!

HUANEBANGO
    O that I might—but I may not, woe to my destiny
    therefore!—   640

626–7 *this?/'Fair* eds. (one line in Q)
630 s.d. *the* ed. (his Q)
634 *peat* (term of endearment) pet, darling
    pigsnie (=pig's eye; term of endearment)
637 *groom* fellow

632–6 A farrago of bombast and nonsense. Binnie thinks 632 'Spanish-sounding nonsense'. 633 is a parody of the style of Richard Stanyhurst, who translated Books I–IV of Virgil's *Aeneid* (1582) into just such amazing verses. Samples (which Peele may have had in mind): 'Lowd dub a dub tabering with frapping rip rap of Aetna'; 'Of ruff raffe roaring, mens herts with terror agrysing'.

637 s.d. *Aside* It may be thought superfluous to indicate this, as Huanebango 'is deaf and cannot hear'. But Zantippa does not know this and would speak the lines to herself and for the audience.

639 *a drum . . . end* Exact meaning unknown. Perhaps a drum with one of its heads or skins broken, producing a dull thump rather than the normal resonant sound when struck on the other, intact head.

640 Dyce pointed out that this line is quoted from Gabriel Harvey's *Encomium Lauri* (1580).

Kiss that I clasp, but I cannot! Tell me, my destiny,
wherefore?

ZANTIPPA [*Aside*]
Whoop! Now I have my dream! Did you never hear so
great a wonder as this?—Three blue beans in a blue
bladder: rattle, bladder, rattle!

HUANEBANGO [*Aside*]
I'll now set my countenance and to her in prose. It may be   645
this 'rim, ram, ruff' is too rude an encounter.—Let me,
fair lady, if you be at leisure, revel with your sweetness,
and rail upon that cowardly conjurer that hath cast me, or
congealed me rather, into an unkind sleep and polluted
my carcass.   650

ZANTIPPA [*Aside*]
Laugh, laugh, Zantippa! Thou hast thy fortune—a fool
and a husband under one!

HUANEBANGO
Truly, sweetheart, as I seem: about some twenty years, the
very April of mine age.

ZANTIPPA [*Aside*]
Why, what a prating ass is this!   655

HUANEBANGO
Her coral lips, her crimson chin,
Her silver teeth so white within,
Her golden locks, her rolling eye,

646 *rim . . . ruff* Q (two copies; rude . . . ruff two copies)
648 *rail upon* utter abusive language against
651 *fortune—a fool* Binnie (fortune, a fool Q)
652 *under one* all in one

643-4 *Three . . . rattle* Proverbial (Tilley B124). Rather a jingle or tongue-twister, used
as a charm, than a true proverb. Learned notes about the prominence of beans in
ritual and folklore are unnecessary. Aubrey recalls that in his boyhood (thus within
a few decades of the date of the play), it was used as a charm against 'an ill tongue'
or evil spirits (*Three Prose Works*, p. 253 n.). Zantippa utters a charm to safeguard
her newfound prize, a husband, or to protect herself against his 'ill tongue'; or else
she is simply trying to converse with Huanebango in language like his own. Jonson
may be alluding to *OWT* when he has Humphrey Wasp speak the words 'Rattle
bladder rattle' and 'O, Madge' in *Bartholmew Fair*, I.iv, 73.

646 *rim, ram, ruff* Huanebango is referring to the verse he has been speaking. In *The
Canterbury Tales*, Chaucer's Parson explains his preference for prose over both
alliterative and rhymed verse: 'But trusteth wel, I am a Southren man,/I kan nat
geeste 'rum, ram, ruf,' by lettre,/Ne, God woot, rym holde I but litel bettre;/And
therfore, if you list— I wil nat glose—/I wol yow telle a myrie tale in prose' ('The
Parsons's Prologue', 42–6). Like the Parson, Huanebango is changing to prose.

Her pretty parts—let them go by—
Heigh-ho, hath wounded me,   660
That I must die this day to see.

ZANTIPPA

By Gog's bones, thou art a flouting knave! 'Her coral lips,
her crimson chin'—ka, wilshaw!

HUANEBANGO

True, my own, and my own because mine, and mine
because mine—ha, ha! Above a thousand pounds in   665
possibility, and things fitting thy desire in possession.

ZANTIPPA [*Aside*]

The sot thinks I ask of his lands. Lob be your comfort and
cuckold be your destiny!—Hear you, sir: and if you will
have us, you had best say so betime.

HUANEBANGO

True, sweetheart, and will royalize thy progeny with my   670
pedigree.

Exeunt

Enter EUMENIDES, *the Wandering Knight*

EUMENIDES

Wretched Eumenides, still unfortunate,
Envied by Fortune, and forlorn by Fate;
Here pine and die, wretched Eumenides.
Die in the spring, the April of my age?   675
Here sit thee down; repent what thou hast done.
I would to God that it were ne'er begun!

660 *hath* (see 159n.)
662 *Gog's* God's
      flouting jeering, scoffing
663 *ka* (=quotha) said he
      wilshaw (meaning unknown; ? will ich ha(ve) (Gayley))
667 *Lob* clown, lout
669 *betime* in good time

664–5 *True . . . because mine* Recalls the Latin word-play at 274–8.
667 *Lob . . . comfort* May your simple-mindedness prevent you from knowing the truth
     about your destiny. But Bullen quotes *The Bachelor's Banquet* (1603), formerly
     atrributed to Dekker, where the proverbial expression 'Lob's Pound' (Tilley
     L403), originally simply 'prison', is used to connote the married man's state of
     entanglement and thraldom. See also Eric Partridge, ed., *A Classical Dictionary of
     the Vulgar Tongue* (1931; repr. 1963), p. 221.

Enter JACK

JACK

You are well overtaken, sir.

EUMENDIES

Who's that?

JACK

You are heartily well met, sir. 680

EUMENIDES

Forbear, I say! Who is that which pincheth me?

JACK

Trusting in God, good Master Eumenides, that you are in
so good health as all your friends were at the making
hereof, God give you good morrow, sir. Lack you not a
neat, handsome and cleanly young lad, about the age of 685
fifteen or sixteen years, that can run by your horse, and
for a need, make your mastership's shoes as black as ink?
How say you, sir?

EUMENIDES

Alas, pretty lad, I know not how to keep myself, and
much less a servant, my pretty boy, my state is so bad. 690

JACK

Content yourself, you shall not be so ill a master but I'll
be as bad a servant. Tut, sir, I know you though you know
not me. Are not you the man, sir—deny it if you can,

684 *good* eds. (God Q)

---

681 *Who . . . me* Pinching is a common way for invisible spirits to manifest their
presence. Here it is not malicious, but see *The Tempest*, II.ii, 4 and V.i., 276.
Eumenides obviously does not see Jack when he speaks at 679 and 681, but does see
him by 689. Peele may have imagined Jack to 'materialize' after 681, but that is
scarcely within an actor's capability. He might come up behind Eumenides,
dodging out of sight until he introduces himself at, say 684. Compare 788 s.d. and
note.

682–4 *Trusting . . . hereof* A formulaic epistolary greeting, puzzling here since no letter is
involved. Perhaps Jack refers humorously to himself ('hereof') in his ghostly form,
released ('made') by Wiggen and Corebus ('your friends') who, thanks to
Eumenides's gift, were able to pay for Jack's funeral. Compare *Arden of Faversham*,
ed. Martin White (1982), sc.iii, 11. 3–4: ' . . . hoping in God you be in good health,
as I, Michael, was at the making hereof'; a letter is being read. See E. Legouis, 'The
Epistolary Past in English', *N&Q*, 198 (1953),111–12.

sir—that came from a strange place in the land of Catita, where Jackanapes flies with his tail in his mouth, to seek 695 out a lady as white as snow and as red as blood? Ha, ha! Have I touched you now?

EUMENIDES [*Aside*]
I think this boy be a spirit!—How knowst thou all this?

JACK
Tut, are not you the man, sir—deny it if you can, sir—that gave all the money you had to the burying of a 700 poor man, and but one three half-pence left in your purse? Content you, sir, I'll serve you, that is flat.

EUMENIDES
Well, my lad, since thou art so importunate, I am content to entertain thee, not as a servant, but a copartner in my journey. But whither shall we go? For I have not any 705 money more than one bare three half-pence.

JACK
Well, master, content yourself, for if my divination be not out, that shall be spent at the next inn or alehouse we come to, for, master, I know you are passing hungry; therefore I'll go before and provide dinner until that you 710 come. No doubt but you'll come fair and softly after.

EUMENIDES
Ay, go before; I'll follow thee.

JACK
But do you hear, master? Do you know my name?

703 *importunate* eds. (impor-/nate Q) insistent
705 *go? For* eds. (goe for Q)
709 *passing* exceedingly

694–5 *Catita ... Jackanapes* Catita is obviously a far-away land, apparently the creation of Peele's imagination, since no trace of it has been found, although the possibility of a misprint (of 'Caria', 'Catina', 'Cataea', 'Carcina', etc.—all real places in the ancient world) cannot be ruled out. There, as in Thessaly, strange things are commonplace. We are not to question how Eumenides knew of Delia if he did not come from Thessaly, nor how, later, he seems to know everyone's name (852–3). 'Jackanapes' too is of uncertain origin (see *OED*). Here an animal, an ape or monkey or some fabulous creature, is meant, with perhaps a glance at Jack's own name, a veiled hint to the baffled Eumenides. See a similar use of both words, probably borrowed from Peele, in Marston's *The Malcontent*, ed. B. Harris (1967), I.iii, 54–5.
711 *fair* and *softly* Proverbial (Tilley S601): 'Fair and softly goes far'. Here it means leisurely, easily.

EUMENIDES
  No, I promise thee, not yet.
JACK
  Why, I am Jack.   *Exit* 715

EUMENIDES
  Jack. Why, be it so then.

Enter the HOSTESS *and* JACK, *setting meat on the table, and Fiddlers
come to play.* EUMENIDES *walketh up and down, and will eat no meat*

HOSTESS
  How say you, sir? Do you please to sit down?

EUMENIDES
  Hostess, I thank you, I have no great stomach.

HOSTESS [*To* JACK]
  Pray, sir, what is the reason your master is so strange?
  Doth not this meat please him?   720

JACK
  Yes, hostess, but it is my master's fashion to pay before he
  eats; therefore, a reckoning, good hostess.

HOSTESS
  Marry, shall you, sir, presently.   *Exit*

EUMENIDES
  Why, Jack what dost thou mean? Thou knowest I have
  not any money. Therefore, sweet Jack, tell me, what shall 725
  I do?

---

715 s.d. *Exit* eds. (Exeunt Jack Q)
718 *stomach* appetite
719 s.d. *To* JACK Binnie
723 *shall you* you shall have it

---

716 *Jack ... then* Eumenides still has not made the connection between the Old Man's
    prophecy about 'dead men's bones' (439), the lad named Jack for whose burial he
    gave money, and this mysterious visitor who has pressed his service upon him.
    s.d. This authorial direction represents a sort of silent interlude, since the actions of
    bringing on the table, and setting it, and of the fiddlers coming in take place before
    the Hostess speaks. Where the 'inn or alehouse' was to be located on the stage did
    not worry Peele. A table (perhaps the one from Sacrapant's magic banquet),
    carried on and set down, and a few chairs would have sufficed. An indefinite lapse
    of time is assumed, for Eumenides to 'arrive', though an impression of the inn's
    coming to him, magically, would be in keeping with the spirit of the play. See
    Hook's discussion of the scene (p. 376), and Chambers, *ES*, III, 48.

JACK

Well, master, look in your purse.

EUMENIDES

Why, faith, it is a folly, for I have no money.

JACK

Why, look you, master, do so much for me.

EUMENIDES

Alas, Jack, my purse is full of money!   730

JACK

'Alas', master? Does that word belong to this accident?
Why, methinks I should have seen you cast away your
cloak and in a bravado dance a galliard round about the
chamber. Why, master, your man can teach you more wit
than this.—Come, hostess, cheer up my master.   735

[*Enter* HOSTESS]

HOSTESS

You are heartily welcome. And if it please you to eat of a
fat capon, a fairer bird, a finer bird, a sweeter bird, a
crisper bird, a neater bird your worship never eat of.

EUMENIDES

Thanks, my fine, eloquent hostess.

731 *'Alas', master? Does* ed. (Alas, maister, does Q)
733 *bravado* gay mood
    dance eds. (daunced Q)
735 s.d. *Enter* HOSTESS eds.
738 *eat* ate

734 *chamber* This suggests that Peele had in mind an indoor setting for this scene. But
    given the non-representational staging of plays in public theatres, no more than the
    table and its accoutrements and the presence of the Hostess were needed to signify
    'inn' (see preceding note).
737–8 *a fairer... eat of* Some eds. quote lines spoken by Dandaline, a hostess, in the
    anonymous *Liberality and Prodigality*:
        A better bird, a fairer bird, a finer bird,
        A sweeter bird, a yonger bird, a tenderer bird
        A daintier bird, a crisper bird, a more delicate bird,
        Was there never set upon any Gentlemans board.
                    (ed. W. W. Greg, MSR (1913), ll. 519–22)
    This play was acted in 1601 and published in 1602, but may have been written
    much earlier, so indebtedness in either direction cannot be affirmed.

JACK

But, hear you, master, one word by the way. Are you 740
content I shall be halves in all you get in your journey?

EUMENIDES

I am, Jack; here is my hand.

JACK

Enough, master. I ask no more.

EUMENIDES

Come, hostess, receive your money, and I thank you for
my good entertainment. 745

HOSTESS

You are heartily welcome, sir.

EUMENIDES

Come, Jack, whither go we now?

JACK

Marry, master, to the conjurer's presently.

EUMENIDES

Content, Jack. Hostess, farewell. *Exeunt*

Enter BOOBY *and* CELANTA, *the Foul Wench, to the well for water*

BOOBY

Come, my duck, come.—I have now got a wife.—Thou 750
art fair, art thou not?

CELANTA

My Booby, the fairest alive, make no doubt of that.

BOOBY

Come, wench, are we almost at the well?

CELANTA

Ay, Booby, we are almost at the well now. I'll go fetch
some water; sit down while I dip my pitcher in. 755

---

741 *be halves* share equally
749 s.d. BOOBY ed. (Corebus Q)
      CELANTA eds. (Zelanto Q)
750 s.p. BOOBY ed. (Coreb. Q; *passim* to 773)
752 s.p. CELANTA eds. (Zelan. Q; *passim* to 772)
      Booby ed. (Corebus Q; *passim* to 772)

---

749 s.d. CELANTA Q's 'Zelanto' may suggest a recollection by Peele of Zelota, the
shrewish wife of the cobbler Rafe in Wilson's *The Cobbler's Prophecy* (see 390–6
n.). She is charmed to sleep by Mercury.

[*She dips her pitcher in the well*]

VOICE [*From the well*]
Gently dip, but not too deep,
For fear you make the golden beard to weep.

A HEAD *comes up with ears of corn*

Fair maiden, white and red,
Comb me smooth, and stroke my head,
And thou shalt have some cockle-bread.   760

She combs [*the corn*] *into her lap.* [*The* HEAD *descends*]

Gently dip, but not too deep,
For fear thou make the golden beard to weep.

[CELANTA *dips her pitcher again*]

A HEAD *comes up full of gold*

Fair maiden, white and red,
Comb me smooth, and stroke my head,
And every hair a sheaf shall be,   765
And every sheaf a golden tree.

She combs [*the gold*] *into her lap.* [*The* HEAD *descends*]

CELANTA
O see, Booby, I have combed a great deal of gold into my
lap and a great deal of corn.

BOOBY
Well said, wench! Now we shall have toast enough. God

755 s.d. *She . . . well* ed. (compare 620 s.d.)
760 s.d. *She . . . lap* ed. (part of 757 s.d. in Q)
   s.d. *The . . . descends* ed. (Descends Binnie; and at 766 s.d.)
762 s.d. *A* HEAD *. . . gold* as in Hook (after 766 Q)
763 *maiden* eds. (maide Q)
766 s.d. *she . . . lap* ed. (part of 762 s.d. in Q)
769 *toast* ed. (tost Q (two copies); just (two copies))

---

760 The offer of cockle-bread does not annoy or offend Celanta as it did Zantippa (625
   and n.). If there is bawdy innuendo, it is lost on or ignored by her.
767 *O see* He cannot, of course.
769 *toast* P. A. Daniel suggested 'toast' to Bullen, who retained his copy's 'just', but
   thought it might be 'grist'. He was on the right track. 'Tost' was one spelling of
   'toast' (see 901 n.); the proofreaders, who improved the BM and Huntington
   copies at 646 and 770, were overzealous here, and the 'uncorrected' Dyce and
   Pforzheimer copies are correct. Celanta's corn would be used to make bread; the
   mundane Booby translates that into toast, as he would translate precious metal into
   spendable coin.

send us coiners to coin our gold. But come, shall we go 770
home, sweetheart?

CELANTA

Nay, come, Booby, I will lead you.

BOOBY

So, Booby, things have well hit;
Thou hast gotten wealth to mend thy wit.

Exeunt

Enter JACK *and the Wandering Knight*

JACK

Come away, master, come.   775

EUMENIDES

Go along, Jack, I'll follow thee. Jack, they say it is good to
go cross-legged and say his prayers backward. How sayest
thou?

JACK

Tut, never fear, master; let me alone. Here sit you still;
speak not a word. And because you shall not be enticed 780
with his enchanting speeches, with this same wool I'll

---

770 *coiners ... coin* Q (two copies; quoiners ... quine two copies)
774 s.d. Exeunt eds. (Exit Q)
777 *his* one's
779 *let me alone* leave it to me
780 *because* so that

---

773 *Booby* As at 551, the substitution alters the metre, but the lines scan comfortably as
tetrameters. The stresses would be on 'So', 'Boo-', 'things', 'hit'; 'got-', 'wealth',
'mend', 'wit'. Even with 'Corebus', this line is a tetrameter; the emendation, made
in the interest of the play's clarity, does scant violence to its poetry.

773–4 The lines echo the Old Man's prediction concerning Booby (322–3).

776–7 *they say ... backward* Going, or sitting, cross-legged seems to have been both an
evil and a good-luck charm (see Hook, pp. 441–2n., and his note to *Edward I*, 1.
2263, in *The Life and Works of George Peele*, II, 199). Gummere and Binnie cite
Milton's *Comus:*

> without his rod revers't,
> And backward mutters of dissevering power,
> We cannot free the Lady.   (815–17)

Saying prayers (as opposed to a conjurer's spell) backward, however, conjures up
the devil (compare Diccon's method in *GGN*, II.i). Eumenides, in his trepidation,
may be recalling the wrong kind of charm, but Jack is in charge.

780–2 *And ... ears* Peele may have had in mind Homer's *Odyssey*, Book XII, where
Odysseus (Ulysses), on the advice of Circe, puts wax in the ears of all his crew so
that they will not hear the fatally enchanting song of the Sirens.

stop your ears. [*Puts wool into* EUMENIDES' *ears*] And so,
master sit still, for I must to the conjurer.

                                          Exit JACK

           Enter the Conjurer to the Wandering Knight

SACRAPANT
    How now! What man art thou that sits so sad?
    Why dost thou gaze upon these stately trees   785
    Without the leave and will of Sacrapant?
    What, not a word but mum?
    Then, Sacrapant, thou art betrayed!

Enter JACK, *invisible, and taketh off* SACRAPANT'*s wreath from his
                 head, and his sword out of his hand*

    What hand invades the head of Sacrapant?
    What hateful fury doth envy my happy state?   790
    Then, Sacrapant, these are thy latest days.
    Alas, my veins are numbed, my sinews shrink,
    My blood is pierced, my breath fleeting away,
    And now my timeless date is come to end.
    He in whose life his actions hath been so foul,   795
    Now in his death to hell descends his soul.

               He dieth [*and his body is removed*]

---

782 s.d. *Puts . . . ears* eds.
794 *timeless date* (supposedly) eternal life
796 s.d. *and . . . removed* Binnie

---

782 s.d. *Puts . . . ears* Called for by 801 s.d.
787 *not . . . mum* Proverbial (Tilley W767).
788 Sacrapant said nothing about a threat from a silent man at 413–19, but he may
    believe that the silent, unhearing Eumenides is the dead man who is destined to kill
    him.
    s.d. *Enter* JACK, *invisible* A delightfully offhand direction. How was it done?
    Compare 679, where Jack is invisible to Eumenides at first, then becomes visible.
    Here he presumably remains invisible to Sacrapant, but is visible to Eumenides. Or
    does Eumenides neither see nor hear him until 802? This too seems to betray the
    author drafting his plot, not yet giving thought to the playing of it.
793 *My . . . pierced* The sense is clear, even if, literally speaking, it would be his veins or
    his body that was pierced, letting out his blood. Hook notes (p. 442) that Peele
    liked the word 'pierced' and used it frequently in other works.
796 s.d. The body must be removed, since Jack enters with the head at 842. It would be
    appropriate for the Furies to carry off Sacrapant's body, as they have carried off his
    victims previously.

JACK

O sir, are you gone? Now I hope we shall have some other
coil. Now, master, how like you this? The conjurer, he is
dead, and vows never to trouble us more. Now get you to
your fair lady, and see what you can do with her.—Alas, 800
he heareth me not all this while. But I will help that.

He pulls the wool out of his ears

EUMENIDES

How now, Jack! What news?

JACK

Here, master, take this sword and dig with it at the foot of
this hill.

He digs and spies a light

EUMENIDES

How now, Jack! What is this?   805

JACK

Master, without this the conjurer could do nothing, and
so long as this light lasts, so long doth his art endure, and
this being out, then doth his art decay.

EUMENIDES

Why then, Jack, I will soon put out this light.

JACK

Ay, master, how?   810

EUMENIDES

Why, with a stone I'll break the glass, and then blow it
out.

JACK

No, master, you may as soon break the smith's anvil as
this little vial, nor the biggest blast that ever Boreas blew
cannot blow out this little light; but she that is neither 815

798 *coil* ado, business
814 *Boreas* the north wind
815–16 *but . . . widow* only she that is . . . can do it

804 s.d. *He . . . light* Compare 588 s.d. and note.

maid, wife nor widow. Master, wind this horn, and see
what will happen.

He winds the horn

Here enters VENELIA *and breaks the glass, and blows out the light, and
goeth in again*

JACK

So master, how like you this? This is she that ran madding
in the woods, his betrothed love that keeps the cross; and
now this light being out, all are restored to their former   820
liberty. And now, master, to the lady that you have so
long looked for.

He draweth a curtain, and there DELIA *sitteth asleep*

EUMENIDES

God speed, fair maid, sitting alone: there is once.
God speed, fair maid, [sitting alone]: there is twice.
God speed, fair maid, [sitting alone]: there is thrice.   825

DELIA

Not so, good sir, for you are by.

JACK

Enough, master; she hath spoke. Now I will leave her
with you.   [*Exit*]

EUMENIDES

Thou fairest flower of these western parts,
Whose beauty so reflecteth in my sight   830
As doth a crystal mirror in the sun,
For thy sweet sake I have crossed the frozen Rhine;

816 *wind* blow
828 s.d. *Exit* eds. (no s.d. in Q)

---

817 s.d. *Hear ... again* This two-line direction describes an action that might consume
several minutes. Such moments of silent action are a notable feature of the play.
Compare, e.g., the narrative directions at 192, 403, 518, 541, 588, 631, 716. Venelia,
who speaks no lines, must rely on behaviour to convey the differences in her state
of mind at 192, here, and at 851.

823–5 *God speed ... thrice* I incorporate a suggestion by G. R. Proudfoot (recorded by
Binnie) that 'sitting alone' should be repeated in each line. It is, after all, a charm,
and 'there is twice' and 'there is thrice' make good sense only if Eumenides is
enumerating repetitions of the magic greeting which will waken the sleeping
princess.

826 *Not ... by* Delia means that she is not alone now, for Eumenides is there.

Leaving fair Po, I sailed up Danuby
As far as Saba, whose enhancing streams
Cuts 'twixt the Tartars and the Russians.					835
These have I crossed for thee, fair Delia:
Then grant me that which I have sued for long.

DELIA

Thou gentle knight, whose fortune is so good
To find me out, and set my brothers free,
My faith, my heart, my hand I give to thee.					840

EUMENIDES

Thanks, gentle madam. But here comes Jack. Thank him,
for he is the best friend that we have.

Enter JACK *with a head in his hand*

How now, Jack! What hast thou there?

JACK

Marry, master, the head of the conjurer.

EUMENIDES

Why, Jack, that is impossible—he was a young man!					845

JACK

Ah, master, so he deceived them that beheld him. But he
was a miserable, old and crooked man, though to each
man's eye he seemed young and fresh. For, master, this
conjurer took the shape of the old man that kept the cross,		850

835 *Cuts* (see 159 n.)

832–5 Editors quote Greene's *Orlando Furioso*, where Mandricard relates his travels to
seek the hand of the emperor's daughter:

> I furrowed Neptune's seas
> Northeast as far as is the frozen Rhene;
> Leaving fair Voya, cross'd up Danuby,
> As high as Saba, whose enhancing streams
> Cut 'twixt the Tartars and the Russians.
>
> (11. 66–70; Dyce, p. 90)

Eumenides's preceding lines (829–31) are similar, though less strikingly so, to
those spoken by the Soldan in Greene's play some fifty lines before those just
quoted:

> The fairest flower that glories Africa,
> Whose beauty Phoebus dares not dash with showers,
> Over whose climate never hung a cloud,
> But smiling Titan lights the horizon—
>
> (11. 17–20)

and that old man was in the likeness of the conjurer. But 850
now, master, wind your horn.

He winds his horn

Enter VENELIA, *the two brothers, and he that was at the cross*

EUMENIDES
Welcome, Erestus! Welcome, fair Venelia!
Welcome, Thelea and Calypha both!
Now have I her that I so long have sought;
So saith fair Delia, if we have your consent.   855

FIRST BROTHER
Valiant Eumenides, thou well deservest
To have our favours; so let us rejoice
That by thy means we are at liberty.
Here may we joy each in other's sight.
And this fair lady have her wandering knight.   860

JACK
So, master, now ye think you have done. But I must have
a saying to you. You know you and I were partners, I to
have half in all you got.

EUMENIDES
Why, so thou shalt, Jack.

JACK
Why then, master, draw your sword, part your lady, let 865
me have half of her presently.

EUMENIDES
Why, I hope, Jack, thou dost but jest! I promised thee half
I got, but not half my lady.

853 *Calypha* eds. (Kalepha Q)
855 *your* (i.e., the brothers')
859 *joy* rejoice

---

851 s.d. *he … cross* Now, with Sacrapant's spell broken, he would enter in his true
shape, as a young man; his name too is restored to him in the next line.

853 *Thelea* The first mention of the Second Brother's name, though since Calypha has
been named earlier (388, 405), no special significance attaches to this fact. But the
addressing of each person by name may be seen as signalling the breaking of the
evil spell and the restoration of their own identities and true status. Eumenides has
also addressed Delia by name for the first time at 836; before the spell was broken
she was 'fair maid'.

861–82 Eumenides's ultimate trial, the friendship or oath-keeping test. It is not
horrible, because it cannot really happen; it is another of the play's many rituals.
Compare Valentine's offer of his love, Silvia, to his friend Proteus in *The Two
Gentlemen of Verona*, V.iv, 82–3. The episode also recalls the judgement of Solomon
(I Kings 3:16–28).

JACK

But what else, master? Have you not gotten her?
Therefore divide her straight, for I will have half. There is   870
no remedy.

EUMENIDES

Well, ere I will falsify my word unto my friend, take her
all. Here, Jack, I'll give her thee.

JACK

Nay, neither more nor less, master, but even just half.

EUMENIDES

Before I will falsify my faith unto my friend, I will divide   875
her. Jack, thou shalt have half.

FIRST BROTHER

Be not so cruel unto our sister, gentle knight!

SECOND BROTHER

O, spare fair Delia! She deserves no death!

EUMENIDES

Content yourselves; my word is passed to him. Therefore
prepare thyself, Delia, for thou must die.   880

DELIA

Then farewell, world! Adieu, Eumenides!

He offers to strike and JACK *stays him*

JACK

Stay, master! It is sufficient I have tried your constancy.
Do you now remember since you paid for the burying of a
poor fellow?

EUMENIDES

Ay, very well, Jack.   885

JACK

Then, master, thank that good deed for this good turn.
And so, God be with you all!

870 *straight* straightaway
879 *my ... passed* I have sworn

886 *this ... turn* Jack may mean simply his sparing of Delia, but 'this good turn' may
also be the whole of his benevolent intervention in the main plot, culminating in
liberty and happiness for everyone.

JACK *leaps down in the ground*

EUMENIDES
    Jack! What, art thou gone? Then farewell, Jack.
    Come, brothers and my beauteous Delia,
    Erestus and thy dear Venelia;   890
    We will to Thessaly with joyful hearts.

ALL
    Agreed! We follow thee and Delia.

                                                    Exeunt

FANTASTIC
    What, gammer, asleep?

MADGE
    By the mass, son, 'tis almost day, and my windows shut at
    the cock's crow!   895

FROLIC
    Do you hear, gammer? Methinks this Jack bore a great
    sway amongst them.

MADGE
    O, man, this was the ghost of the poor man that they kept
    such a coil to bury, and that makes him to help the
    wandering knight so much. But come, let us in. We will   900
    have a cup of ale and a toast this morning, and so depart.

FANTASTIC
    Then you have made an end of your tale, gammer?

888 *gone? Then* eds. (gone?/Then Q)
894 *shut* eds. (shuts Q)
901 *toast* eds. (tost Q; see 769 n.)

---

887 s.d. JACK ... *ground* A trap is needed for this. It would probably be used for the well
    scenes also, with the well built over the trap for the Head to rise from, and with the
    person speaking the Voice's part stationed under it. At some point, the well would
    have been removed, perhaps immediately after 774, leaving the trap open for Jack
    to leap into here.
894–5 *my ... crow* My eyes are still closed; they should be open by now. The window
    metaphor for the eyes and eyelids is common from the fourteenth century. Madge
    is replying in the affirmative to Fantastic's query.
900 *let us in* Madge and the pages were 'in' her cottage already, and have not come out
    since the beginning, nor would we expect her to 'depart' from her own home with
    the others. But this is being perversely literal-minded. The effect of the words is to
    suggest, indirectly, that they—and we—have been somewhere else, in the land of
    romance and folktale, watching the events of the inner play unfold. And, at the end
    of the play, Madge's invitation to her audience to go 'in' is literally an invitation to
    the actors to go 'off'; the play that all of them are in is over. Clunch and Antic are
    forgotten.

MADGE

Yes, faith. When this was done I took a piece of bread and cheese, and came my way, and so shall you have too before you go, to your breakfast.   [*Exeunt*]   905

FINIS

905 *to* for
      s.d. *Exeunt* eds. (no s.d. in Q)

903–4 *was done . . . took . . . came* Madge's sudden shift of tense and her reference to 'coming her way', as if she herself had seen or heard the tale somewhere else at some other time, is the final disorientating wrench. Dislocation is now temporal as well as spatial: we shift from the dramatic present, not simply to the narrative past of Madge's 'Once upon a time' (106), but to the implied pluperfect, when she was the auditor/spectator, not the teller. The effect is similar to that of Milton's unexpected shift to a framing, narrative past tense in the final verse-paragraph of *Lycidas*.